"...a consciousness-raising self-help detective story that can lead you to examine the everyday details of your life."

Peter Michalos,
Author of *Psyche, a Novel of the Young Freud*,
(Nan A. Talese, Doubleday)

"Truly brilliant work, *The Key of Life* is certainly a story that needs to be told. The comfort I felt reading this was like nothing I've ever experienced. ...Thank you for the reminder of how glorious this existence can be."

Michael Schlau, Producer - Los Angeles

"*The Key of Life* has changed my beliefs about life and death forever. I met Randy on Aug. 23rd and my father passed away just a few weeks later, on Sept. 14th. This book eased my pain so much during this difficult time. And I could not believe the significance of these dates with those in the book! If you have ever even thought about the possibility of reincarnation, you must read this book."

Trudy Clarke, Butte MT

"*The Key of Life* is a frank, insightful chronicle of one man's spiritual odyssey. Everyone can relate in some way to his experiences. We may interpret them differently, yet Randy's ability to pull us in and share his drama takes us, in fact, to the same spiritual home."

Lynda Neff, West Virginia

"*The Key of Life* is an intriguing and captivating true story that demonstrates the importance of understanding the wisdom of previous generations. Randy's numerous revelations throughout his journey are provocative and builds the anticipation throughout the book toward the final pages. The synchronistic events in this story are amazing to witness and validates the significance of paying close attention to the signs in our own lives."

Shirley Barnett,
Healthcare Operations Consultant,
San Bernardino, CA

"...An incredible present-day journey about how our lives are touched by the living and deceased with Randy Rogers' connect-the-dots experiences. Warning: you won't be able to put *The Key of Life* down after starting it!"

Jim White, former NBC News cameraman,
Chatsworth, CA

"Amazing! excellent! well written, did not want it to end. A must read for those who are looking for their *Key of Life*. A journey in life through the lives of the soul, Past, Present, and Future."

Kevin Clarke, Butte MT

"*The Key of Life* is another true account of the existence of the many levels and realms where we go to and come from in life. If you have ever wondered what some of those dreams were about, this book is for you. I recommend this read to anyone looking for inspiration, information into the unknown and those who question their own existence. Which key will unlock your door?"

Alexandra Holzer, Paranormalist and
Author of *Growing Up Haunted*

"I highly recommend this book for anyone who asks the question 'Am I on the right path?' This story will undoubtedly help open many doors in your own search for *The Key of Life*."

John Dietsch, Founder/CEO of Hook.TV and
Author of the award winning *Shadowcasting*

The Key of Life

A METAPHYSICAL INVESTIGATION

Randolph J. Rogers

Bloomington, Indiana, U.S.A. 2009

Published by Transformation Media Books, USA
www.TransformationMediaBooks.com

An imprint of Pen & Publish, Inc.
Bloomington, Indiana
(812) 837-9226
info@PenandPublish.com
www.PenandPublish.com

Visit the author at
www.thekeyoflife.net
www.randolphrogers.com

ISBN: 978-0-9823850-9-8

Library of Congress Control Number: 2009936365

This book is printed on acid free paper.

Printed in the USA

In memory of Kathy Lynch,
her spirit lives on forever!

Contents

Preface

Who am I? For most of my life, I never asked that question, so it never haunted me. Sure, I thought about it from time to time, but I didn't make it my life's passion to find an answer. That is, until now.

My upbringing may have had something to do with me suppressing the question of who I am. It's amazing what happens to a young person's natural curiosity after years of repression by nuns, priests and parents, threatening eternal damnation for even thinking there may be answers to the mysteries of life other than the traditional orthodox teachings of the Catholic Church. The Catholic Church buries that curiosity by covering it over with so many rules and doctrines that most people never can dig themselves out. I didn't know it at the time, but I was one of those people.

The story of my Catholic upbringing will have to wait for another time however. It would take a separate book, and possibly years of therapy, to open that issue. I will touch on parts of it though. Suffice to say, I'm glad I experienced it now, but at the time I was living it, I felt that going to hell and going to a Catholic grade school were parallel experiences.

I eventually discarded my faith in religion after a divorce from my first wife. Religion had let me down when I needed it the most so what good was it exactly. I quit going to church, but the church and its dogmas hadn't left me. They remained buried under years of guilt and regret, regret that maybe I hadn't done everything I should've to make my personal life turn out just a little bit better.

As I relate the story that follows, I want you to remember one thing. Everything in it is true. No matter how fantastic parts of it may sound, nothing was made up, created, enhanced or altered to make the story better. I came from a news background, so notes, journals and recordings were kept as this story unfolded in my life. Everything is verifiable by these documents or the parties involved.

Thinking about it now, the events that transpired couldn't have happened to someone with a more skeptical personality. I spent twenty years as a photojournalist, committed to always uncovering the truth and only believing something that was backed up by multiple pieces of information. After all those years of covering the news, I couldn't help but become keenly aware when one event synchronized perfectly with another. It was ingrained into my personality to sit up and take notice the minute I heard or witnessed the same information presented by two different sources. This story begins exactly that way, with the subtle awareness that my feelings and thoughts were meshing just a little too "coincidentally" with events in my life… too coincidentally for even me, with my Catholic background, to accept blindly.

I.

AN AWAKENING

Chapter 1

It was June 23rd, 1995. I'm sure of the date as I've gone back over my calendar and phone records to verify *everything*. At the time the date meant nothing to me, just another day like any other. The only difference was that my wife Susan and I had just completed construction of a new home with a separate office building out back, above the garage. We lived on a bluff in Westchester that gave us a great view over Marina del Rey, Santa Monica Bay and the entire West Los Angeles basin.

I remember it being a cool, clear day heading into evening. The foggy marine layer usually present that time of year was gone and I could see all the way along the coast to Malibu. I stood up from my desk, walked over to the window and lifted up on the lower pane, cracking it open a few inches to let the soft ocean breeze spill in.

Susan was over in the house unpacking, and still fuming from an argument we had an hour earlier. When she got like this I found it was best to just leave her alone so I had retreated to the safety and solitude of my office space, her words still ringing in my head.

"I don't know why I ever let you talk me into building a new house in this white trash neighborhood with these white trash neighbors."

I wondered if she actually meant what she said. She seemed happy when we first moved into the area eight years earlier. I chalked her comments up to the tension and stress of building a new home and all the work of moving into it. Standing there now, gazing out to the mountains off Point Dume, the sting of her remarks dissipated as my mind quickly cleared of everything. I was focused on the sun's brilliant yellow mass as it diffused into a soft orange glow slipping quickly towards the horizon.

I don't know where my next thought came from. It was just there, out of nowhere – the memory of a girl I'd known in grade school. Her name was Kathy Lynch, and what I was thinking was so disturbing I tried to push my thoughts of her out of my mind. But it came back again, stronger and through my inner voice, telling me Kathy had passed away. Kathy was dead. I felt it… I knew it!

A feeling of immense sadness washed over me quickly and with such force that my body shuddered, causing my knees to buckle, snapping me out of my daydream. I quickly grabbed onto the window sill to regain my balance. Looking out again, the sun had vanished and my haunting thoughts echoed the loss through my own emotions as well. Kathy was gone…forever!

I sat back down in my chair, trying to understand what had just happened and hoping to shake this feeling of losing my friend.

Why am I thinking this? I'll just make it go away. I won't think this thought anymore. I tried once again to shove the idea out of my mind.

If she's not dead, then what happened to her?

Who keeps asking these questions I hear bouncing around loudly in my head? It's as though Kathy herself was prodding me for the answers. The thought to ask my mother about Kathy the next time I talked with her crossed my mind.

No, you have got to call your mother now!

My inner voice had begun taking over, demanding action tonight. I had always lived by that inner voice, my conscience; something my parents had always told me would be there to guide me through life. It had never failed me before through my career as a photojournalist. Listening to it often gave me the extra edge of being in the right place at just the right time to get the perfect shot.

I looked down at my watch. It was eight minutes after eleven in Pennsylvania. I started to hesitate, but then picked up the phone and dialed my parents' number.

"Hi Mom, it's Randy." I always identified myself when I called even though my mother could usually detect the subtle voice differences between me and my brothers' Jeff and Tom.

"Oh, hi Randy. Bob, pickup the other phone it's Randy." My mother called out for my dad.

"How's the new house going? Are you finished moving in?" My dad was now on the line.

"Everything's in, and we've made good progress of getting it put into place but it feels like a never ending job."

"How many moves does this make for you now? Have you kept count?" My mom laughed as she brought up the subject.

"It's an even dozen now Mom, but I'll never catch up to Jeff." We all chuckled. My brother Jeff definitely held the record for a life in constant transition.

"How do the kids like it?" My dad was asking about Dana and Phil, Susan's two children from her previous marriage.

"They love having their own bathrooms. I guess I won't be hearing Phil arguing with Dana about that anymore."

"And how's Susan holding up with all the turmoil?" Mom asked.

I paused for the briefest of time but enough to drive home my next statement. "She's over in the house and I'm in my office, trying to stay out of her way. It's a little tense and that's all I'm going to say on the subject." They both laughed and didn't push me any further about Susan.

All the time I was talking to my parents, my inner thoughts kept bubbling to the surface, pressuring me from the background to get creative, change directions and work my questions about Kathy into the conversation. I finally got my chance when I brought up the topic of an old friend of mine from high school.

"I talked to Dave Lang the other day. He's still working down in Wallops Island with the rocket launches," I said. "He's the only guy from high school that I still talk to anymore."

"You two did spend a lot of time together hunting and fishing back then," my mom said.

"I used to stay in touch with Kathy Lynch too, but her Christmas cards stopped coming a while back. I always wondered how she's doing. You wouldn't happen to know anyone to call who might know where she is, would you?"

"They moved down to Florida years ago, Randy. But I could ask Rita Sheehan – she was Caroline's best friend when they lived up here. She may know where they are now. I'll mention it to her the next time I see her." Caroline was Kathy's mother. My mom and Caroline were friends but never stayed in touch after the Lynch family moved.

I wanted to say more. I wanted to ask my mother to make sure to call Rita tomorrow and find out for me but I didn't. I didn't want to bring on a lot of questions from my mom asking why I was so interested in finding Kathy right now. I didn't have an answer for her that made sense, just my feelings and I wasn't ready to reveal those feelings to anyone. I just moved on to the next subject and hoped my mom would see Rita Sheehan in the near future. The funny thing was the constant demand from my inner voice to find Kathy now subsided. Events were in motion that I hoped would eventually lead me to an answer to all these thoughts of her passing away.

♋ ♋ ♋

Within a few weeks I had all but given up on my mother coming through with any information. I did continue to ask, but at the same time turned my attention to a different kind of search. The Internet was still in its infancy when I hooked up my computer to it in August 1995 and began spending countless hours late at night searching for Kathy. I had a feeling she was listed somewhere out on that vast web, but finding out where was going to be another problem. I never gave up hope that Kathy was still alive, yet couldn't bring myself to tell anyone that I had fears she wasn't.

The hardest part of all was keeping my feelings to myself. I'm usually a very open person with most people, but what I was dealing with had me confused, unsettled and driven to find an answer I thought might lie deep within feelings for Kathy that I had buried a long time ago. I couldn't tell a soul, especially my wife Susan who I knew would never understand the connection I had to this girl.

Also high on my list of fears was the fear of being wrong. I may have been living in California now, but my personal character and values were molded in a totally different environment. Having thoughts and feelings about someone passing away was new to me. Was I losing my mind? What kind of person has these kinds of thoughts? As I sat in my office night after night repeatedly typing her name into various search engines, I was beginning to wonder about my sanity myself.

♋ ♋ ♋

Kathy and I met in the early '60s. My family had just moved out to the "country" from the city of Johnstown in western

Pennsylvania, famous for its great flood of 1889. More than 2,200 people perished when the South Fork Dam on the Conemaugh River collapsed during torrential rains on the morning of May 31st, 1889.

Western Pennsylvania was a region rich with a mix of Eastern European immigrants working hard in the steel and mining industries that dominated the landscape. Great clouds of red smoke billowed daily from the dozens of stacks scattered around the town. These steel and coal mining industries made industrialists, like the Forbes, Carnegies and Mellons, the richest people in America.

These same industrialists owned a secluded sportsman's lodge near the South Fork Dam where they spent weekends hunting and fishing. Engineers had been warning them that a height modification they had added to the breast of the dam would dangerously stress the structure if the water level continued to build up behind it. Instead of removing it, the club ignored their warnings and gambled that the dam would never reach that level. It was a gamble they were destined to lose.

A severe storm centered over the Johnstown area in late May of 1889 and refused to move. It unleashed a downpour that filled the dam to the brim. The structure failed, just as the engineers had predicted and the resulting flood forever changed the landscape and the character of Johnstown, Pennsylvania, which was now host to the greatest "natural" disaster ever to strike this country.

Even with all the death and destruction caused by the flood, many good things occurred. The American Red Cross started service at the Johnstown Flood; Clara Barton herself was present to help in the recovery, and most importantly, the local people became determined to rise above the situation and work together to rebuild the area.

The character, history and work ethic of the region was ingrained in me from my earliest memories. We had Polish, Slovak, Serbian, Hungarian and other European heritage in our backgrounds. Like our ancestors who settled the area, many of us came from large families. Our fathers all worked in the steel mills or the coal mines, and if we didn't do something with our lives, so would we. I imagine breaking this trend was one catalyst prompting my parents to send all five of their children to a private Catholic school. That's what happened when we moved from renting a house in the city to building our own place in the country. One day we were in normal public school classrooms, just like everyone else, and the next day we were in parochial school. The differences were startling for me, my two brothers and two sisters.

It was the fall of 1961, I was 8 years old and starting third grade at Sacred Heart School in Conemaugh, Pennsylvania. Sacred Heart's pastor was Father Kelly, a very large, no-nonsense Catholic priest of Irish heritage. His mere presence caused a nervous quaking among the students that never really settled down until he was out of sight again. The sisters who taught grade school ran the gamut from loving, caring souls everyone wanted to be near, to what I can only describe now as Marine drill instructors disguised as nuns.

Going to school everyday was a conditioning exercise for me and my younger siblings. I was the oldest and had to set an example but no matter how hard I tried, my efforts were just not going to be good enough in ways I'd never foresee. As Sister Josita paced up and down the rows of desks, I would quiver in my seat, my head bent over, braced for a slap to the back of it or a hard tug on my ear. A sharp, unexpected, crack across the knuckles with her steel ruler was another attention getter. She liked to mix them up, keep you off guard so you couldn't protect yourself. If you were unlucky enough to catch her full wrath, you could expect it flying violently from all directions.

It was in this setting of strict discipline, fear of damnation for impure thoughts and general loathing of nuns and priests in general that I met Kathy Lynch. I remember the moment I first laid eyes on her, standing on the playground among a group of her friends. They all looked the same dressed in their green and white uniforms and giggling among themselves, but Kathy stood out above the rest. Her light brown hair was parted down the middle, long and straight with a slight curl up at the ends where it fell just below her shoulders. Kathy's neck was long and slender matching her slim body with its long arms and legs.

I was standing there, attracted like a magnet to steel, when one of her girlfriends whispered something in Kathy's ear. She immediately looked up to catch me staring in her direction. It was

Kathy's sparkling, steel blue eyes that captured me that morning and though she looked away, feigning shyness, a connection had been made. She looked up again and this time our eyes lock together and in that brief moment, volumes were said. Her spirit emanated from a place very close to mine, radiating an instant association through those eyes, and pulling on my heart. I can only describe my initial feelings for Kathy as pure love.

We were only 8 years old, but my feelings of love and a bond to Kathy never left me. By the time I reached 7th grade at Sacred Heart, my parents had finally heard enough complaining from the five of us kids about the excessive physical abuse and humiliation by the nuns. We were all taken out of Sacred Heart and put back into the Conemaugh Valley public schools.

Kathy finished grade school at Sacred Heart and then went off to Bishop McCort High. She had four siblings as well, one brother and three sisters. Kathy was the youngest. I never knew any of them at the time. They were all much older than Kathy and gone from their parents' home. In that respect, Kathy was an only child growing up. That was the image that played in my mind when I thought of her. I held my love for Kathy close to my heart, and viewed myself as her protector, a guardian she might need someday. One thing I knew, nothing would ever happen to her while I was around to do something about it.

I never dated Kathy – never even kissed her – but I had this feeling of responsibility for her well-being that stayed with me as we grew up. One day after we graduated from high school, I heard she was in a hospital in Pittsburgh with Hodgkin's disease. It was the fall of 1972 and I had been working as a news cinematographer at WJAC-TV in Johnstown since my graduation from high school in 1971. As soon as I heard Kathy was sick, I took my first day off work and drove the eighty miles over to Pittsburgh to visit her.

"You've got the entire congregation praying for you now, thanks to Father Kelly," I said jokingly as I walked into her hospital room. "He made a special request to pray for your speedy recovery during his sermon last Sunday but I thought a personal visit might work better." Kathy's face lit up when she saw me enter the room.

"I know it will definitely help," she replied. Kathy looked tired from all the blood tests and injections she had been receiving.

Hodgkin's disease is a cancer of the lymphatic system that causes your cells to grow abnormally, weakening your immune system and if left unchecked, spreading to other parts of your body. Kathy's initial symptoms were mistaken for the flu, but combined with a sudden loss of weight and then swelling in her lymph nodes, the diagnosis was finally made. Treatment back then was with radiation.

"I can see the prayers are working already – you don't look sick to me," I replied, smiling back at her.

"I've felt better, that's for sure," Kathy answered in a soft, sedated voice. Kathy's mom was in the room with her when I arrived and took the opportunity to go out for a break while I visited with Kathy. There was only one IV bottle hanging above her bed with the line running into a needle in Kathy's arm. Kathy had just begun her radiation treatments, so the full effect hadn't yet shown in her face although she was noticeably thinner than normal.

"I know you have a battle ahead of you but you'll be out of here before you know it. Everything will be fine after that." I could see a good spark of energy still burning in Kathy. She was young and ready to fight this disease, and all she needed was some encouragement and support from everyone around her. I told her I was working as a photographer in the television news business now and relayed a few short stories about the news I had been covering lately. I finished up by telling her about my latest love.

"I just got a '69 Javelin that I'm dying to give you a ride in when you get out."

"I'd really like to do that," Kathy replied. Her voice was upbeat now and I could feel my visit having the desired effect of giving her the energy to carry on.

"I promise I'll call as soon as you're back home and feeling up to it."

"I'm looking forward to it," she said.

I didn't realize it but I had been holding her hand the whole time I was talking to her and now it was time to let go. We both seemed to notice it at the same time and as I pulled my hand back she gripped it one last squeeze reaffirming to me that she would soon be back to normal.

Chapter 2

It was January of 1973, after a heavy snowfall, that I picked Kathy up at her home and took her with me to the Blue Knob ski area to shoot some weather footage for the news that night on WJAC-TV. Her hair was gone from all the radiation treatments and she was wearing a wig, but Kathy was full of life and anxious to enjoy a day out in the weather.

"There ought to be a lot of snow up on Blue Knob today, look at those clouds." Kathy pointed out the front window at the remnants of last night's storm ahead of us as we drove over the back country roads east of Johnstown. We were headed to the highest ski area in Pennsylvania nestled among the peaks of the Allegheny Mountains in Bedford County.

"Yeah, I was a little worried the roads might not be opened but they seem okay so far," I replied. The highways had been cleared by the plows but many were still snow covered where the salt trucks hadn't made it.

Kathy and I drove along enjoying the scenery of a pristine winter wonderland. Stands of hemlock and pine, leaden with snow, created a tunnel effect through the forest that would suddenly break out into a rolling meadow, free of any human tracks and glistening like a field of diamonds in the mid-morning sun.

At the ski resort, Kathy seemed pensive. I remember watching her as she leaned against the railing on the viewing platform, bundled up with layers of undergarments, a heavy coat, warm mittens and a tousle cap. I turned my camera lens towards her to get a cutaway shot from the action on the slope. The steam from her breath was barely noticeable compared to other people around her. She was conserving her energy and just trying to stay warm. I hit the button on my Bell & Howell and as the film started to crank through the camera, a broad smile broke across Kathy's face. She had just won the battle of her life and it was time to enjoy it.

The Hodgkin's disease had really beaten Kathy down, but her doctor said it was in remission. Kathy's immune system however was far from recovered so I didn't want to keep her out in the cold too long. The last thing her mother had warned her was not to overdo it. I wrapped up my shooting quickly and got Kathy back into the car.

"That cold really took it out of me," she said warming her hands in the hot air blowing from the heater.

"It was freezing, that's for sure. I didn't want to stay out there any longer myself. I'm just happy the film didn't break." She laughed and I was glad to see I hadn't completely worn her out. "I have to get this into the lab anyway and you look like you've had enough for one day."

"I'm definitely ready to go home," Kathy said.

That was the last time I can ever remember seeing Kathy Lynch. That image of her sitting next to me in the Javelin as I drove back out of the mountains is all I can recall when I search my mind and think about her now.

Funny thing about my relationship with Kathy, the greatest thing I cared about was her well being. It was so strong of a love that it somehow transcended the romantic part altogether. Sure I would've kissed her if the situation would've presented itself, that day or any other day, but our lives passed by each other, so close but somehow just out of reach. Being with her that day and thinking she was going to be okay was somehow all I needed to move forward with my life.

Back at my job at WJAC-TV, the photo staff had been receiving letters from Bob Barndt, a friend and former co-worker of ours who had moved to Phoenix recently and opened up a camera shop. Bob's reports about the warm Southwest winters sounded like paradise to a nineteen year old guy who had just spent a frigid night at the TV station with most of the crew. We were stranded there because we couldn't find or move our cars buried under the yards of snow.

♋ ♋ ♋

In May of 1973, I put a hitch on my Javelin and packed up a rental trailer with my worldly possessions. These consisted of my clothes, a guitar, an amplifier, my recently purchased 1972 Yamaha 350 Enduro motorcycle, and several boxes of things my mother knew I'd need to survive on my own. I was off to Phoenix, Arizona, looking for a fresh start, away from my family for the very first time.

An Awakening

Within three months of getting settled in Phoenix, I managed to pick up a job working at KPHO-TV in their commercial production department, processing the station's news and commercial film and shooting various promotional projects. I wanted to get back into the newsroom as soon as they had an opening but for now I had my foot in the door. I hadn't been in Phoenix eights months when I went through the first of several life altering events.

On January 11th 1974, I was on my way home from work at the television station. It was Friday night, shortly after 9 p.m. I was riding my motorcycle east on Thomas Road, passing in front of the Phoenix College campus when a guy decided to turn left directly in front of me. I had no warning and no time to react. My bike crashed into his right rear quarter panel, stopping instantly and launching me off the seat. Everything went into slow motion. I was floating peacefully along, out of my body and thinking, *so this is what it's like to be dead*...when suddenly, the violent impact of landing back onto the pavement, knocked the wind out of me, jolting me back into my body and the realization I wasn't dead. Sliding and bouncing my way down the roadway, my helmet dragged along the asphalt, grinding huge gashes into the surface where my head would've been without it, I finally came to rest lying in the gutter, thirty-five feet from my crumpled motorcycle.

The accident happened in full view of dozens of college students. They rushed across the street to check on me. I was still conscious but couldn't see my right foot when I looked down to where it should've been.

"Is my foot ripped off?" I asked the first person that came up beside me.

"No, it's still there but your shoe is gone and your ankle is pretty messed up. Just lie there and don't try to move until we can get an ambulance."

My hip was killing me and my right leg seemed tangled under my body and over where my left leg should be. I didn't know it but I had broken my hip and everything was out of place.

I was rushed by ambulance a few blocks down the street to St. Joseph's Hospital where an orthopedic surgeon would perform the first of multiple surgeries on my right ankle and hip. I had lost a lot of blood and the last thing I remember before being given a pain killer that knocked me out was having an argument with the hospital staff.

"Can you give me your parents' phone number so we can call them and let them know what has happened?" An emergency room physician was looking directly over me waiting for the number.

"They live in Pennsylvania. It's late back there, I'll call them in the morning," was my reply.

"I think it's best if we call them now, you're in serious condition and I think they would want to know," he replied.

"I don't want to wake them up and have them worrying all night. Can't I just call them in the morning?"

"You may not be here in the morning to make that call." His sober response drove home the seriousness of my injuries. I begged him to give me some kind of shot to take away the pain and put me to sleep but he held off waiting for the number. I finally relented and gave it to him.

It was 2 a.m. in Johnstown when my parents got the call informing them I was going into emergency surgery immediately. I didn't know it, but my life was heading down another new path.

One of the people taking care of me in the hospital was Judy Myrick, a young nurse's aid. I spent three weeks at St. Joseph's and got to know her well enough to ask her out a few months later when I had recovered. She and I dated solidly for a year and married on June 14th 1975. I continued working at KPHO-TV, moving back into the news department as a cameraman again, while Judy quit her part time job to get a registered nursing degree at Phoenix College. Two years later she was a full fledged RN working in the pediatrics intensive care unit of St. Joseph's Hospital. About a year after getting back into the work force, Judy began to have second thoughts about wanting to be married. She moved out of our house during the summer of 1978 while having an affair with a pilot she had met. I took her back that fall, forgiving her indiscretions and hoping that would be the end of it. Two years later it happened again and we divorced in July of 1980.

♋ ♋ ♋

After the divorce I began questioning my own beliefs in religion, praying and in particular, marriage vows, especially the line "until death do us part." I knew for sure that wasn't true. Years of praying and going to church didn't seem to make any difference when you were dealing in real life situations. I stopped going to church but didn't stop praying. I still felt connected on some level to whatever higher power there was controlling all this.

Kathy Lynch and I had continued to stay in touch yearly with Christmas cards. She and her parents had moved down to Orlando a few years after I left Johnstown. Now my latest card to her was returned as undeliverable. She had moved again and the forwarding address had expired. I didn't feel the need to search Kathy out and burden her with my problems. I thought of her often, but always felt she must have gotten married herself. I knew that I should just move on with my life and let Kathy live hers. That was December of 1980.

In February 1982, I met Susan, a management compensation analyst and divorced mother with two small children. Our meeting was happenstance, I asked her to dance in a country western bar one night after a friend of mine pointed her out to me. She said yes, and at the end of the evening I asked for her number.

Susan was thirty years old when we met and I was twenty-eight. Dana, her daughter, had just turned three and her son Phil was only one and a half. My first date with Susan was really a double date, taking Dana with us to the Phoenix Rodeo. Susan had great kids that were fun to be around and many of our outings included the whole family. I remember watching Phil for her one time while she went out of town on a business trip. She was more than a little nervous about leaving him in my care for the weekend but could also see I was someone she could trust to handle any situation.

Susan was everything I wanted in a woman, energetic, outgoing and could hold her own keeping up with my skiing, scuba diving, hiking, camping and boating. She was five feet eight inches tall on a thin build with medium length brunette hair full of body. She had brown eyes and thin lips with sharp facial features. If you saw us together you would think we were the perfectly matched couple. I felt very comfortable with Susan and her children. Being part of a family was something I was very familiar with and it was easy for me to quickly fall in love with my instant family of Susan, Dana and Phil. Susan and I dated for less than six months and married in July of 1982.

Susan was just the spark I needed to push my life down the right path. We built a new home together in Phoenix, vacationed on our boat at Catalina Island and moved to Los Angeles in 1986 when NBC offered me a job as a network news cameraman out of the Burbank bureau. It was the crowning highlight of my fifteen years in the television news business when I got the call. I now traveled wherever the news was happening on a much wider scope, shooting images that millions of people watched on the NBC Nightly News and Today Show. I covered Dick Rutan and Jeana Yeager's quest to become the first pilots to circumnavigate the earth non-stop and without re-fueling in their aircraft the Voyager. I climbed Mt. Whitney with ninety year old Hulda Crooks, documenting her accent as she became the oldest person to climb the mountain. On March 24th, 1989 I was one of several crews sent on assignment to Alaska for the Exxon Valdez oil spill. Later that year I was dispatched to another disaster, the earthquake in San Francisco on October 17th.

It was an exciting life in its heyday, carrying a suitcase of clothing with you at all times, ready to leave for anywhere in the world at a moment's notice, but by the end of the '80s I could see it was all but over. NBC had been sold to GE and the news business would never be the same again. It was then that I started my own production company and began doing promotional work behind the scenes of many of the major motion pictures coming out of Hollywood in the early '90s.

In 1993 I branched out into what are known as press junkets. Press junkets are publicity interviews with the stars of a movie, set up by the studios to promote the release of their motion picture. I ran the junket venture under my corporation, Telefilm, Inc. supplying the crews, cameras, lighting, sound and set design for the promotion of dozens of major motion pictures every year. I lit and photographed nearly every major star of the day including Clint Eastwood, Tom Cruise, Sylvester Stallone, John Travolta, Tom Hanks and Jim Carrey just to name a few.

An Awakening

♋ ♋ ♋

It had now been a year since my first thoughts of Kathy passing away had swept over me. I was busily engaged with all my promotional work yet discreetly continuing the Internet search for any record of her with no luck at all. As fate would have it, events were about to change for me.

One June morning in 1996 I received a call asking if I would produce a video to be shown at the Fire & Ice Ball in the fall. This ball was held annually to raise funds for breast and ovarian cancer research funded by Revlon. The host of that year's ball was Jane Semel, wife of Terry Semel, Warner Bros. studio chief at the time. The request to do the video had come from producer Joel Silver. The very first junket I had worked on was Demolition Man, a Joel Silver picture starring Sylvester Stallone. It was Joel's movie that gave me my start at Warner Bros. so I immediately signed on for the project. They wanted a short, documentary style video about the latest breakthroughs in breast and ovarian cancer research at the Jonsson Comprehensive Cancer Center at UCLA.

I called Nancy Williams, the best medical writer/producer I knew. Nancy and I had known each other since working together in 1976 at KPNX-TV in Phoenix. She has a shelf full of Emmys and was now living in Los Angeles freelancing for a variety of clients. To say Nancy was extremely excited when I told her about the project would be an understatement – she has an energy about her that is off any Richter Scale. She immediately began to research the project and line up shooting for later that summer.

When the mail arrived one day in late June it contained a letter from the reunion committee for my Conemaugh Valley High School Class of '71. It had been 25 years since I graduated from high school. *If I'm having a reunion then Kathy's class should be having one also,* I thought to myself. Had I finally gotten a break in my quest to find what had happened to her? It didn't take me long to come up with the name of someone who would know when and where their reunion was going to be.

I called Chuck Mamula, a photographer friend of mine who shot almost every reunion in the Johnstown area. It was July 1st 1996.

Chuck had a name and number for the place Bishop McCort High School would be holding their reunion, and through them I found Mary Pat Sheridan, the coordinator. I called her at work and, on my second attempt, got through.

"Mary Pat, this is Randy Rogers, I'm a director out here in Los Angeles." I said, explaining that I grew up in Conemaugh. "I was wondering if you could help me. I understand you're in charge of the reunion party for the class of '71 at McCort and I'd like to get a current address list of your alumni for that class." I explained to her that I was working on a short film about growing up there and would like to talk to some of the kids I had gone to grade school with at Sacred Heart.

"I knew a few of the kids that came from there," she said. "Who are you looking for in particular?"

I decided to cut to the chase. I had gotten nowhere beating around the bush before with my parents. "Well in particular, I'm looking for Kathy Lynch."

"Oh, well, I heard that Kathy passed away over a year ago."

I nearly dropped the phone. It seemed like an eternity until I finally answered her.

"Where? When? What happened?" I asked. A cold chill was sweeping over my body.

"I don't really know," she said. "I can't remember where I heard it and I don't know what she died from. I just remember hearing it."

"Do you happen to know where she was living?" I asked, grasping for any shred of information to help in my search.

"I think somewhere out in California, some town with desert in the name. She got married and changed her name to Winger, I do know that."

"Is there someone else that can help me find out about her? Do you have a list of your alumni you could send me?"

"You can call Charlie Hagins. He's in charge of alumni and could get you a copy, he may even know more about Kathy."

"So you're not even sure she died, just that you heard it from someone and can't remember who?" I asked, surprised.

"Right," she said, "I wish I could tell you more."

I thanked her and got Charlie's phone number to try to find out more about Kathy.

After trying to reach Charlie for several days, I finally spoke with him on July 3rd, but he knew even less than Mary Pat. He was not aware that Kathy had died, which gave me hope that the rumor I was hearing may be just that: a rumor. He did have the alumni list but there wasn't an address for Kathy. Her forwarding order had expired. I asked him to send me the list, thinking I would call everyone on it if necessary to get the information I needed. One of her classmates must know where Kathy was, I just had to figure out which one.

I was having quite a morning. Here it was the day before the 4th of July, 1996. I had been searching for Kathy for a year now and still no solid answers. All I could think about was Kathy's fate; she was possibly gone. I felt that it was true, but I still tried to push the thought away. It could all be a big mistake. After all, it's easy for rumors to get started – at one time people had heard I was dead. I had plenty of them flying around about me during my life. Nevertheless, I decided to keep an open mind.

But who was I fooling? I was the one that felt she had died over a year ago, now I was just denying that feeling. How did I feel this? How did I know this? I know what torment I had gone through the past year, driven to search for the answer and now here it was, staring me in the face and I still didn't want to accept it. My news background was demanding positive proof. Even though I constantly relied on my intuition as a news photographer to be in the right place at the right time, I wouldn't listen to it now. I had to hold on to any last hope that it was all a mistake. I knew I would just have to wait until I received the alumni list. When I did, I would call every person on the list if I had to until I found out what happened to Kathy Lynch. As it turned out, I was not going to have to wait as long as I thought.

II.

A VOICE FROM THE PAST

Chapter 3

I went to bed about 10 p.m. on Friday, July 5th 1996. I was thinking of Kathy as I drifted off to sleep, still hoping it was all a mistake. I was sleeping soundly until around 2 a.m. when I was awakened by a dream; not an ordinary dream by any means. The clarity of it helped me to remember it in remarkable detail.

I'm standing out in the desert – Palm Springs to be exact – in front of a single story, white stucco building with palm trees in front of it. Suddenly, I'm inside this same building, looking out of a window into a landscaped courtyard. As I turned around from my view out the window, I see I'm seated in a wood paneled office, talking with Kathy's husband. He's telling me that Kathy died peacefully in her sleep. Other people begin to appear and collaborate on his story. She didn't suffer at all, they are saying, but none of them can even show me a picture of Kathy when I ask to see one. From the distant background, I can hear Kathy calling out to me.

"No, no, no!" she cried. "Find out what happened to me! Tell all my friends what happened to me – Karen Vickroy, Joan Wojnarowski, Bonnie Mutch, and Lee Ann Vautar. They don't know what has happened. Find out and tell them."

She kept repeating those same names. The last thing I remember her saying was, "Don't forget me! Wake up! Wake up and write this down. You won't remember it if you don't wake up and write this down."

At 2:13 a.m. on July 6th, I found myself downstairs with a pencil and paper writing down the dream I'd just had. I thought I was losing my mind. This was the first time in my life I was writing down a dream, let alone waking up at two in the morning and doing it because someone who might be dead has asked me to.

It's amazing how quickly the details started to fade once I was awake. I jotted down the important parts quickly, the people I saw and the women I should contact. I then took the paper and pencil back upstairs to the bedroom with me and placed it on the nightstand.

Susan was still sound asleep and never even heard me go downstairs. I slipped back under the covers and lay there, looking up at the ceiling. It had been an emotional dream and

I had awakened crying out in my sleep. I relaxed back into the pillows and found myself staring up at the fast-moving ceiling fan overhead. As I watched the mesmerizing motion of the blades blurring past, one after the other, I became aware of a strange lifting sensation. My body remained in the bed as I felt myself start to float upward and pull away from my body. I was clearly not asleep but in a very relaxed state. The relaxed feeling increased as I floated higher and higher until I realized I had no sensation at all of being in the bed. It was incredible. I had drifted completely free of my body and could now look down at myself in the bed next to Susan.

I was hovering over my bed at approximately the height of the ceiling when I sensed the energy of Kathy's presence next to me. I would know her anywhere and there was no mistaking that she was beside me as I floated above the bed. I didn't see her physically, nor could I sense anything physical about her or myself for that matter. I was in some kind of energy state of being, very fluid and free flowing with her spirit spiraling around mine high above the bed. This separation from my body didn't concern me – a feeling of love and warmth was now washing over me in waves.

Kathy began speaking to me immediately, in a rapid flow of thoughts so loud that I felt they would wake my wife for sure. The first thing she said to me was that she was not "dead."

"You never die," she told me. "I see you every night when you fall asleep." Her statement overwhelmed me. I had so many things happening at once, I didn't know what to think.

"I'm surrounding you, Randy, and the whole universe as far as you can imagine," Kathy said. "If you were a sponge in water, I would *be* the water. All life in the universe comes from a spiritual world that surrounds and penetrates us. From the center of the earth with every object and creature on it, to beyond the end of space with every planet and star in the sky, it's all absorbed in that same glass of water – the spiritual world which I'm part of now."

I was so confused I didn't know what to understand. Why was she contacting me? Why was this happening now?

My questions to her went unanswered as she finished by saying, "Just remember this. Feel my spirit, that is what makes us as one."

The warmth and love surrounding me was intense. It felt like every ounce of love I have ever had in me magnified a billion times over, engulfing my very being. Love was my being and it was building like a tornado, drawing me higher and higher. I just wanted to float off forever with her, but I could feel myself gently sinking down into my body again. All the time she kept repeating, "Just remember this. Feel my spirit, that is what makes us as one. Write this down or you won't remember. Feel my spirit that is what makes us as one… Write this down…"

As I returned to my body, I remember talking aloud to her, actually crying out to her. It was an extremely emotional experience and I was sure I woke up Susan with all the talking going on, but when I looked over she was still soundly asleep. I reached over and wrote down Kathy's final words on the same sheet of paper on which I had recorded the dream.

The next morning I woke up and looked over at the paper on my nightstand, wondering if it had really happened. As I read the notes on the page, I remembered everything that had occurred. I was still trying to make sense of it all when Susan woke up.

"Did you hear me talking in my sleep last night?" was the first thing I asked her.

"No, I didn't hear anything. Why, were you having trouble sleeping?" she replied.

"I just got up once and couldn't get back to sleep. I thought maybe I woke you up getting in and out of bed."

"No, you must have been pretty quiet about it because I never heard you." Susan's last reply trailed off as she went down the stairs for breakfast. I walked into the bathroom to shave.

Looking into the mirror I saw a different person looking back at me. My reflection was the same but I could sense an inner presence now, my true spirit, something indestructible and more powerful than my physical body. Last night had certainly changed me, in ways I never could've imagined. Suddenly I was not afraid of dying and I now knew for certain that Kathy was reaching out to me from beyond this physical world. I had more questions than ever that needed answers quickly. I headed over to my office to think about what to do next.

Debating my options for most of the day, I finally decided to tell someone what was happening to me. That "someone" was going to have to be my parents, for several important reasons. The first being they were the only people I knew I could tell that would believe me without question. The second reason was that my mother would now know why I had asked about Kathy for so long, and help me find someone who knew where she was. I thought about telling Susan but knew that would only bring more questions at a time when I had no answers besides there was nothing she could do to help me find Kathy anyway. I decided to wait and see how my parents reacted to the news first. Something would tell me when the time was right to share it with Susan.

The dream had an energizing effect on me. I never experienced anything so intense in all my life. The feelings of the previous evening's meeting, with Kathy asking me not to forget her, were playing strongly in my head. I picked up the phone and dialed my parents. When my mother answered, I got straight to the point of my call.

"Mom, you know how I've been asking you to find out what ever happened to Kathy Lynch?"

"Well now that you mention it, you have asked me about her quite a few times," she replied.

"There's a reason I've been asking you," I said. "I've been having premonitions that she passed away for over a year now and a few days ago I finally spoke with an old classmate of hers. She told me she had heard Kathy died over a year ago. She didn't have any details, though, and couldn't even remember who told her. Then last night I had this intense dream where Kathy came to me and told me all the secrets of what life is about." I was sure I sounded completely off the deep end. My mom, however, listened patiently to the rest of my story and then I made another request to find Kathy's relatives.

"I'll start making some phone calls and see what I can find out for you. This may take awhile. They've been gone a long time."

"Thanks Mom, I'm sailing over to Catalina tomorrow and staying for my birthday. If you find out anything just leave a message. The machine will be on or Phil should be home. He has to stay here and work at the bagel shop all week."

"Have a happy birthday Randy and I'll call you as soon as I hear anything." My mom and I finished up our call and then I sat back in my office chair, looking out the window and wondering how long this new search would take.

I considered the possibility that my dream and out of body experience the previous night was the result of hidden feelings that had built up during my search for Kathy. Now that I was nearing an answer, had my subconscious mind created this early-morning meeting of our spirits? That was a possibility, but if my inner mind was looking to soothe a feeling of loss, why didn't my dream play out that Kathy died peacefully in her sleep and leave it at that? Why was she calling from the background, pleading for me to find out what happened, not to forget about her and tell all her friends? Why continue with the out of body experience after I had written down the dream?

I was increasingly certain what was happening was real, not my imagination. Being with Kathy last night was not something I could make up in my mind. It was a true feeling that I experienced. During our short time together, every ounce of Kathy's energy, love, and emotion poured into my very soul. She gave me a slight glimpse and understanding of how the world works and who we really are when you take away the body. She cared enough to come to me after all these years and I was not going to let her down now. I had to know the complete story of what happened to Kathy Lynch.

♋ ♋ ♋

As I sailed off for Catalina Island the next day, I felt I would finally have some closure on my search. The end was near, or so I thought. In reality, what lay ahead was a quest that would take me to the beginning of time itself.

Susan, Dana and her high school friend Diva Zappa were along on the sail. It was a beautiful Southern California day with a moderate breeze moving us along at seven knots, nearly hull speed. The ocean was calm, no swells and light wave chop, making a very pleasant haul to the island. About midway across the channel Dana and Diva went to the forward deck to lie down and sunbathe. Susan and I were alone in the cockpit so I decided to take a chance, throw caution to the wind, and tell her everything I had been experiencing.

"I've been having some interesting dreams lately." I started off the conversation with a statement I felt anyone could relate to as everyone had dreams.

"Oh really, what kind of dreams have they been?" The dialog was opened now so I jumped right in.

"They're a little more than just dreams. They started out more as a premonition about a girl I knew back in Catholic grade school. Her name is Kathy Lynch and the last time I saw her was 23 years ago." I let the first bit of information sink in waiting for a response.

"What kind of premonitions were they?" Susan asked.

"I felt she had passed away. I don't know what exactly happened to her, but I've had these feelings for a year now, and then last Friday night she came to me in this dream asking me to find out what happened to her. I got up and wrote down the dream, and then when I got back in bed I had some kind of an out of body experience where she told me what life is really about."

"Wow, is that what you were talking about when you said you couldn't sleep?"

"Yeah, it was like she was reaching out to me now and I couldn't just ignore her. I called my mother to see if she can find any of Kathy's relatives."

Susan wanted more details so I told her everything I had learned in my search for Kathy. Her reaction was about what I expected.

"I'm sure it's just some kind of coincidence all this has been happening," was all she said.

"I think it's more than that. There has to be a reason she's contacted me and I want to find out why."

"Well I don't see the purpose of you pursuing it any further." Those were Susan's final words on the subject.

Sensing Susan's negativity on the subject, I felt the less said the better and dropped the topic - at least for now.

Chapter 4

My 43rd birthday on Catalina Island was a low-key affair. Susan, Dana and Diva sang happy birthday to me on board our boat that afternoon as I blew out the single candle on a small cake. Susan had clipped out my horoscope from the newspaper and put it into a birthday card for me. It was a simple gift with a prophetic message: *What appeared long ago and far away will be practically at your doorstep. Focus on spirituality, publishing, journey that leads to soul mate.* I made a mental note to start keeping a record of events from that point forward.

After spending my birthday on the island, we sailed back to Los Angeles. No word had come from my mother yet so I went to work trying to contact the few people Kathy had mentioned in the dream. The alumni list arrived while I was gone and I looked it over. I found the women Kathy had mentioned during my out of body experience, and two were listed with phone numbers. The first one I was able to reach was Bonnie Mutch.

"Hello, Bonnie, this is an old classmate of yours from Sacred Heart – Randy Rogers." There was a long pause as she searched her memory.

"I can't seem to remember you," Bonnie replied, making what I had to say next even harder.

"Well, I did go to school with you at Sacred Heart, but what I'm calling about is Kathy Lynch. You do remember her?"

"Of course I remember Kathy," she replied.

"I'm calling to see if you've stayed in contact with her, or know where she is now."

"No, I haven't spoken to her since we graduated."

"I'm trying to find out what became of her. I'm having visits from Kathy in my dreams. She's asking me to find out what happened to her and to tell some of her friends. I feel she has passed away but I haven't found anyone that knows what happened."

There was another long pause as Bonnie absorbed everything I was telling her.

"I can't really help you. I don't even know anyone you could contact who might know where she is." Bonnie apologized, asking me to let her know if I discovered anything. I promised her I would call the minute I knew something.

My conversation with Bonnie did confirm part of my dream was correct. So far, one of the women Kathy asked me to contact didn't known what had happened to Kathy; of course neither did I. I moved on to the next name I had written down from my dream.

Joan Wojnarowski remembered me very well when I finally reached her on July 16th. She was shocked to hear Kathy may have passed away. She had also lost touch with her after high school. I realized I was probably sounding like a complete lunatic to these people, calling unexpectedly after 30 years, relating stories of premonitions and dreams. They had to have been thinking, "This person's been living in California way too long." A driving force that I felt was coming from Kathy kept me pushing for an answer, and now I had two people she named that didn't know what had happened to her. So far, at least that part of my dream was correct.

I was trying more numbers from the alumni list to no avail, planning for my own class reunion and doing my promotional work all at the same time. Something had to slip through the cracks and on July 18th I realized my wife's birthday was the next day and I hadn't shopped for her at all. Since we just moved into our new home a year ago, we both had agreed any gifts for each other would be something we could use in the house. That evening I drove up to Santa Monica to search for Susan's gift. I pictured finding some cobalt blue vases to match the drinking glasses she recently purchased. I figured a few pretty vases and maybe some candles would make a nice, simple gift this year. I got to Main Street in Santa Monica and couldn't find a place to park near any of the shops I wanted to look in. After two trips up and down the street, I ended up parking at the very south end of town and walking.

After not finding a single thing I had in mind, I started back. I was ready to cross the street to my car when I felt my inner voice tell me what I wanted was just a little farther down the street in front of me. I looked down Main Street and could see some light spilling onto the sidewalk from the open door of a shop a few hundred feet ahead of me and just about directly across from my car. I didn't think I would be interested in any shops down there but decided to look anyway.

As I approached the open doorway, I looked up at the sign, *Psychic Eye Book Shop*. I thought, "There's nothing in here that I need," so I walked a few feet farther to another window with a full display. A wind chime made up of brass suns caught my eye. All I had ever bought for Susan since we married were sun images of one sort or another. Not only were they her favorite, but they also attracted me. Whenever I spotted something with a sun that she might like, I brought it home for her.

I walked into the store and realized it was a second entrance to the psychic shop I had passed a moment ago. The first entrance was for the reading rooms and book section. This one was for all kinds of items, from incense to crystals. I went down an aisle and promptly found the blue vases, exactly as I had pictured. I gathered up a few and some candles to go with them. Since I was there, I decided to look around to see what else they had. Strolling among the aisles, I soon came upon a long, single bookshelf labeled *Dreams*. A large red cover next to a muted grey one blurred together as I quickly ran my hand across them, even pulling a blue-jacketed one out to look at. It didn't interest me, none of them did. I gathered up my vases and headed for the cashier.

As I walked up to the checkout counter, my inner voice was saying: *You didn't get what you came in here for. Go back to those books again.* I turned around and went back to the shelf. This time, as I scanned across the row of titles, one book in the very center jumped out at me. I would've sworn it wasn't there the first time I looked through them but there it was now, standing out like a sore thumb, *Dreams and Premonitions*. The author's name at the very top of the spine really stood out, *Rogers*. "That's the same as my name," I thought as I reached for the book.

It was a thin book and upon initial inspection appeared to be very old. I could see from the copyright page it was a 1992 re-print of a much older book. It had a yellow cover with a lithograph on the front. The title, *Dreams and Premonitions*, was above the artwork printed in simple Roman style type. The drawing depicted a young woman, all clothed in white, clinging to a white steed flying up into the heavens. Her long, flowing hair was streaming in the wind as a coven of faceless spirits, dressed in black robes, hovered about her. Beneath the picture on the cover it simply said *by L.W. Rogers*. The publisher listed on the inside was Sun Books, Sun Publishing. I flipped it over and saw it was just $12 so I added it to my other purchases. I left the book in the bag when I got home and wrapped up the other gifts for Susan's birthday.

The next day we had a little celebration and I presented her with the gifts. She loved the blue glasswork and put the pieces up on the mantle above our fireplace. As she was picking up the wrappings, she grabbed the bag from the store to use for the trash. Before I could stop her, she had the book in her hand.

"Oh, are you going to try and interpret your dreams now?" Susan teased me as she made the connection to my purchase.

"It just kind of jumped out at me so I had to buy it," I replied. "Look at the name of the author. We have the same last name, even spelled the same."

That bit of information was just more coincidence to her. She couldn't see what I noticed. Things were starting to happen just a little too frequently for it all to be a coincidence. Besides, she had no idea what was going on in my head. It wasn't that I was hearing voices, but I felt someone or something was definitely guiding me. I took the book from her and put it on my nightstand to read later.

In bed a few hours later, we both started reading. Susan was wrapped up in a magazine on home decorating tips and I was examining *Dreams and Premonitions*. The book had nine chapters and in the preface said its chief purpose was '*to present a reasonable explanation of the phenomena of dreams and premonitions*' and '*to present a large number of authenticated cases for study*'. I noticed the language seemed very old fashioned. I didn't pay much attention until I got about a dozen pages into the first chapter.

I immediately sat upright and shouted, "This is what she told me! This is exactly what Kathy told me in the dream! Listen to this: '*As a ball of fibrous matter might be immersed in liquid matter, saturated with it and completely surrounded by it, so the physical globe is interpenetrated and enveloped by the matter of the astral world. The astral world then, is not remote but is here in the midst of us, about us, through us and beyond us.*' 'Like a sponge in water, she would be the water,' that's what she told me!"

I read further, becoming quite loud in my excitement as more information matched what Kathy had given me.

"He says that sleep and death are the only times we enter this astral world. Kathy said she sees me every night when I sleep and she's there now because she has passed on!"

"Calm down, calm down. I'm sure it's just a coincidence. Don't get so excited about it." Susan was not sharing in my enthusiasm.

"You don't know what is going on in my head," I said. "This is no coincidence. I know things contained in this book because I heard the same explanation from Kathy two weeks ago. How can this possibly be happening? When was this written?" I fumbled through the front of the book looking for the date. "Copyrighted 1923!"

The feelings rushing through me kept my mind racing. Kathy had given me the same information L.W. Rogers believed and wrote about back in 1923! Why and how could I be directed to find this book now? I became quite agitated as I struggled to understand exactly what was happening to me. Whatever it was, I was sure finding out what happened to Kathy would help answer many of my questions.

Chapter 5

On July 26th 1996, my sister Diane came out to Los Angeles for a visit. She and her thirteen year old son William were going to sail over to Catalina Island with us for a few days of rest and relaxation. Diane was in the Navy stationed down in Key West. Her husband had passed away when William was very young and Diane managed to raise him alone, while continuing to rise through the ranks to become a senior chief.

I didn't fill Diane in on what was happening with me. I still wanted to have proof that what I had been saying was true. I wasn't even thinking about the consequences if this all proved a mistake. For one thing, I would have to call several women and apologize for upsetting them about Kathy. I was trying to relax and enjoy myself on Catalina while back in Pennsylvania my mother was continuing to look for Kathy's relatives.

The answers to my search for Kathy Lynch came while I was still over on Catalina Island. We had taken our dinghy into the island early on the morning of July 31st for a quick breakfast at Doug's Harbor Reef Restaurant at the Isthmus. We then planned to pack up and return to Los Angeles. When I called home to check for any messages, our son Phil told me that my mother called from Pennsylvania with some information for me. With my heart in my throat, I thanked him for the message and placed a second call back to Pennsylvania from the pay phones at the Isthmus. Cell phone service hadn't reached this part of Catalina Island yet.

When my mother answered I said, "I got a message that you had some information, what did you find out?"

"Randy, I just want to let you know that I did find Kathy's sister near Pittsburgh. Her name is Sister Carleen and she's a nun at a convent in Baden. I told her you were interested in getting in touch with Kathy and would like to know where she was now. Sister Carleen told me that she was very sorry to tell me, but Kathy passed away over a year ago from ovarian cancer."

As I heard the words coming across the phone line, it was as if an electrical charge jolted through my body. All my senses began tingling as Kathy's message came screaming out to me.

"See why I wanted you to find out? Can you see the connection now?" Kathy's voice echoed in my head.

"Oh my God, that's what I'm working on right now! I'm producing a video to raise money for breast and ovarian cancer research at UCLA."

My mind raced as the words left my mouth, trying to grab onto any idea how this could all be occurring around my initial thought of Kathy passing away. As I opened my mind, Kathy's thoughts came, telling me she's been calling out to me all along. I didn't tell my mother that Kathy was talking to me. Right now, even as I was on the phone, I had no doubt her thoughts were blending into mine. I clearly recognized the inflections of Kathy's voice. Her thoughts were my thoughts. It was as if she was right inside of me. For all I knew she had been, since the day I first felt she passed away.

"Kathy was in a hospice out in Palm Springs when she passed away," my mother added.

"Mom, that's where my dream took place," I said. "I was in a building in Palm Springs. I don't know how I knew it was Palm Springs but I just knew that's where I was."

"Well, I told Sister Carleen that you have been having dreams about Kathy and she said she would talk with you when you come home for your class reunion, if you'd like."

She gave me the number to the convent so I could set up a meeting. I thanked her for finding Kathy's sister and told her I would talk to Sister Carleen when I returned to Los Angeles. I hung up the phone, stunned by the information I had just received.

When I relayed the news to Susan a few minutes later she took it as just another coincidence. I was really starting to become annoyed that she couldn't see the puzzle starting to assemble in front of me.

I didn't know what the final picture would look like, but I did know that I had to follow up with a visit to Sister Carleen. My questions for Sister Carleen were about what Kathy had gone through right up to the end. What was it making her contact me now? If I could just have those answers, then maybe I could rest. In truth, my search for Kathy had now become an obsession. The more I learned, the more I wanted to know. I didn't realize that

I had barely scratched the surface. The rest of the answers I was searching for were buried in the past, deep in the past. I had no idea my digging was just beginning.

♋ ♋ ♋

We sailed back to Los Angeles later that morning and the next day gave Diane and William a whirlwind tour of the usual Southern California tourist sites. Venice Beach, Grauman's Chinese Theatre, Hollywood Boulevard, Beverly Hills, we hit all the ones they wanted to see before taking them to LAX on August 2nd for their trip back to Key West.

August 2nd was also the day we started shooting the video for the Fire & Ice Ball. Nancy Williams had set up some of the interviews with the various doctors and patients at UCLA's cancer center. It felt great to finally get started on the project. We had two months to write, shoot and edit the piece before it premiered on October 17th. That seems like plenty of time, but the days shrunk quickly when I started trying to coordinate doctors' and patients' schedules together for shooting. Added to that I had to find a day that would work for filming the host on camera segments with Annette Benning. Annette had been asked to narrate the mini-documentary and graciously accepted the non-paying job. Her duties consisted of appearing on camera for several segments of the story along with recording all the audio narration tracks of the script. It was going to be a very tight schedule with very few options.

That's where Nancy Williams' talent really helped. Doing documentaries is not at all like shooting a movie. Nancy and I both came from the same news background and knew the story comes to life as you interview the people. These doctors, patients and loved ones' interviews would be pieced together with our narration until the story flowed seamlessly. This documentary on cancer research at UCLA was like getting back on an old familiar horse again. Nancy asked all the right questions and by the end of the week, a good picture was starting to come into focus as to how the story would look.

♋ ♋ ♋

On August 7th, Nancy, my sound man Ron Siegel, and I were in the offices of Dr. Beth Carlson near Cedars-Sinai Hospital. We were there to shoot cover footage and interview a young woman undergoing treatment for ovarian cancer. It was your typical doctor's examination room, tiny and now crowded with the lights, camera and audio equipment needed to make the shots. The conditions were nothing new to me though and soon after I finished setting up, the patient, Donna Isman walked in.

The minute I met Donna I felt as though I must be looking at what Kathy looked like during the same stage of her ovarian cancer. Donna's hair was just starting to grow back from the chemotherapy treatments and she was noticeably underweight for her height. I could sense an immediate connection between us and knew at some point we would become close friends.

Nancy began the interview with Donna by asking a simple but direct question. "What's it like battling cancer?"

"It's very scary," Donna said. "You lose your hair, you lose your appetite and you lose your self-esteem. Lucky for me the one thing I never lost is the support of my friends, my family and my co-workers."

"What does the future look like for you?" Nancy asked.

"I'm scared, I'm scared about the future. I sometimes have trouble sleeping… going to sleep at night "cause I'm afraid it might be my last night. I try to appreciate every day. I try to treat the people I love with more patience and be there for them. I feel the biggest legacy I can leave for people is a part of me, so when I'm gone, they can just think of me and they can have part of me with them. That's the biggest legacy I can give to anybody is love."

Donna finished her interview with a story about her dad who passed away from cancer while she was undergoing her initial surgery. Donna felt his spirit was with her now, watching over her and giving her the strength to fight the disease.

Donna's physician was Beth Carlson, a young, energetic and compassionate doctor who radiated love for all her patients. During our interview you could see the emotion Beth held inside knowing, that although she was doing her best for Donna, it was never going to be enough. She told us Donna was a very special person who had a very good attitude about her situation, but the statistics showed the odds were not in her favor. After interviewing Donna and Beth, I knew we had the driving force for our piece. I had to leave the next day for my class reunion but felt confident Nancy had all she needed to write the story.

♋ ♋ ♋

On Sunday, August 4th, I had called Sister Carleen at the convent back in Baden, Pennsylvania. I wanted to tell her my story in person so I kept the conversation brief. We set a time for Monday, August 12th that I would come to visit her.

Susan and I flew back to Pittsburgh on Thursday, August 8th and on Saturday morning we went down to the banquet hall to set up the decorations for the party that evening. It was great to see a few of my high school friends who were there to help. Rick and Karen Pudliner, who had been high school sweethearts and married just after graduation, were there along with Linda Partsch, Norma Johns and Tina Russo. We didn't have a large turnout coming for the reunion, about 25 classmates, but it was going to be a fun group of people. I brought along all the promotional hats, T-shirts and other Hollywood studio giveaways I had collected during the past few years. Since the turnout was small, I had enough gifts to handout one to each classmate. I tied a personal story from high school to each of the gifts. Some of the girls had wanted to be flight attendants so they received the flight bags from the movie *Executive Decision*. One of the guys liked to hunt and fish so he got the shooting vest from the movie *The Rock*. I was able to find enough stories from old junior high and high school newspapers to tell a funny story about everyone there. It was a great party and everyone stayed on 'til the end, around 1 a.m.

During my conversations, I asked a few classmates that had also gone to Sacred Heart Church if they had heard what happened to Kathy Lynch. None of them had, and they were shocked to find out she had passed away. I didn't get into the story of what was happening to me but was sure they would've been even more surprised if I told them how she had spoken to me after her passing. With the reunion over, I was more than anxious to drive to Baden and visit Sister Carleen.

As it worked out, Susan wanted to visit Doty, another friend of ours who lived over in State College. I drove her over on Sunday to spend the night and return sometime on Monday, with Doty driving her back to my parents. This left me free for my trip to the Pittsburgh area the next day. I knew Susan was not interested in listening to me tell the story again and I didn't feel comfortable telling it when she was around.

Chapter 6

Around 10 a.m. on Monday August 12th, I left my parents' home outside of Conemaugh for Baden, a small town just north of Pittsburgh. I had never been there before that I could remember, but I knew it wouldn't be too hard to find. The convent was right off Route 65, which winds its way alongside the Ohio River that flows out of Pittsburgh. The drive from my parents' house took about two and a half hours. It was a beautiful sunny day, the kind of day I loved to spend alone, driving through the Pennsylvania countryside.

The Sisters of St. Joseph convent was part of a large and immaculate eco-setting. Acres of neatly groomed lawns with large trees lined the long drive onto the property. The black topped road wound its way past the church, a school and several new buildings under construction. The entire campus was built out of that classic old red brick. I thought to myself how I would love to see this place in the fall with all the trees ablaze in color.

The convent Sister Carleen lived in was an old, restored, farmhouse nestled at the top of the property, surrounded by fields and overlooking the campus. It was a large, white clapboard house with a banister front porch, typical of Pennsylvania farm architecture. Its contrast to the brick buildings led me to believe that it was the oldest structure there. Only a very meticulous caretaker could keep it looking so lovely.

I had stopped earlier and purchased a small audiocassette recorder at Radio Shack so I could have a recording to transcribe from later. I didn't feel like writing down notes while I was trying to tell a story and listen to what she might tell me. I've found that reviewing an event on tape later, will always tell me something I missed – the way a person says something, maybe a simple inflection I may not have noticed.

To have decent audio to listen to later, I setup the recorder in my pocket and wired an external microphone to the front of my shirt. I decided not to make a big point of the fact that I was recording our conversation as she could clearly see the microphone. I felt it might make her self-conscious to put the microphone on her directly and since I was only using it for the information, not broadcast, the quality was not that important, as long as it was there.

I took a deep breath, walked up the stairs onto the front porch and rang the doorbell. It didn't take Sister Carleen long to answer the door.

"Hi, you found it I see."

"Yes I found it… I'm Randy."

"I'm Carleen, come on in."

She was a stout woman with glasses, gray hair and a friendly smile. She didn't remind me a lot of Kathy, but when she spoke I heard the undeniable Pennsylvania accent Kathy and I shared. She did seem familiar to me in some way. I'm sure it was my memory reaching back to a day when I had seen her at Sacred Heart Church with Kathy and her family.

"You're house is in a beautiful area."

"Isn't it nice out today!"

"Yes, I had a beautiful drive here."

She led me into the foyer of the lovely turn of the century home. Decorated with a few antiques and pictures on all the walls, the house was stone silent except for the ticking of a grandfather clock. There were no other nuns to be seen.

"So, how are you?"

"Good," she replied.

More silence, the same quietness that pervades a home when all of the children have grown up and gone. The effect was heightening the subject at hand.

"How long have you been living here?" I asked.

"In this house, it will be my third year. I was in Atlanta for five years and Columbus, Ohio for five and Altoona for ten so I've been around." She laughed, helping to break the silence that was, in my mind, creating the eerie feeling that Kathy had passed away yesterday instead of a year and a half earlier.

"Come on into the parlor so we can sit down." Sister Carleen led me into the living room and I took a seat on the couch facing a chair opposite it. There was only a coffee table separating us physically, but spiritually I felt we would be in two different worlds when it came to our beliefs. As Sister Carleen settled into the chair, I began to tell her my story from the beginning.

"It all started with these thoughts I had of Kathy passing away. It was the strangest thing to be thinking but I couldn't get them out of my head for over a year. It all culminated with this dream I had, a month ago now, where I was out in Palm Springs meeting all of these people. They kept telling me Kathy died peacefully in her sleep, but I could still hear her calling out to me from the background telling me not to forget her and find out what happened."

Sister Carleen cut in at this point. "Kathy was living out in Desert Hot Springs with our other sister Chris just before she died. Chris had moved her into a hospice in Palm Springs when she was near the end. I was out there with her the night she passed away. She did go peacefully… just stopped breathing in her sleep around 2 a.m." Sister Carleen's voice faded out softly.

"Do you remember what date that was?" I asked.

"It was last year on February 26th."

The phone began ringing in the convent.

"Could you excuse me while I get the phone? I'm the only one here today. Everyone else is down on the campus." Sister Carleen disappeared into another room.

I was feeling a little awkward in the beginning, telling a complete stranger about my dreams, let alone Kathy's relative. I had a feeling she believed what I had told her so far but I didn't expect her to understand or accept the entire message Kathy had given me. I did want her to believe what I was telling her was the truth.

Sister Carleen came back into the room a few minutes later with a slip of paper in her hand.

"That was my sister Chris from out in California. I told her what a coincidence it was that she called right now while I was just sitting here talking about her with an old friend of Kathy's from grade school. I also told her you've been having dreams about Kathy visiting you. She wanted me to give you this."

Sister Carleen reached over and handed me the yellow post-it note she had in her hand. On it was written Desert Hospital Comprehensive Cancer Center and a phone number.

"It's Chris' number at work. She asked me to have you call her when you get back out to California."

I folded over the piece of paper and stuck it in my shirt pocket. To me this was just one more event in an ever-expanding series of "coincidences," as my wife would call them. Here I was sitting in a convent in western Pennsylvania and just while we happened to be here talking about her, Kathy's sister Chris calls from Palm Springs.

Sister Carleen was not very descriptive in her storytelling but with a little prodding she was able to reveal a glimpse of what Kathy's life was like since I had last seen her.

"The last time I saw Kathy was in '73… back in Johnstown," I said. "She was recovering from Hodgkin's at the time. Do you remember what year she moved down to Florida?"

"It must have been '78. Our parents were moving down there to be with my brother Jim. He had built a separate place for them on his property so Kathy went down there too."

"I heard she'd gotten married at some point. Who was that to?"

"Kathy had met this fellow by the name of Terry Winger back in Johnstown. He moved down to Orlando and they lived together for a while before they decided to get married."

"When was that?"

"I remember it was in July of '83. Our mom had passed away two months earlier in May and Kathy wanted to postpone the wedding but Mom made her promise not to change it. They got married on the 9th of July in 1983."

"What happened to your mom?" I asked her about Caroline so I could bring my mother up to date as well.

"She died from liver and lung cancer. Dad had died four years earlier so this was especially hard on Kathy with neither of our parents there."

"So she got married that July then what?" I continued looking for details.

"Well, she started having problems with her husband Terry a few years into the marriage…" Sister Carleen stopped and didn't elaborate.

"What kind of problems?" I wanted all the details to get a complete picture of Kathy's life.

"It wasn't working… It just wasn't a good situation she was in." That was as far as Sister Carleen would go and I didn't push any further.

"So she got divorced in…?"

"Sometime in the spring of 1989, I remember because it was the same year she was first diagnosed with ovarian cancer."

"So that's when her cancer began, 1989?"

"Yes, I believe it was August of '89, she was living by herself, going through a series of surgeries and chemotherapy sessions, it was extremely hard on her, even with the support of our brother Jim down there... she struggled to keep it all together."

"Was she working too?"

Sister Carleen nodded yes. "She had a job at an insurance company in Orlando. They treated her great though, kept her job open while she was gone for months at a time, even promoted her two years later. She moved to another office in Jacksonville just as her cancer was going into remission, I think it was the spring of '91."

"How did she end up in California?"

"Chris was living out there already. She had offered Kathy a place to stay while she got her feet on the ground. I think Kathy was just looking for a change in her life so she turned in her notice at work and made plans to move out to be with Chris."

"She must have felt good about starting over in a new place for a change," I said remembering my own trip out West for the first time.

"She was really excited about going, but just before she left Florida she got a call from her doctor's office. Her last lab tests showed that the cancer had returned."

"She must have been devastated."

"She didn't know what to do at first. Kathy was a fighter, but those last two years really took their toll on her. She was just getting back on her feet when she was knocked down again. She knew she didn't have it in her to stay and fight it on her own again, but she didn't want to be a burden on Chris either. Ironically, Chris was working at the cancer center in Palm Springs so she had access to some of the best physicians for Kathy. She ended up convincing Kathy that she would be better off out there with her."

"So she moved out to California when?" I asked.

"I believe it was in the summer of '92. She and Chris really bonded out there, together. Kathy went through so many treatments... chemo... and the drugs... She never gave up hope, but in the end it just proved too much for her."

Sister Carleen stopped there and the clock's ticking dominated the silence.

♋ ♋ ♋

Sister Carleen still clung tightly to the fears and beliefs imbedded throughout her years of service in the Catholic Church. That was evident in her one last comment as we walked across the front porch towards my car.

"I was just concerned Kathy's soul might be in hell, because Kathy had gotten a divorce and had left the church."

I stopped and turned to look at her. The statement brought back memories to me of the strict rules I had to adhere to in the Catholic Church. Day after day, they had driven this pure nonsense into each of us at Catholic grade school. Anything we did that wasn't in accordance with church laws put us one-step closer to hell. Go into another church and you're on hell's front door step. Get a divorce and you've just opened the door. Leave the church… well you're eternally damned now; everyone knows only Catholics go to heaven.

"Let me tell you something, Sister, Kathy's nowhere near hell. She's in the most beautiful place you can ever imagine. She doesn't want us to be sad about what happened to her. She just wants us to remember her and think good thoughts about her."

"I don't even know if there is such a thing as hell anymore," replied Sister Carleen.

Her statement caught me off guard. I never in my entire life thought I would hear those words coming from a nun, much less that I would say any of these things to one. "There is no such thing as hell, Sister, we create our own hell right here on earth. Right now Kathy is in the place that all life comes from, and where you and I will also be once we pass on."

I didn't know if I went over the top with a statement like that but I could feel Kathy's presence around me. I was hoping Sister Carleen could also feel that these words were coming directly from Kathy. For her to believe in them though, would take something greater than anything I could say. As I parted company with Sister Carleen, I told her I would stay in touch, and visit with her when I came back this way again.

♋ ♋ ♋

My visit with Sister Carleen was not quite what I had expected. I hadn't learned anything about Kathy's state of mind in her final years. What kind of beliefs did she have after she left the church? Why did she leave the church? Sister Carleen was not very enlightening in those areas, after all she and Kathy were not close in age growing up. During my visit, I definitely learned who was close to her in her final years. That phone call coming from Chris was no accident. I knew my search for answers would continue, though how much longer was anybody's guess. Back in Los Angeles, my boat and Catalina Island were calling to me for a much-needed rest.

III.

SEARCHING FOR ANSWERS

Chapter 7

When I arrived back in Los Angeles on August 15th, the first thing I did was call Kathy's sister, Chris Russell, in Palm Springs. I told her briefly about everything that had been happening and then received some very interesting information from Chris.

"You know Randy… Kathy always believed she was reincarnated from an Indian. She'd also tell me that she knew she was a very old soul and had been here before."

"I can't believe you're telling me this. Carleen never even mentioned anything about it."

"Carleen didn't live with Kathy like I did. Kathy was a very internal person… she liked to keep things to herself… but living with her I got to know her pretty well so she would open up and tell me about these feelings of hers all the time."

"No wonder you wanted me to call you when I got back to Los Angeles. It sounds like we have a lot to talk about. I'd really like to come out to meet you soon."

"Yes, that would be great. I'm off every weekend so just let me know what works best for you."

I knew a trip out to talk with Chris would give me a much better picture of what Kathy's life had been like. With all the summer movies already released, August was usually my down time for work Even though I was chomping at the bit to run out to Palm Springs, I knew I had to get some vacation time in or I would miss my opportunity for the rest of the summer. Susan was also becoming more argumentative anytime I brought up the subject of Kathy so I decided it was probably a good idea to give the whole thing a rest and go over to Catalina Island. I told Chris I would call her after I returned and set up a time to visit. I hung up the phone and headed straight for my boat.

♋ ♋ ♋

Sailing had become a passion of mine ever since I moved out to Los Angeles in 1986. Back in November of 1995, I had purchased the best boat I've ever owned. She was a 1984 Choey Lee Pedrick designed 41-foot sloop rig with an aft cockpit. The minute I saw it I fell in love with her. I remember driving back from Ardell Yachts in Newport Beach with Susan on the day we signed the papers. She asked me what I wanted to do about the name.

"I think we should call her *Déjà Vu*." The name just popped into my head and out of my mouth as we drove north on the 405.

"What about *My Darling Susan*? I think that has a nice ring to it," Susan joked.

"Ed McMahon named his boat after his wife but I keep seeing workers out there repainting the stern every time he gets remarried. Do you really want to take that chance?"

"Maybe *Déjà Vu* isn't a bad name after all," she laughed. "At least we stand the chance of having our relationship repeat over again."

At the time, I had no idea how prophetic my words would become.

♋ ♋ ♋

I sailed away from Marina del Rey alone on the afternoon of August 15th 1996. Susan was going to come over on the ferry in a few days. She had to catch up on her work that had built up during our trip to Pennsylvania. I tried to relax and clear my mind of all the clutter. I had read the book *Dreams and Premonitions* and was trying to practice some simple suggestions from L. W. Rogers. The book said to just relax and empty your mind of all thoughts. This would allow me to hear more clearly and get a better picture of what was trying to reach me.

I wanted to send out a simple clear question and see what kind of answer I would get. A beautiful orange sky surrounded me, and a stiff breeze was moving Déjà Vu along nicely when I put her on autopilot and stretched out on the deck. I focused my thoughts into two short sentences to send out to my friend.

"How do I know you? Why do I feel so close to you?" The questions were barely away from my mind when the answers hit me.

"I've known you since the beginning of time," the reply came softly. "I've known you since the beginning of time."

There wasn't any mistake. I was clearly feeling the answer from my friend. I could sense her voice inflections as they played inside my mind. It was a clear recognition of the way she once spoke to me and how she sounded. The only difference being Kathy had never said any such words to me while she was alive and now I was feeling her very essence repeating in my mind. "I've known you since the beginning of time."

I instantly thought back, "How can I have known you since the beginning of time? I've only been here since 1953. How is that possible?"

"I've known you since the beginning of time."

I sailed on, watching the sunset and trying to make sense of what I was feeling. By 10 p.m., I had reached the island and moored my boat in Cherry Cove. As I settled in for the evening, I was hoping some kind of answers would come during sleep, but as morning broke I couldn't remember any of my dreams.

About mid-morning, I was resting in the cockpit, just lying there gazing across the water at the shoreline. The trees on the mountain were swaying gently in the breeze. I was watching a pair of seagulls soaring in circles over the rocky cliff top when I heard that familiar voice come drifting into my mind again.

"Get the book out and look at the title," Kathy said very strongly. I went down below and pulled out the copy of *Dreams and Premonitions* from my briefcase.

"Look at the title," she said. "The title," kept repeating in my mind.

The title was straightforward *Dreams and Premonitions.* As I looked at the cover, the picture was the only thing that stood out to me. "This young girl riding on the horse, is that you, Kathy?" I asked as I let the question bleed from my mind.

"No, no, no, title, title, title!" kept echoing in my head.

I looked again at the whole book this time and I realized that the only thing I hadn't focused on was the part that read *By L. W. Rogers.* As soon as I saw those initials, the words passed through my mind, "Those are Kathy's initials and my last name together." Her last name was Lynch then she got married and now it was Winger. Lynch, Winger, Rogers.

As soon as I made the connection, it was as if a floodgate opened. "If you find out about the author, you'll find out about us. If you find out who he was, you'll find out who we were." The information was flowing freely inside my head now. I knew

I had to find this author but there was nothing in the book about him. I didn't even know his name, just his initials. I looked through the book again and verified that he was indeed a man. A letter from a previous reader reprinted in the book started out with Dear Mr. Rogers. The copyright was dated 1923. I knew that even if the author was in his early 20s when he wrote it he would have to be nearly 100 if he were even still alive.

As I held the book in my hands, thinking about what kind of man wrote this, the first thing that came to me was the author was in his 60s when he wrote this book. I knew it had to have been written by a much older and wiser person.

The second thing I knew was that he passed away in 1953, the same year Kathy and I were born, and just before we were born. I was born on July 8th. I didn't know when Kathy's birth date was but I felt it was very close to mine. If my feelings were correct, L.W. would have been at least 90 years old when he died. This was quite a long shot prediction to make by just holding a book in my hand, but I knew when I found him these feelings of mine would prove to be true. It was the same kind of knowledge I had from my youth when I always knew I would be a photographer. I never *wanted* to be anything. I only *knew* what I would be.

♋ ♋ ♋

Susan came out to visit for a day or two, and while she was there I decided to get up early one morning and go snorkeling out at Ship's Rock. I left by myself at dawn in the inflatable dinghy and dropped anchor in the calm shallow reef on the south end of the rock. The water was exceptionally clear as I slipped into the kelp forest to go exploring. It was extremely peaceful to have the place to myself. Diving down among the Garibaldi and Kelp Bass I noticed everything seemed more colorful, like the chroma on a picture tube turned up to maximum. I spotted a small seal on one of my dives down to the bottom and began a series of circling maneuvers to work my way closer to him. We were at arms length when we surfaced after about the sixth dive. It was my first time staying that close and that long with a seal and it not darting off in fear. It was like having a dive buddy with me.

I had to laugh at his comical expressions each time we surfaced for air. He would look at me and then scan the surface for any sign of trouble. On one of our surfaces, I was next to him, shoulder to shoulder when he whipped his attention around to look behind us. I could see a look of panic when he turned to face me again.

I turned around to see what was startling him. On the horizon, several hundred yards away, was an armada of Boy Scouts in kayaks paddling like mad for our position. My little friend decided that was enough for this spot and took off like a bullet. We hooked up again later on the other side of the rock, but the noise from the scouts was too much for him and he disappeared into the deep.

After spending the morning snorkeling, I got back in the inflatable and headed over to my boat to take Susan into the Isthmus. She had to catch a ferry to the mainland and get back to the work still waiting for her. We stopped and had a "Buffalo Milk" at the bar before she jumped on the express for the hour and a half ride to San Pedro. I escorted the ferry along as it departed the dock, waving goodbye as she sped out to sea. As I made my way out into the harbor, I noticed a black hulled ship standing off to my starboard. Something about this boat drew my attention. Maybe it was the fact she sat moored all alone.

I turned my inflatable towards where she was lying and cruised over to have a look. As I approached her port side, I could make out the name *Whistlin Riggin* and remembered having met her owner several years earlier when she moored next to me in Cherry Cove. I circled around her stern and saw the owner lying in the cockpit resting. I decided to pass by, quietly. She spotted me though and called out for me to pull up alongside.

It had been three or four years since I had met this woman. Strangely enough I remembered her name, Donna Matson. It may have been that I had just met Donna Isman on the cancer shoot, but her name just shot into my head. I reminded her about our meeting years ago. She invited me onboard so I tied off and climbed her boarding ladder. We started talking about how great it was to be over on the island, away from the craziness of L.A.

"I was in these horrible business meetings all week that just drained every ounce of energy out of me, but when I finally got down to my boat and cleared the breakwater out of the marina, it was as though a band of angels were surrounding me as I made my way across the channel. Have you experienced anything like that?" Donna asked.

"It's funny you should ask me that question," I said, and then related all the strange things going on with me. Donna's expression changed to a smile as I ended my story with the question, "So, have you ever had anything like *that* happen to you?"

Donna looked at me very seriously. "Why do you think you stopped at my boat just now?" She held up a book resting on her lap. I hadn't noticed it while I was telling my tale but now she was pointing to the title, *The Celestine Prophecy.*

I asked her what she meant by this. I had never heard of the book.

"A lot of what you've just been telling me is explained in this book."

I tried questioning her further to find out exactly what the book was about, but she told me I would have to read it for myself. All she would say was that I was becoming aware and that was the first sign. I didn't understand what she was talking about.

Before I left she told me to stop by tomorrow evening and she'd be done with the book and lend it to me. She also said I was right in believing that there was no such thing as coincidences.

I got back to my boat just as the stars were starting to come out. I was lying back in the cockpit taking in the beauty of the evening when I started to notice an odd glow from the plants along the ridge of the island. A fluctuating halo effect seemed to sway and extend for a foot or two beyond the branches. I attributed it to some kind of atmospheric condition combined with the moonlight, then noticed the moon itself seemed to radiate a solid stream of light right down to my boat. I passed my hand through the light shaft. That's when I noticed my hand also had the glow around it. I spent hours playing with the moonlight and watching the different glows off various objects.

The next day I spent reading and working around the boat. About 5 p.m., I jumped in the dinghy and headed over to Donna's boat to see if she wanted to get something to eat. As I pulled along side, she was just closing up her hatches before going into the Isthmus. She was glad I had stopped by and took up my invitation to dinner. Motoring away from her yacht, I asked her about the events of the previous evening.

"Did you happen to notice a strange glow coming off the plants on the island last night?"

"No, I didn't see it," Donna said smiling, "but you've just got to read this book. I'll tell you more about it at dinner." We wound our way through the dozens of boats moored at the Isthmus and coasted smoothly up to the dingy dock.

The Harbor Reef Restaurant was the only game in town for dinner at this end of the island. It is a beach shack style structure with weathered wood siding and an exterior patio for lunch and weekend evenings. Since the patio was closed that night, we walked inside to be seated in the dining room. I immediately picked up our discussion about the book.

"So, what is this *Celestine Prophecy* all about?"

"It's about all the things you're describing, Randy, they're all in this book. There is a transformation taking place with you and you are becoming aware."

"Aware of what?" I asked.

"That's the first insight, becoming aware of the synchronicity surrounding your life." Donna had excitement in the tone of her voice.

"Well I've certainly had my share of those lately, synchronistic events I mean… in fact that's all I see anymore. What's the second insight?"

"That's when you begin to wonder how life works, what really makes this place run." Donna motioned her hands around the space above her head, signifying what I took to mean the world and everything in it.

"Okay, that seems like a logical thing to ask once you pickup on the synchronicity part."

Donna's face broke out into a wide smile. "There are nine insights in all, one leading to the next and you'll progress gradually through each one of them as you grow spiritually."

"So what's the third?" I asked, trying to get a jump on what possibly lay ahead of me.

"That's the exciting part!" Donna was beaming from ear to ear now. "The third insight is a heightened sensitivity to beauty and the ability to see an energy field hovering above everything. Randy… you're already up to the third insight!"

Donna didn't want to tell me anything else about the book until I read it. She certainly had my interest. The rest of the dinner was spent talking about diving at Catalina Island and other interesting places in the world. She was an expert on the subject, having spent the better part of her life doing just that.

Dropping Donna back at her mooring, she handed me the book in a plastic bag to keep it dry. I thanked her for the loan and promised to get it back in a couple days.

I headed back to my mooring and jumped straight into bed. It didn't take me long to find out what Donna was talking about. Many of the things I had been describing were indeed various prophecy stages James Redfield had written about in his book. I couldn't figure out how or why these things were happening to me but according to the book, there was some kind of evolution taking place. I read late into the night until I was too tired to continue.

The next day I finished the book and took it back over to Donna. I was only half way up the boarding ladder when the questions started.

"Did you like it? What did you think?"

"I can't believe these signs are beginning to happen to me. I could understand it if I had read the book *then* had the experiences, but I'm having the experiences and then reading the book. Where is all this taking me?"

"Randy, you've got to continue on your path. You have a very special gift you've been given with your ability to sense things other people don't readily see. You've got to let it develop… let it grow… see where it takes you."

"Well, thanks for all the advice… and the loan of the book." I smiled and handed Donna back *The Celestine Prophecy*.

It was time to go home and begin my search for the mysterious L.W. Rogers. I had this strange feeling I knew him somehow, but I couldn't understand how that could be possible.

♋ ♋ ♋

The first thing I did when I arrived back in L.A. was call Chris Russell to set up our meeting. We decided the best day to get together would be Saturday, August 31st. I would drive out to

Cabazon where Chris was living now and we'd spend the day together visiting the ranch and areas where Kathy had spent her last years of this life.

After speaking with Chris, I turned my attention to the search for L. W. Rogers. I began by typing his name into the same search engines I had used to no avail in my search for Kathy. I was getting the same results for L.W. Rogers; not one bit of information seemed to be out there on the web.

I hadn't told anyone about the events taking place in my life other than my parents, my wife, Kathy's sisters and now Donna. I felt I would have to tell the story to a few close friends so that as it unfolded they would see I had been telling the truth. The first person I told was Ron Siegel. Ron started out as a summer intern, working with me for several years before he pulled up roots from Virginia Beach and moved permanently to Los Angeles. During that time, we had become quite close. Susan and I were the closest people to family for him out here. When I relayed the story to Ron, he was amazed to say the least, especially coming from me. I was not the kind of person to whom he would expect something like this to be happening.

I told Ron how I had to find L. W. Rogers and when I did, he would have died the year Kathy and I were born, just before we were born. I also told him I was searching on the Internet and hadn't had any luck in finding him. I asked Ron not to tell anyone else about what I had been experiencing. I didn't want to turn this into a circus with everyone cracking jokes about it. It's not that I didn't love to joke. I have made plenty of them about this whole affair, but at the time I just needed to find some answers. Ron promised to keep it confidential.

♋ ♋ ♋

As the day to visit Kathy's sister Chris grew near, I noticed that Susan was becoming more agitated when I brought up anything about my investigation. One day in particular, she began by prodding me into another debate. She believed all these events were nothing more than simple coincidences. I responded quite heatedly that there are no such things as coincidences.

"It's been 23 years since I've seen Kathy!" I shouted. "Why would I pick her out of anyone else to start thinking these things and then find them to be true?"

"Well, if there aren't any such things as coincidences, there's another one for you," she shouted back.

"What do you mean?"

"Do you know how many times you've used the number 23? It's been 23 years since you've seen Kathy, the book was written in 1923 and I can't remember what else you've said but you keep using that number!"

"Exactly," I said. "Now you're helping me. I never even looked at the numbers. Chris just told me that Kathy's birthday was June 23rd."

"It's not the number 23, Dad," our daughter Dana chimed in. "It's really the number 5, that's Kathy's number. Everyone is born with one number so Kathy's is a 5 because you add the 2 and the 3. Your number is an 8 because you were born July 8th."

"How do you know this?" I asked.

"I read it in one of the magazines I get," she said. "It's called numerology and it's a whole study of numbers and how they affect your life."

"Yes, look at the numbers." I could feel the message strongly. "Take a good look at the numbers and you will see the connection." I could hear the instructions clearly but didn't know what numbers to look at yet. My education in that field was yet to come.

Ironically, now my arguments with Susan were actually helping me to branch off my search in more directions along a path that was still pointing out to Palm Springs as the main starting point.

Chapter 8

On Saturday August 31st, I rose early, packed some fruit and water in a bag and drove east towards Palm Springs. I've always been an early riser. It started as a child when I would get up at 5 a.m. to watch old Tarzan and Robin Hood movies. For some reason they always played them at the crack of dawn, but I would always watch them faithfully every Saturday, at least during the school year. In the summers I would be sleeping out somewhere in the old "pup" tent my father had given us to use. Even if it were just the backyard, my friends and I would make an adventure of a night away from the confines of our parents and siblings. We would tell ghost stories all night until no one could fall asleep, for fear the headless horseman would come calling in the dark.

Now I had my own personal "ghost" to deal with and it wasn't at all like the stories we scared ourselves with in my youth. I could feel Kathy's presence surrounding me as I drove into a beautiful sunrise that cast its orange light across the buildings of downtown L.A.

As I made my way along I started the tape recorder rolling to capture my thoughts about what was happening so I would have them for future reference. I knew Kathy wanted me to remember her and I thought the best way to do that would be to write a book or make a movie about her life.

This trip to visit Chris would shed some light on what Kathy's life had been like in the 23 years since I had last seen her. She was only 41 when the cancer took her away. It may have ended her existence as Kathy Lynch, but from what I was feeling, that was just a vehicle she had used in this life. According to Kathy and L.W. Rogers, the true spirit that drives each of us lives on forever and returns again to gain another experience.

It was a little before eight a.m. when I reached Cabazon. It wasn't hard to spot our meeting place off Interstate 10. It was the only one surrounded by life-size dinosaurs. I had always wanted to see what they looked like up close and now I had my chance while I waited for Chris to show up. Like everything in life, especially flying down a freeway, they looked a lot better from a distance. Los Angeles, Hollywood in particular, is the capital of making things look great on the outside.

Chris came wheeling into the parking lot in her little pickup truck with a camper shell on the bed. It was easy to recognize her by the description she had given me on the phone.

Chris didn't look a bit like her sister Kathy. Standing about five foot six with a shock of medium short bleached blonde hair spiking off her head, she was wearing sky blue, knee length shorts with an Indian beadwork belt in a multitude of colors, sash tied across the front. It separated her white polo top nicely and, combined with the turquoise pendant hanging around her neck, painted an immediate picture of someone who loved the desert and its Native American culture.

Meeting her for the first time, I could see she had gotten the majority of her family's outgoing personality gene. She immediately hugged me, radiating an affection that made me feel like I had known her forever. She invited me to ride in her truck since she knew where she was going and it would be easier if she drove. I grabbed my camera and tape recorder and climbed in.

We headed out Highway 14 to visit the place where she and Kathy last lived together. It was a ranch in the Morongo Valley and getting there required going off the beaten path. Along the way, Chris was a fountain of information about Kathy's life.

"Kathy just loved the desert, she and I used to go out on the weekends to gem and mineral shows or just doing this and that. We lived over there in Desert Hot Springs, up against those foothills," Chris said, pointing out towards the mountains in the distance.

Chris lived with Kathy during the last three years of Kathy's life. During that time, she was able to get to know her sister better than anyone else in her family. Kathy was a very private person and didn't share many of her feelings with people. Chris on the other hand had no problem talking about anything with anyone. As we discussed our religious upbringing, both Chris and I agreed it played a big part in warping our view of what life was supposed to be like. For her sister Kathy, it hadn't been any different.

"After Mum and Dad died, Kathy quit going to church. The only reason she had gone up until then was because of Mum."

I could easily relate to the feeling. My mother and the Catholic religion had a bigger hold on my life than anything else I could think of. Even two thousand miles away from my mother wasn't enough to break that bond. It took a divorce to do that for me, and in Kathy's case her mother's death.

I could start to get a feeling of what was going through Kathy's mind. I was sure that Kathy felt as I did. The real world does not function the way the Catholic Church thinks it should.

It's not the principal of trying to live a good life with your fellow man that is the priority in the Catholic Church, but the demands that you *must* follow all these rules and regulations in order to find salvation. Kathy and I both broke free of the hold the Catholic Church had on us in the early '80s. If Kathy went through anything like I did, her separation from the church and its teachings was never clean. The Catholic religion had one last virus they imbedded deep inside each one of us; guilt. People joke about it, but that is the one last root that refuses to be pulled from my Catholic past. I was sure it caused some trying times for Kathy as she struggled down her path in life.

We made our way through the desert washes and up to the ranch property where Kathy had spent her final years. Chris told me the story of how Kathy came out to stay with her. Kathy had already battled through the first bout of ovarian cancer alone in Florida. She didn't feel like she had the strength to do this second round by herself.

After arriving in Desert Hot Springs in July of 1992, Kathy settled in with Chris and her husband. Chris' own marriage was on shaky ground. Shortly after Kathy's arrival, Chris divorced and she and Kathy were left with each other. Through a friend, Chris found this secluded little spot in the desert for rent. Their home consisted of a trailer on the property with running water and electricity. Kathy loved being out in the desert even though it was a far cry from the forests and mountains she had grown up around in Western Pennsylvania.

It was easy to see what Kathy loved about this place. I had spent 13 years living in a desert climate. There was a calm peacefulness about the doves that cooed from the Palos Verde trees near the wash. Unlike most desert washes, this one had an underground stream that surfaced on the property. It had water running in it year round. The little run emptied into several large marshes just below their home on the ridge. Plants and animal life were abundant and the view from what Kathy called "her lookout" was of a green oasis in the desert below.

"This was her favorite spot," Chris said, taking me behind the property to a deck overlooking the springs. It was a deck only in the sense that it had a covered wood beam ceiling about twenty-five feet long and ten feet wide supported by six large, rough sawn timbers. The ground was bare desert and the far end of the open patio was closed off by a bench. It consisted of two long boards for the seat and a single plank across the back. On the other end was another short, freestanding wood bench sitting catty-corner to the end post. In front of it was a large, old wooden cable spool they used as a coffee table. There was a three-foot long pipe wind chime hanging over the table, and two brown padded, tubular chrome, easy chairs sat facing out to the wash.

"Kathy would spend hours upon end just sitting out here, looking over this. One of the reasons she liked it out here so much was there was no one to judge you by your money or your looks.

"We had these two dogs, Magic, who was a black Lab and was Kathy's dog, and Missy, a German Shepherd that was mine. I came home one day and I said, 'It looks like there was somebody here today.'

"Kathy said, 'A couple of those Jehovah's Witness.'

"I said, 'What'd they want?'

"She said, 'I never got a chance to find out.'

"Now she had lost all her hair from the chemo, and she was extremely thin…. So Kathy said, 'I was trying to hold Missy and Magic back but Missy got out and started nipping at the back of the one guy's pants, when I opened the door and said, that's okay they won't hurt you, they took one look at me and ran off.'"

Kathy laughed and Chris told her, "See. It's for a reason! It's for a reason."

Kathy knew the odds were against her surviving. She knew that only 5% of ovarian cancer patients lived beyond 5 years after their first diagnosis. Five years were almost up since her first diagnosis in 1989 and the cancer hadn't gone away for very long. It was back now and stronger than ever.

As I hiked around the property looking at the sights Kathy saw and listening to the sounds she heard, I could feel her spirit surrounding this place. It was the presence of one unified, living being. The very essence of life itself and Kathy was the soul of its existence. As I felt her spirit encompassing us, I had an even better understanding of her words the night she came to me. "Feel my spirit, that is what makes us as one," she had said.

In her final days on earth, Kathy had come to know that soon she would truly be one with the universe. Not the universe as we view it, but the spiritual universe that engulfs everything we think is so infinite in this place. Kathy wasn't gone now, it fact it was quite the opposite. Somehow, she had become larger than in life, and in so doing, was now a part of everything surrounding me. I could feel her reaching out to me, trying to explain who I am and how it all works. As I listened to the wind rustling through the cattails in the pond, I opened my mind to hear more of her story.

Chris and I finished strolling around the property then left the ranch about mid-morning and drove north towards the high desert and Yucca Valley. Chris said Joshua Tree National Park was one of Kathy's favorite places to visit. She asked me if I would like to stop off there for a while. I had never been in the park before and was anxious to see any place Kathy liked to frequent.

After paying our entrance fee, Chris and I drove through the park into a camping area surrounded by giant sandstone boulders and Joshua Trees. We found a shady spot at one of the picnic tables and Chris brought out an old photo album of Kathy's. The pictures spanned back to her childhood in Pennsylvania. It was great looking back at the ones taken during our grade school days at Sacred Heart. There was a photo of Kathy in her cheerleading uniform. I had forgotten she was even a cheerleader back then. Lee Ann Vautar, Bonnie Mutch, Joan Wojnarowski and Karen Vickroy, all the girls Kathy had mentioned in the dream, frozen in time before me now. Seeing them all again brought back a flood of memories. The photos and Chris' stories moved forward through Kathy's life painting a tale of a very brave woman who never gave up her fight with ovarian cancer.

"Here she is at a costume party after she had her spleen taken out. She painted her scar from the surgery into a snake and put that big gem stone in her bellybutton," Chris said, showing me a picture of Kathy in a harem outfit.

Kathy was five foot nine inches tall with light brown hair and blue eyes. She had a long, slender neck that accentuated her facial features, especially her beautiful, broad smile that was always present.

After Kathy lost her hair, she wore several wigs. A favorite was one she called her "Carol Channing." It was a platinum gray bob cut that, combined with Kathy's facial features, made her look like the spitting image of Carol Channing. Kathy had always been a tall, thin girl but now the pictures showed her looking anorexic. There were photos of her in a hospital bed, needles and IV's attached to both her arms and not a lick of hair on her head, including her eyebrows. Kathy's blue eyes and smile still grabbed your attention the most in those photos. They sparkled with life and radiated a confidence that she would beat this cancer.

"Did Kathy have any friends from work or back in Johnstown that she talked to?" I asked Chris after looking at all her photographs.

"You know, she only kept touch with two of her girlfriends as far as I knew. One was Bernie, a girl she had gone to high school with and the other was named Tammy. She was a co-worker from Kathy's last job in Florida." Chris then gave me the details on how Bernie and Kathy became lifelong friends.

Bernadette Punako and Kathy Lynch ran into each other by the strangest of circumstances a year after graduation. It happened one day in 1972 while Kathy was in the hospital in Pittsburgh receiving her treatments for Hodgkin's disease. As Kathy was lying in her hospital bed, she saw Bernie walk past the doorway to her room and quickly called out to her. When Bernie came back in to see who was calling her, she was surprised to find her high school friend. Even more shocking was the fact Bernie was there to start *her* treatments for Hodgkin's disease. This "coincidental" meeting started a friendship between the two of them that stayed strong until the end.

Bernie came out to California to visit Kathy in the fall of 1994. The photos in Kathy's album showed the two of them smiling and enjoying each other's company for one last time. Chris' story made me wonder what strange twist of fate would put two girls from the same high school together in the same hospital and diagnosed with the same disease. I was sure it had to have been more than a coincidence. The fact that they both grew up in a heavily polluted steel town certainly didn't decrease their odds of having some kind of health problems, but why these two people together, at this time in their lives? I would have to talk with Bernie to find out more about their relationship.

Chris and I finished looking through the photo album and then she brought out a few pieces of Kathy's artwork. One painting represented Kathy's favorite place, and it reminded me a lot of Alaska. An eagle soared over a tranquil lake surrounded by towering mountains. I had seen many places like that when I covered the Exxon Valdez oil spill. Alaska impressed me as the most beautiful and peaceful spot on earth I had ever visited. Chris told me that Kathy had never been to Alaska, but from what I could see she had the scenery playing in her mind when she painted her favorite place on earth. Another one of her art pieces was a mask with a mountain scene painted across half of the face. Kathy's escape from the life she was living showed clearly in her artwork, and in the stories Chris told me of Kathy's final years of her life living in the desert.

One story started with an evening when Kathy had been sitting playing solitaire for hours on end. Chris never had the patience to play card games but Kathy had become a pro at it and had accumulated quite a few books on different types of games to play. The repetition of game after game finally got to Chris that night and she decided to try to break up the monotony.

"Why don't you just cheat and get it over with?" Chris asked her.

"Nah, I can't do that," Kathy replied, and continued to lay out the cards.

"I don't see how you can sit there playing that! Let's go up to Yucca Valley and get an ice cream cone," Chris said, trying another approach to get Kathy away from the cards.

"I'm gonna finish this game first." Kathy replied.

Chris looked over at all the cards Kathy had laid out and knew the game would take her some time to finish. She decided to speed things up a bit, so she took her hands and mixed up all the cards.

"There, it's done! Now let's go get an ice cream cone."

"I can't believe… I can't believe you did that," Kathy stammered to her sister. "I can't believe you did that!"

The next day, Chris was sunbathing in a lounge chair when she heard a rustling coming from somewhere behind her. Dismissing the noise as just the dogs, she never turned around to investigate. A few seconds later, a steady blast of ice-cold water shocked Chris from her tanning session, courtesy of the garden hose in Kathy's hand. "Towanda!" shouted Kathy, unmercifully dousing Chris. She was quoting a line from the movie *Fried Green Tomatoes* that Chris and Kathy had recently seen together. In the movie, Kathy Bates' character, Evelyn Couch, finally snaps in a grocery store parking lot when a car load of young girls takes her parking space. Shouting "Towanda," Evelyn rams their car repeatedly as she gets payback for their impudence. The story of Towanda, a warrior-like alter ego created by a woman in a previous generation, wove itself through the current day events of the movie. Towanda always materialized to stand up for her friend's rights during a time when women's rights were being suppressed.

Kathy used the line as it was used in the movie, a battle cry as she exacted her revenge on Chris. On another level however, Kathy related completely with Bates character. She felt trapped in a life that didn't have many options but she still had her self-respect. She wasn't going to roll over for anyone or anything. The cancer may have had her on the ropes, but she was never going to give up the fight. "Towanda!"

Kathy's determination remained strong right up to the very end, and actually caused a part of Chris to think Kathy wasn't ever going to die from the disease.

"I just thought she'd keep doing what she was doing," Chris said. "When I saw her changing, that's when my panic came in... so I went out and dyed my hair blonde and got a tattoo." Chris laughed to lighten the moment, but I could clearly feel the love she had for her sister and how deeply it troubled her that she was powerless to help Kathy beat the disease.

Kathy always felt she would lick this thing if she could just manage to gain some weight. However, the combination of the cancer and the toxic chemotherapy drugs were taking a toll on Kathy's body, and try as she might, there was no way to reverse the damage they were causing. Kathy's weight dropped steadily until Chris could no longer take adequate care of her out in the desert. She decided it would be best if she moved Kathy into a hospice in Palm Springs to provide her with twenty-four hour nursing supervision and keep her closer to Chris' work at the Breast Cancer Center.

Kathy now had to face the cold reality; she knew the hospice was a place people went to spend their final days. That truth was driven home for Chris one day, just before Kathy left the desert. Kathy had received a call from her friend Tammy Maier back in Florida. During their conversation, Chris overheard Kathy telling Tammy she was moving into a hospice in Palm Springs. Tammy must have asked how long she would have to spend in there.

"I won't be coming back out," Kathy said softly to her friend as her tears began to flow. She then gently explained that hospice was a place where they cared for people who were terminally ill.

"It was the hardest conversation I ever had to listen to," Chris said. "Kathy had to tell her friend that she was dying."

Chapter 9

In January of 1995, shortly after Kathy moved into the hospice in Palm Springs, Chris took her outside one day for a breath of fresh air. Chris bundled her from head to toe as Kathy's weight had dropped to where she couldn't generate any heat to keep herself warm. As Chris pushed her wheelchair around the grounds, Kathy soaked in the beautiful blue sky on that clear winter day in the Southern California desert. On their way back to the building, Chris momentarily lost her grip on the wheelchair. It started freewheeling down the grade towards the traffic on the street below.

"Whoo-hoo!" shouted Kathy as she felt her speed begin to pick up.

Chris caught up to her, managed to regain control and slowed her down after a few tense moments.

"Kathy, I almost lost you!" Chris said after catching the runaway wheelchair. "You'd have been going down Via Miraeste," she added as Kathy sat there smiling.

"Let's go for it," Kathy said to Chris, looking for a way to liven up the outing she was enjoying with her sister.

Chris decided she had had enough excitement for one day and turned Kathy around to take her back to her room. As they made their way back to the door of the building, Kathy broke the silence with one last question.

"How long do you think this is going to take?" she asked.

Chris was unprepared for her question. "I don't know… as long as it's going to take… I guess."

They continued on to her room in silence. It was the last time Kathy would enjoy the feeling of being in the outdoors. Around two in the morning on February 26, 1995, Kathy passed away. Chris was at home when it happened. Sister Carleen was at Kathy's bedside keeping watch over her. She had been in and out of consciousness for the past few days.

"In the end, she simply stopped breathing in her sleep," Chris said.

Chris and I went through the photographs in the album one last time. She pulled a few of the more recent pictures of Kathy, along with some of her artwork, aside for me to photograph. We then drove out of Joshua Tree and stopped off at Kathy's favorite diner to get some lunch. I felt like I was still missing something in this story so I asked Chris if Kathy had kept any kind of diary. Chris told me that she did have a journal of Kathy's, along with a family tree she had started just before she died. They were packed away in storage but Chris promised to find them and ship them off to me. There was one more thing she was also going to include in the package. An Indian friend had given Chris a bracelet to give to Kathy. The Indian told Chris it was very powerful medicine and Kathy wore the bracelet all the time. After Kathy passed away, Chris kept the bracelet. She now thought it was something that I should have.

We climbed into Chris' truck one last time and headed back towards the Cabazon exit where I had left my Bronco. As we drove along Chris asked me if I would like to swing by the hospice where Kathy had spent her last days. I immediately answered yes. Chris continued into Palm Springs eventually turning left onto Via Miraeste. As Chris drove down the street towards the facility, she didn't have to point it out to me.

"There it is!" I pointed out the front windshield to our left. "It's exactly like I remember it in my dream." My eyes were locked onto a single story white stucco structure with palm trees in front of it.

Chris pulled to a stop in front so I could get out and take a closer look. The building sat back some thirty feet from the sidewalk. A grass lawn sloped up the four-foot grade to the foundation, with a wheelchair ramp winding its way out from the center. Running along both sides were private courtyards attached to each of the patient's rooms. I walked up and looked in through the open block walls of one of the patios to see the small trees, potted plants and other greenery inside the patio area.

An eerie feeling swept over me – I had definitely been here before, not physically, but during my dream on July 6th. Chris was amazed that I had picked out the facility as we were driving down the street. The image was so firmly implanted in my mind though, that it seemed I could never forget it. It was confirmation that what I saw in my dream really did happen and somehow I experienced events in a place of which I had no prior knowledge. I had too many details exactly right to explain it away to mere coincidence.

I thanked Chris for spending the day with me and told her I would let her know what happened next. As I drove back to the coast I felt like I had a much better feeling of what Kathy's last few years must have been like. I was blaming myself for not being there when she needed me, and I felt in my heart that I could've done something to help her. The more emotional I became over what had happened, the more I could feel Kathy telling me that everything went the way it was supposed to. It was very soothing to feel her presence on the drive home. Her calming spirit helped to lift the sorrow I was experiencing. I knew I had to keep looking to find out who L.W. Rogers really was.

♋ ♋ ♋

Back on the Internet, I had finally gotten into the Library of Congress. This may not seem like much of an accomplishment now, but in 1996, modems were slow and Internet access was terrible. Just staying online was a chore. I typed in L.W. Rogers to the search query. It returned my request with too many parameters. I decided to try just W. Rogers and the screen came back with 58 solutions to my search. As I paged through them one at a time I came up to response number 41. It read Rogers, Louis William, born 1859, died 1953. My heart skipped a beat. Nineteen fifty three, the year I was born – this had to be him! There was the first line of a paragraph that started out "His Elementary Theosophy…" and then the rest of the sentence was cut off.

I quickly grabbed a dictionary to look up the word Theosophy; a movement based on the belief of reincarnation. Now I was sure I had my man! With no apparent way to get any further information out of the computer at the Library of Congress, I printed out the page and logged off.

Now that I had L.W.'s full name I decided to call the Los Angeles Public Library. They referred me to the religion section where one of the librarians ran a quick computer search and found they had two books by Louis William Rogers. One was *Elementary Theosophy* and the other was *Gods In The Making*. He pulled them aside to reserve for me and I drove downtown to try to learn more about my mysterious author.

The downtown library was a place I hadn't been to very often. I had done a public service announcement film shoot with the state librarian there a year earlier and since then I hadn't been back. I remembered a fire gutted the building around 1986 just after I moved out to Los Angeles. After an expensive renovation, it was looking better than ever. I guess something good comes out of everything, even though there is some loss along the way.

I had to stop at the front desk and get a library card first. The last time I had a library card was in high school, and it was kind of fun to be doing something different. After finding my way to the religion section, I asked the librarian at the desk for the two books held for me. He turned out to be the same person I had spoken to on the phone and after he gave me the books, I asked him how I could find information about the author. He told me a good place to start would be to search through the Who's Who in America yearbooks.

I took his advice and after a short search starting in the early 1900s, I located L.W. listed in the 1920 yearbook. In a brief biography, it listed his birth date as May 28th, 1859 near Cedar Rapids, Iowa. It also listed him as president of The Theosophical Society of America in Wheaton, Illinois beginning in 1920. As I looked through yearbook after yearbook, he remained president until 1931. The later bios also included his wife's name, May, and two sons, Stanley and Grayson. After a few years his listing disappeared and I could only surmise that he had retired or quit writing, after all he would have been well into his 70s by then. I did manage to get several addresses for him in Los Angeles so I thought it would be fun to look them up sometime and see if there was anything left of his homes.

As I left the library with the latest information in my hand, I felt the next place to check would be the Theosophical Society in Wheaton, Illinois. I didn't even know where Wheaton was located but I knew I had heard of it before. It sounded like one of those places they ask you to send donations to for various charities or to write to for more information on whatever kind of addiction you may have. When I got home, I found out it was just outside Chicago. I called information and asked if they had a number for the Theosophical Society there. The operator came back quickly with a listing and I started to feel like some of the answers to my many questions were just a phone call away.

Who was this mysterious author, L.W. Rogers, and did he die just before Kathy and I were born? These were the latest pieces of a puzzle revealing itself one piece at a time. It started out with one simple question. What happened to Kathy Lynch? The answer, death by ovarian cancer, hit too close to my charity video project to stop asking questions. And the more questions I asked, the more my eyes were opened.

Somehow all these inter-twined events were related. Me, Kathy, the dreams, her cancer and now L.W. Rogers, had become too many coincidences to just write them off. What really hooked me was my visit to Palm Springs. When I saw the exact place I had been in my dream, the hospice, where Kathy had taken her last breath of life… I couldn't let it go. I had to know how and why all these events were connected… and they were connected. The puzzle was growing and L.W. Rogers was now the latest piece within my grasp.

♋ ♋ ♋

I reached the Theosophical Society's switchboard and asked if they had a library, they did, and after putting me through, I had a pleasant conversation with a woman by the name of Lilly. I don't know how old Lilly was but judging from the tone of her voice she sounded quite elderly. I explained that I was looking for an obituary on L.W. Rogers, a former president of their organization. I told her that he would've passed away in 1953, possibly sometime before June 23rd. I was still sticking to my feelings but I needed to find the truth what ever it was. Lilly didn't have the information off the top of her head. She asked me to call back in a few days, giving her time to search for his obituary. Lilly was very friendly on the phone but my feelings told me I was going to have to make several calls just to keep her on track.

I went out to dinner one evening in mid-September with my friend Ron Siegel and his girlfriend Renée Stauffer. Renée worked at Disney Studios and met Ron at one of our junkets the previous December. They had been inseparable ever since their first date. Renée likes to relate the story about how they met, the time when a little voice inside of her stopped her at the elevator, made her go back down the hall to the room Ron was in and ask him out on a date. Their relationship was truly meant to be and I knew it wouldn't be long until the two of them were married.

Ron and Renée were anxious to hear the latest details of my story. Their support for what I was going through helped me to weather the storm building at home. After I filled them in, Renée had a suggestion of her own.

"Randy, you've got to go see this acupuncturist I go to! Her name's Lucy and she can do the most amazing regression therapy with you!" Renée was excited as she began to tell me about a Russian doctor she had been seeing.

"What's regression therapy?" I asked.

"She puts these needles in you and then takes you back into a previous lifetime so you can experience it. When I did it, I saw myself as this huge, fat woman sitting on the back of a wagon being pulled by some horses across a field. It felt like I was in some Scandinavian country back in the 1800s."

Renée revealed to me that she had an obsession where she felt she had to stockpile several weeks' worth of food for fear of running out. Lucy was trying to help her find out why she worried about this. After her session seeing herself as this massive person in a past life, they concluded her previous incarnation just might be one of the underlying reasons.

I immediately dismissed the idea of a regression session. I felt the answers to my questions were somewhere in our family trees, some distant connection between the Lynches and the Rogers. Renée didn't press the issue but told me if I ever changed my mind to call her and she would put me in touch with Lucy.

♋ ♋ ♋

I scheduled the editing on the Fire and Ice project for September at Face Video Productions. Ron and Jaime Malvin were the owners of the postproduction house. I had known Jaime from NBC where she had been an editor for many years before starting her own business. The two of them were close friends and I had done all of my projects at their facility. I had already edited the offline version on my non-linear computer editing system. All I had to do now was supervise the final cut. By the end of the first day, we had assembled the entire piece, leaving only the graphics and audio mixing for the next day. I hadn't seen Ron and Jaime for quite a while so that evening we went out to dinner together. I was now starting to feel more comfortable sharing my story so I filled them in on everything that had been happening. When I was through Jaime told me she had a book I should read. She promised to bring it in the next day.

I had been calling the librarian in Wheaton for two weeks now and not getting anywhere. Lilly was the sweetest person on the phone but the minute I hung up she forgot what she was supposed to do for me. Week by week, I had slowly gotten her to at least remember who I was and now I was hoping she would also remember what I wanted. I was going to try back again with her on the second day of my editing session.

Chapter 10

I arrived at Face early on September 23rd 1996 and Jaime came into the session with a present for me. "Here," she said. "This may help you understand what is happening to you."

The book she handed over to me was titled *Many Lives, Many Masters* by Dr. Brian Weiss. I thanked her and sat down in the chair behind Ron who was editing the Fire and Ice video. It wasn't a very thick book so I started reading it while Ron made the edits and played with title designs. It didn't take many pages for me to get caught up in the true story of psychiatrist Dr. Brian Weiss and his young patient by the name of Catherine.

Dr. Weiss was treating several of Catherine's problems with hypnotherapy sessions. They were the type of ailments some people would call phobias. He was trying to get to the root of her fears by taking her back to the earliest memories of her childhood and, in the process, attempt to find anything that may have scarred her at a very young age. She had an overwhelming fear of water and confined spaces. The simple act of swallowing a pill was extremely difficult for her.

While under hypnosis one day, she was relating events that had taken place when she was three years old. He still couldn't find anything significant enough to have caused the problems she was now experiencing in her life. Thinking her trauma may have occurred even earlier in her life, Dr. Weiss asked the patient to go back to when her problems first appeared. Suddenly she started describing another life in the 1800s, her name was different and she began talking about making butter in a churn. She told a detailed story of that life and how it ended when a raging flood swept her away. Dr. Weiss found it hard to believe that she could've really lived this other life. However, as the treatments with her progressed, she told story after story of her different lives and different deaths and each one she relived helped her to understand why she had her fears in this life. She was quickly overcoming all her problems but Dr. Weiss, with his Yale training, still had trouble believing her stories of multiple lives.

One day, during another session under hypnosis, she started to tell Dr. Weiss about his son who had died a few weeks after being born. She said she was with him now and proceeded to tell Dr. Weiss how and why his son died. The psychiatrist was taken completely off guard. He and his wife never told anyone about the death of their newborn. His patient giving him this information, including details of his son's fatal heart defect, convinced him she truly must be operating on another plane of existence. The patient even went a step further and told Dr. Weiss that his father was also present and he too had died from a heart problem. She was now communicating directly with their spirits. Dr. Weiss listened intently as she relayed the information to him. He finally believed that his patient was somehow able to bridge the gap between this plane of existence and another world.

After I finished reading the book, I realized I had very little knowledge on the subject of reincarnation. Events, however, seemed to be quickly steering me towards exploring this new direction. Renée's dinner story was also a regression session, done with acupuncture instead of hypnosis. Looking into a past life helped her understand why she had an obsession in this one. Another similarity was my communication with Kathy who was on another level of existence. In the book *Many Lives, Many Masters*, the patient, coincidentally named Catherine, did the same type of thing, communicate with the son of Dr. Brian Weiss and bring back details only the doctor would've known.

Kathy Lynch also believed in reincarnation.

At lunchtime, I decided to try calling the Theosophical Society in Wheaton again. When Lilly answered the phone, she actually remembered me this time and told me she found the obituary on L.W. Rogers. I listened patiently as she started to paraphrase the entire article. I finally cut in and told her that I was mainly interested in the date he died.

"It was April 18th, 1953," she replied.

L.W. had died just two months before Kathy and I were born! I thanked Lilly for finding the article and she said she would mail me a copy. I could barely contain myself after I hung up the phone. I told Ron and Jaime what had just happened. This was the first time I had ever done anything like this.

How did I know these facts about this man? The questions began to race through my mind. Who was L.W. Rogers? Could Kathy Lynch have been his reincarnation or had I been L.W. in a previous life? Maybe he was a separate spirit altogether?

♋ ♋ ♋

Unfortunately, my wife was not sharing my interest in exploring the subject further. An argument would break out every time I tried to share something new. I finally reached the point where I wouldn't discuss anything with her that had to do with the events I was experiencing. This new problem in our relationship left me feeling cold and distant. At social gatherings I would have to stop talking about it when Susan would approach a group of our friends listening to my story. I was constantly dodging the awkward situation, changing topics when someone would ask me about it in her presence.

After a cocktail party in Venice one evening the battles really started. I had just walked into the place when a producer friend spotted me and came over with several of her friends.

"Randy, what's the latest on your search for L.W.?" Diana asked after she had introduced Susan and me to the group.

"Well, I found him, and he died just two months before Kathy and I were born." I could sense Susan doing a slow burn. Before I could say anything else, she excused herself and moved off into the party.

I explained that Susan was not happy about me continuing to investigate my connection with Kathy and L.W. However the damage was already done, so I continued telling the group my story as they were peppering me for more details. I was having a great time, sharing all the events that had taken place, and everyone seemed genuinely interested.

Leaving the party that evening, I could sense Susan was less than happy with me. I had no idea just how unhappy until we were both in the car and driving home.

"Can't you talk about something other than that same old boring story?" Her voice was harsh and as demeaning as it could possibly be. "You're boring the hell out of everyone forcing them to listen to you and that stupid story."

I sat stunned for a moment. I searched my memory back to how the evening had started before answering her attack.

"I didn't bring it up. They asked me!"

"You could've changed the subject but no, you kept right on going, telling the whole thing over and over again to anyone who would listen." Susan was fuming now and nervous as she continued her barrage. "Those people were just being polite staying there and listening to that garbage."

"If I'm really forcing this story on them then why do they ask me more questions about it? Why don't they change the subject or walk away if they want me to shut up?" I waited a moment for her reply.

"Because you don't give them a chance." Susan snapped back at me in a vile, cutting tone that left me shaken.

We drove the rest of the way home in silence.

Our relationship was beginning to fall apart. All I wanted was her support, but that was the one thing she would never give me. We became two people living together but without sharing anything intimate or personal. I stayed at work longer and longer each day, searching on the Internet or talking with my friends. The longer I was away from her, the more distant I became when I did see her at home.

♋ ♋ ♋

One evening in mid-September, I had gone to bed early to try to get some extra sleep. I had just settled into a light state of semi-consciousness when I felt someone was telling me to look for a cardboard box in my closet. I got back up and went over to the closet and indeed, there was a cardboard box sitting in the bottom of it. The box was left over from moving, odds and ends that had no place else to go. I had no idea what I was looking for but I started digging.

After searching down through various legal papers and other documents I had kept over the years, I found another smaller cardboard box. Inside was a notebook diary I kept during 1986, the first year I worked with NBC. I had forgotten I had even put it in there. When I lifted it out of the box, I saw a yellowed newspaper clipping lying underneath it. I opened it and recognized an astrological forecast I had clipped that same year from the Arizona Republic.

I could clearly remember reading it out of the paper to Susan at breakfast that morning.

"*What seemed a "no exit" proposition will be brighter. You will have more love and money as result. Get ready for new start. Display pioneering spirit.* Maybe I'll get a call from the network today," I said as I headed out the door for the television station.

An hour later I was walking into the newsroom when the receptionist handed me a phone message. Edwin Croft from the NBC Burbank Bureau was calling to offer me a job! I had forgotten I clipped out the forecast after my prophecy came true. What grabbed my attention next was the date at the top of the newsprint… **April 23rd, 1986!**

Now, look through the other papers. Kathy's thoughts were with me again. I began rummaging through the other documents. My wedding to my first wife, June 14th 1975, my divorce from her, signed by the judge on July 23rd 1980, the motorcycle accident court settlement, April 5th 1976, all 5's… every one of these life changing dates in my past broke down to the base number five. *Now do you understand the importance of the numbers?* Kathy's spirit had just given me another road sign to watch for as I continued my search.

♋ ♋ ♋

At the end of September, I had to take a trip back to New York to set up and shoot a press junket for *The Associate*, a Disney movie starring Whoopi Goldberg. Ron Siegel was along on the shoot and I gave him the book *Many Lives, Many Masters* to read on the plane. I told him to watch how the number 23 kept appearing around me as I went though my life. He read most of the book on the plane and as I walked off the jet-way into the terminal in New York, I turned around to wait for him. As he approached me, I said to him, "Look at what gate we landed at!" It was gate 23.

The shoot in NY was relatively uneventful but as we were departing JFK Airport on Sunday night, the mayhem started. Normally I was able to easily upgrade to business class on American Airlines from flying so many miles each year. That was not to be the case this time though.

The terminal was a crowded, noisy mess; flights delayed, then cancelled. The one I was taking was overbooked and late. As the ticket agent handed me my seat assignment I was thinking about Renée and the acupuncturist back in Los Angeles. Maybe I should give her a call and see if she could help me. Just as the thought passed through my mind a young woman, standing in front of me and carrying a backpack, turned around and began talking to me. With all the things going on with me lately, I listened carefully as she told me she had just gotten back from Prague in Czechoslovakia. Right away, I picked up on the connection to me. My great grandparents were from Czechoslovakia, as were Kathy's.

I thought to myself, *Is this some kind of sign? Should I see this acupuncturist?*

No sooner had the thought crossed my mind than an old familiar voice came back to me with a reply: *Look at her seat assignment, what number is her seat?*

The girl was holding her ticket in her hand right in front of me so I could see it quite easily. It was seat 23! I pulled my boarding pass out of my pocket: seat number 32. I had to call Renée the first thing Monday morning.

Chapter 11

When I arrived home in Los Angeles, my relationship with Susan hadn't improved. She was leaving for Washington and Oregon to look at colleges with our daughter, Dana. It seemed I would have the perfect opportunity to see this acupuncturist without causing major strife in my home environment. Also waiting for me when I arrived was a package from Kathy's sister Chris Russell. I hurriedly took it out to my office to examine the contents in privacy.

Inside the box were three articles. The first was the bracelet Kathy had worn. It was a thin strap of leather with a simple Indian red and black beadwork across the center of the strap. As I grasped this last piece of Kathy's jewelry in my hand, I felt close to her, yet so far away at the same time. I now had something that would be with me to my final day. As I tied the leather thongs of the deer hide around my wrist, I knew I would think of her every day of my life.

The next piece of paper I opened was a copy of Kathy's family tree she had started to build. I quickly glanced over it and nothing unusual caught my eye. None of the names stood out, but I had yet to receive anything from my parents about our family history.

The last item I removed from the package was a thin journal of Kathy's that Chris had told me she would try to find. As I held it in my hands I knew that this was going to be a very personal glimpse of Kathy she may have never revealed to anyone. I opened to the first page and started to read. The book was old and there were no dates entered in the beginning so I could only guess when she started to write in it. It appeared to be sometime after high school and maybe even after she had left Johnstown. Whenever it was, Kathy had definite answers for two of her own questions about life, God and reincarnation.

What is God to me?

I find it hard to put a definition on something that is everything. There are an infinite amount of definitions I could use to express what I feel him to be. I do not picture him as a being. To me he is a spirit as I will be a spirit upon death.

What about re-incarnation?

I would like to think it's possible. I wouldn't want it to be mandatory. I don't want to check out and check in, in the blink of an eye. I would like a little R & R in order to relish what I have experienced in this life.

I sometimes meet a person and there is a certain familiarity about them. It would be nice to think that perhaps our spirits were acquainted and even loved in some other existence.

What if the existence of "Kathy Lynch" would always be the same, as characters in a play? Juliet will always be Juliet, her life will always be the same and her death will always be the same. It is the actress-spirit that gives her dimension and that is what we experience. Perhaps Shakespeare knew more than we think when he said "All the world's a stage and all the men and women merely players"

Of course my ego takes over and says that there couldn't possibly be another Kathy Lynch. But perhaps there have been and will be many more Kathys but I intend to thoroughly enjoy my jaunt at it.

As I read further into her journal, the ups and downs of living this life were boldly splashed across each page.

I am not an older spirit. I am "nothing". How stupid of me, to write, to think, to care. I am worthless.

And on the next page…

…and another butterfly evolves, one more lovely than the last!! How glorious it is to be part of and experience this thing called life!

Each setback Kathy suffered was followed by a short period of somewhat good times. "Peaks and valleys" she called them and her next valley appeared to be the one into which her marriage had crumbled.

I'm tired. Why do I try? Why do I care? Why do I dream? Why do I hope? My life remains empty…I try not to notice. But, again I begin and ask <u>why</u>?

I had thought I left it behind, behind with the foolish dreamer, but it haunts me still. Ah, the serenity. Ah, the fulfillment. As wisps of fog on warm mornings, there, but on approachment...gone. How do I grasp it? How do I hold it? How can I make it envelop me? I wish I hadn't remembered!!! I haven't known pain such as this in quite some time. I was perfectly happy, then ajar, now the pain! If only it wouldn't remind me that it could be so good.

On the day after her 36th birthday, she dated her entry.

6/24/89

What a ride! I think I may have finally come to a stop. It's called co-dependency. I've always envied people who enjoyed life, people who are able to just take it all in and enjoy it. They run into things they have to work through but they simply absorb them and move on! Piece of cake! Meanwhile I sit in my boarded-up shell, completely bricked-in, encased in high tempered steel just to make sure nothing gets in – and I never get out. I'm miserable, I'm lonely, unloved, afraid, feeling guilty and ashamed. Only I can take down the steel, brick, and wood shell, but it's everybody else's fault that I'm stuck here.

What's wrong with this picture???

Well, I'm gonna try to find out. I guess the next ride's about to take off. I have a feeling this is going to be a pain-in-the-ass but it will be exciting and best of all – fun!

Two months later a second dated entry was made.

8/26/89

Fun? Fun? You call this next ride <u>Fun</u>!? Pain-in-the-ass, yes (literally even), but "Fun"?... In your dreams!

Well, Well, Well…

It appears I am a "double winner". I never thought – in my wildest nightmares – I would ever be going thru this again. Fallopian Cancer.

I'm scared – what if I don't make it this time?

I see people on T.V. with Alzheimer's, Cerebral Palsy, even people waiting on death row and I feel I could be worse off. Even at the center there are times – people I see – I know I could be worse off.

I really keep trying to have a good attitude. I know how important that is. Sometimes I hit bottom though. That's when I really start thinking how much worse it could be. It helps.

One thing that really scares me is Chemo. I have no idea what to expect from that. But that's in the future and I don't have the time or energy to worry about that now.

At least I'm mobile - that's great, to be able to get around where & when I want. Also, I'm at home for this one – much better than the last time. Also it's only 10 miles to the center. Beats the hell out of a bus! Luckily this time I'm not nauseous and my taste buds aren't going bananas. I do have a problem with diarrhea but I've gotten medication for it. I've lost some weight but this medication should allow me to put it back on. That's a big concern right now. I need to get as much weight on as soon as possible before Chemo and I know how tough it was when I wasn't even sick!

Sandra (Sister Carleen) *came down and stayed for a week. That was really great. I didn't feel quite so alone.*

One of the hardest things I've had to learn to do is to allow people to do things for me. Everyone's been so great.

And of course my medical bills are dribbling in. So far they've dribbled a total of about $22,000. Ain't it great! Oh well, another thing to worry about some other time.

Oh yeah – I had a hysterectomy! ...Minor detail.

The thing that really pisses me off is that things were starting to really look good. It was a bit of a struggle but I was making it. I was happy. Damn!

Oh well – moaning & groaning won't do any good. "Attitude Kathy Attitude".

At points my tears were flowing as I found myself wanting to do anything to go back and help her cope with the loneliness and helplessness she had sunken into as life threw her one hard pitch after another.

After reading her story, I was more determined than ever to call Renée and try anything I could to find out why Kathy was reaching out to me.

Monday morning I went to my office around 8 a.m. to get an early start on the paperwork from our trip to New York. I was planning to call Renée just shortly after 9 a.m. to get the doctor's number from her, but I didn't have to wait that long. At 8:30 Renée called me from her office with excitement ringing in her voice.

"Randy, you'll never guess what happened to me on Saturday!" she blurts out to me on the phone.

"What happened to you on Saturday?" I asked.

"I was at my acupuncturist Lucy's office and she told me that I have to read this book called *Many Lives, Many Masters*! I told Lucy that it was such a coincidence, because my boyfriend had been given the book from a friend who was having a lot of psychic things happening to him. It's no coincidence that this is happening Randy."

"I know it isn't." I said. I related the events that had happened in New York and how I was just going to call her to get the doctor's number. "I'm being led to her by something that is beyond anything I have control over. I need to see this Lucy and find out what is going on with me."

Renée gave me Lucy Postolov's name and phone number. She asked me to call her as soon as I had my first meeting with Lucy.

I hung up with Renée and dialed Lucy's number. Dr. Postolov was with a patient so I left a message. Less than an hour later, she returned my call. Lucy had a very strong Russian accent but her English was perfect and easily understood. She didn't ask me any questions about what was happening to me but told me I could come in the next day for a session. I marked my calendar for noon on October 1st 1996, my first meeting with an acupuncturist. Maybe tomorrow I would start to get some answers to this ever-growing search that had taken over my life.

♋ ♋ ♋

The next day I arrived at Lucy's about five minutes before noon. She was in a medical building off Wilshire Boulevard in West Los Angeles, just on the border of Santa Monica. It was a small building with an even smaller parking lot. I had to squeeze my Bronco into the last tight space.

The sign outside her office had two other doctor's names listed along with Lucy's so I assumed she was sharing the space with a few colleagues. I had to ring a buzzer and wait for a few minutes but when the door opened, I finally met the doctor Renée had been talking up a storm about. Lucy was about five foot five inches tall and mid-thirties in age. She had a warm smile and friendly face that reminded me of many of my friends I had grown up with in Pennsylvania. Her hair was a medium cut and auburn in color.

She shook my hand and had me take a seat in the waiting room while she collected some papers for me to fill out. It was your usual medical paperwork, asking for a background of everything that had ever happened to me during my 43 years on this planet. I quickly breezed over it and spent the most time filling in the details of the motorcycle accident that almost took my life in 1974. I listed my allergy to penicillin and handed back the paper work for her to look over.

Lucy called me back to a treatment room a few minutes later and we sat there discussing my previous health history before changing the conversation to why I was there. I began by telling her the story of my obsession to find Kathy. When I got to the part about working on a cancer video for the Fire & Ice Ball, Lucy interrupted me to interject a story about her own mother's struggle with breast cancer.

"She is so lucky though," Lucy said, "because she's just one of a handful of women enrolled in this special UCLA program that's testing a new cancer therapy."

I stopped Lucy before she could go any farther. "You don't have to tell me about the program," I told her. "That is the video I've been shooting for the Fire & Ice Ball. It's no accident that I'm here in your office right now. There are over 14 million people in this city and it's just a coincidence I'm sitting here with you while your mother is in the program I'm shooting? I'm being led to you for some reason, and I just want to find out why."

She agreed it was too much of a stretch for this to all be a big coincidence. After a quick check of my pulse, eyes and tongue, Lucy had me remove my shoes and socks and then lay back on the acupuncture table. She told me she wanted to start with what she called a cleansing session. During this time, I would lie on the table with some needles placed in me. I was to reflect back on my entire life and try to understand why key events in it had occurred to me. She especially wanted me to think about my motorcycle accident, since it had the biggest effect on my health as well as my personal life. I agreed I would try, so Lucy began to place the needles into my wrists and the arches of my feet.

I was lying perfectly still on the table when she finished placing the last of the four needles in my body. There had been a definite electrical shock with each one, but it was only momentary and there was no pain at all coming from where she had inserted the needles. In fact, I couldn't even tell where the needles were any more. Lucy came around to the head of the table and told me she wanted me to see something before we started. She asked me to look where she had placed the pins in my body. To help me do that she lifted my head so I could see down the length of my body. I started by looking at my left wrist, which had a needle sticking straight out of it. As I glanced down to my body I could see there was also one needle in each of the arches of my feet, but as I looked over at my right wrist I could see that the needle in it wasn't acting like the others. This one needle was vibrating like a divining rod. My hand and arm were perfectly still and flat but the needle looked like it was going to shoot out of my arm at any second.

"Can you feel that?" Lucy asked me as I watched the pin moving as if it were in an earthquake.

"I can see it," I replied, "but I can't feel a thing. What is causing that?"

"That is the Chi," she answered. "It is the energy in your body and I find it amazing that it is flowing so strongly out of this point on your wrist next to this bracelet you're wearing."

It was true that the other points seemed calm and normal but the wrist with the bracelet was flowing as if a valve had opened below the needle.

"I don't find anything amazing anymore," I said to Lucy. "I just want to try to find out why this is happening to me."

"OK," she said, "we'll start by relaxing while you review your life."

Lucy turned off the lights and left me alone for twenty minutes. I was very relaxed and, as I started to think about my life, it was as though a movie projector turned on in my head. I could see events as clearly as if they had happened yesterday. Tears began to trickle uncontrollably down the side of my face as I went back to my previous marriage and divorce from my first wife. I began to see the relationship between everything I did and how good always came from what appeared on the surface to be bad.

The motorcycle accident was the catalyst needed to meet my first wife. I grew so much because of that relationship, and even left the Catholic Church because of it. The divorce from my first wife moved me to new highs that I would've never achieved if I had stayed in that relationship. Things were starting to make sense now. The bitterness I once had for my first wife leaving was being replaced with a knowledge that my relationship with her was only supposed to last that long.

I could now feel a presence in the room on either side of me. Holding onto my right hand was Kathy and holding the left was my grandmother who had passed away from cancer in the early '70s. My emotions were at a peak now and, as I held onto them, they gave me the energy to continue with my quest. Many of the pieces were still missing but the puzzle had become suddenly clear. I was searching for the Key of Life!

IV.

REUNION OF SOULS

Chapter 12

Lucy re-entered the room and walked up next to the acupuncture table. "Did you learn anything about yourself today?" She asked as she brought the lights back up and reached over to check my pulse.

"It was so emotional, the whole experience. I began to understand why different things happened in my life, my motorcycle accident, my first marriage… they were all important events that had to happen to move me forward."

"Your heart rate is very relaxed now compared to when we started." Lucy pulled her hand away from my wrist. "Did you see anything else that was important during your cleansing session?"

"I had the strangest feeling just before I came back to the present. I felt like Kathy and my grandmother, were in this room holding onto each of my hands. I could feel their energy on both sides of me." I replied.

"The needles do open a link for you to allow those kinds of feelings to come through. I'm sure their spirits are close to you right now."

"May I try the regression session now? I want to see what that is like as well."

"I don't normally do the regressions so quickly on a new patient," Lucy replied. "It usually takes several sessions just to get your energy balanced and flowing correctly."

"I feel fine, actually better than ever right now. You said my heart rate was relaxed. I really want to at least attempt it today. If it doesn't work then I can come back again to work on my energy flow."

"All right, I don't see any harm in trying it today. Let's see what happens." Lucy left the needles in me then sat down on a stool off to my right side and near the end of the acupuncture table. She reached over to turn off the lights again and then began the regression session.

"Take a deep breath… hold it…now let it out," Lucy said as she began to set a pace for my breathing. After repeating this phrase slowly for half a dozen times or more, I settled into a very slow rhythmic breathing pattern.

"I want you to imagine yourself standing in a hall that has many doors leading off of it. There are all types of doors around you, every shape, size, color and material you can imagine. In a moment, one of these doors is going to open for you and when it does, you will be able to walk into another time and place and experience another life you have lived. When you do, you will observe everything happening to you during that time and you will describe those events to me. Are you ready to find your door?"

"Yes, I'm ready," I replied softly. I was so intrigued by my surroundings that Lucy had become just a voice in the distance. I don't know if it was just my ability to visualize easily or if she had actually guided me to this other place, but I suddenly found myself standing in the center of a dimly lit hall. It was circular in shape and about 50 feet across with all kinds of doors lining the perimeter on all sides. Directly ahead of me, and dividing the room, was a long hallway that also had doors on both sides. This hallway seemed to continue into darkness or infinity, but I didn't study it long as I was looking at a white door with a simple brass knob just off to my left. I walked to the door and extended my hand to grab the doorknob. It turned easily and I pulled the door open towards me. I was describing what I was doing to Lucy. After the door was open, she encouraged me to walk through it.

I stepped through the doorway and immediately found myself surrounded by an intense color of green. "It's so intense," I said. The color was so saturated I couldn't tell where I was.

"Where are you?" she asked me.

As soon as she asked, everything suddenly came into focus. "I'm in a forest. It's so green and dense. I'm on a path and I can't get off. I must stay on this path."

"Stop a minute. Is anyone around you?"

"No, there's no one around me." I was standing alone on the path.

"Well, can you see yourself?"

"No, of course I can't see myself." I didn't have a mirror or anything around me to see my reflection.

"Look down at your feet. Can you see your feet?"

"Yes, I can see my feet," I said.

"What color are your shoes?" she asked.

"They're brown shoes. But they're not really shoes, they're moccasins."

"Are you a Native American?" Lucy asked.

"Yes I'm young and I'm a Native American boy. I feel like I'm 18 and I'm very strong. I must stay on this path that I'm on," I said as I continued walking through the forest.

I looked up at the towering canopy of trees on both sides of the trail. The color was so vivid it was almost surreal. I hadn't taken many steps when I came up on a clearing. Directly ahead of me I could see a stream flowing down the hill to my right.

"I'm coming up to a stream and there is a woman on the opposite side of it," I told Lucy. "She's kneeling down and washing her face with the water."

I was about 50 yards away from the woman when I first saw her. Her long black hair flowed onto a dress made of buckskin. She was on her knees with her hands cupped, splashing water on her face and looking up at me between each splash. Lucy asked if I knew her but I had to get closer to see who she was. I made my way to the water's edge within 15 feet of her. Lucy asked again if I knew her. I was trying to study her face between splashes and couldn't get a clear view.

"I've got to talk to her." I was just about to say hello when I felt a strange lifting sensation and now found myself floating up into the sky. It was as though I was in a cloud.

"I'm with Kathy now," I said to Lucy, as I felt the immediate presence of my friend beside me. The event was very similar to my out of body experience the night in my bedroom. I couldn't see Kathy but her thoughts came smoothly into my head, and I repeated them to Lucy as Kathy spoke to me.

"Just stay on your course, listen to what is in your head and you will not go wrong." Kathy repeated this over several times to me as I felt myself getting heavier and heavier. I was suddenly aware that I was on the table in Lucy's office.

Lucy asked me if I was coming back and I quietly told her I was. She said she was going to count backward and when she got to one I would be completely back in her office. She counted slowly down from three and now I felt like my body was made of rock. I was so heavy I didn't feel like I could lift my head. Lucy walked around me, taking out the needles, and told me it was normal to feel much heavier. She had me rest on the table while she sat down and gave me her interpretation of what she felt my vision meant.

"Where did you find yourself when you first opened the door and entered this other life?" Lucy asked me.

"I was on a path in a forest," I said.

"Yes, you said you were on this path and you couldn't get off, you had to stay on it. Then what did you see next?"

"I saw a woman at a stream."

"And what was she doing?" Lucy asked.

"She was washing her face."

"She was cleansing herself," Lucy said. "I feel like this was a very symbolic session in that you found yourself on this path that you couldn't get off of, and when you talked with Kathy later she told you to stay on your course, which translates to staying on your path. This path led you to a woman, not a man, but a woman, and this woman was cleansing herself very purposefully for you to see her. I think this relates very strongly to the women you have been around that have cancer. There is some kind of cleansing process going on and you need to be near them."

I finished my session with Lucy and made another appointment to try again tomorrow. I still didn't have the answers I needed about Kathy, L.W. Rogers and what our relationship was all about.

♋ ♋ ♋

There was no one home when I got back from the session. Susan was in Washington State with our daughter Dana looking at potential colleges. I wasn't sure I wanted to tell her about it anyway because I knew she would just shrug it off as meaningless. Going to sleep that night, I hoped tomorrow's session would reveal something more tangible.

Chapter 13

I arrived about 15 minutes early for my 11:30 appointment. Rather than go inside right away, I sat in my Bronco and reclined the seat to relax and think about everything happening to me. I started to think about the previous day's session and wondered if I had actually been in that forest or if I had created the scene. After all, I had been wearing the Indian bracelet that Kathy's sister had sent me. Did I subconsciously create these events because of outside stimuli? Maybe this was all a waste of time and I should just stop my searching now. I needed some kind of sign from Kathy that I was on the right path. As soon as that last thought ran across my mind, I had an instant response.

"Get out the book. Get out the book," Kathy whispered in my ear.

I reached into my briefcase and pulled out the book *Many Lives, Many Masters*. I had brought it with me to leave at Lucy's for Renée to borrow. She was going to pick it up when she came in for her acupuncture session later that evening. As I placed the book on my lap, I could feel Kathy's spirit in my thoughts again.

"Open it up, open it up," came clearly into my head.

As I opened the book, it fell to page 55. With my new awareness of numbers, I immediately recognized the double fives as having a special meaning being Kathy's number repeated twice. I figured she must want me to read this page, and I quickly realized this was the part where Dr. Weiss was gaining belief in his patient's story after she told him about his son that had died shortly after he had brought him home from the hospital. Halfway down the page my heart nearly skipped a beat. There, spelled out in full, was the word twenty-three. He was only *twenty-three days old!* As I read these words, a chill shot through me. How are all these events lining up with so much synchronicity? This can't just be a coincidence.

Dr. Weiss wanted some proof the stories his patient told were true and he got it. I wanted a sign that I was on the right path and it came as the page of the story where Dr. Weiss had gotten his proof. This interlocking of one story to another was a great mystery to me. How could all these events mesh so easily, tying one with another almost seamlessly? Were other things happening in my life also tied to people I didn't know or at least thought I didn't know?

I began my session with Lucy by telling her what had just happened in the car. I was more excited than ever to start the acupuncture session with her. I pointed out the fictitious name given the patient in the book was Catherine, another version of Kathy and actually my grandmother's name. Lucy told me Catherine was also her grandmother's name.

Lucy began to place the needles in my wrists and feet. With each initial puncture I felt a slight shock of electricity that quickly subsided. The needles were comfortable once in, and I lost all awareness of them after I started concentrating on my breathing. Lucy dimmed the lights and started again by asking me to breathe in, hold it, and then let it go. As I listened, her soothing voice paced my breath and soon I reached a very relaxed state. Lucy then asked me to imagine myself standing again in the hall of doors. This time as I looked at the doors, she said I would find a very special one to open.

I was standing in the subdued light of the hallway once again but couldn't see the door I was to open. I told Lucy I couldn't find it but she told me to keep looking and it would be there somewhere. I walked along looking to the left where I found the door yesterday but nothing jumped out until I looked back over to my right.

There it was, a massive structure made of rough-hewn timber at least 8 feet tall and 5 feet wide. The thick lumber was reinforced with several wide bands of steel that wrapped around its width. It had a giant bolt of wood that had to be slid from left to right to allow the door to swing free. The bolt felt very coarse as I lifted it. I strained under its weight. Pushing the door open took every bit of strength I could gather. I described to Lucy how hard it was to get to move as it slowly opened and I stepped across the threshold.

"I'm standing on a drawbridge in front of the most beautiful castle I've ever seen. It has white stone walls and twin towers on each end of the parapet running around it."

I stood there in silence for a minute just looking. Directly in front of me, there was a huge vertical gate made out of wood and steel, closed tightly to the ground. I was standing on the bridge with a stone wall running alongside me. I touched the wall as I leaned over to get a view of the scene below me.

"Wow, I'm so high up," I said to Lucy. It seemed I was a good 100 feet above the ground. "It's so massive."

Lucy asked me if I could see myself and again I told her I couldn't so she asked me to look down at my feet. "I can't see my feet." I replied.

"Look again," she said.

I looked down and exclaimed, "I'm wearing sandals!"

"You're wearing sandals?" she asked surprised. "Are you a man or a woman?"

"I'm a woman," I whispered. "I'm wearing a long dress with many layers."

My feet appeared and disappeared by the movement of the dress. I told Lucy I had a babushka tied under my chin and I was carrying a basket of bread under my left arm. Lucy asked me if there was anyone else around. I told her I couldn't see anyone.

"How old are you?" Lucy asked as I stood looking all around me.

"I'm twenty-eight years old and I'm in England in the 1560s."

"Can you move ahead ten years in your life?" Lucy asked.

I replied I could, but when I thought about moving ahead ten years in my life, I found myself suddenly standing in complete blackness. I related this to Lucy, and she told me I had probably died before then. Lucy then asked me to go back to where I had been standing on the drawbridge. Just the thought instantly transported me back and once again, I was standing by the wall looking down at the steep terrain that surrounded the castle.

"Would you like to go into the castle?"

"No, I can't go into the castle. I have to go to the village." I turned around and started to walk down the road leading away from the bridge.

I hadn't gone far before reaching an open-air market, filled with horses, carts and people. The first person I passed off to my right was a giant of a bald man holding a dead goose up by its neck. His arms were as thick as tree trunks. He was so big the goose looked like a chicken in comparison to his size. He smiled and nodded at me as I passed, and I thought I knew him from somewhere. Something caused me to look to my left, breaking my stare. There, moving out of the crowd of people, was someone very familiar.

"She's my sister! She's my sister!" I yelled, as I ran towards my friend Kathy. She was also running toward me and when we reached each other, she grabbed a hold of my hand and held onto it tightly. "She's my sister, she's my sister," I repeated again as we looked into each other's eyes smiling with happiness.

"Is she your older sister?" Lucy asked.

"Of course she's not my older sister," I responded, as if Lucy could see Kathy.

"Then she's your younger sister?"

"Well, no, we're very close in age," I said.

"Are you twin sisters?" Lucy asked, surprised.

"When I see her, I see myself."

She didn't look anything like the Kathy Lynch I knew growing up in Pennsylvania. In this life, she had black, medium-length hair covered with a scarf like mine. Her facial features were very sharp and attractive, and she was wearing a dress similar to mine in its layers and pattern. I had no mirror around me, but I somehow knew that when I looked at her I was looking at me. Kathy continued holding my hand in hers as we walked around the market square. As we passed by the large man with the goose, he waved goodbye to us and it was then I recognized him.

"It's my Uncle Bob," I said to Lucy, meaning my uncle in this life, not in England. "He was the butcher."

"It's time for us to go home now," Kathy said as she spoke her first words to me.

We continued holding hands as we walked down the road away from the market square.

We hadn't walked far before the scenery changed and we were out in the countryside, approaching a small cottage. It appeared to be a single room structure with a thatched roof and a rickety fence of crooked sticks surrounding the front. Off to the right I noticed a man chopping wood by an outside fire but I didn't pay him any attention. I was concentrating completely on the front of the house as we approached the front door. It was old and gray with a black metal bolt that I slid open. When the door swung forward, I could see a woman inside.

"It's my grandmother," I said to Lucy as I described the scene to her. "But she was my mother back then."

The vibration I was feeling was definitely from my grandmother's spirit. She quickly stepped aside, disappearing into the shadows as we entered the room. Kathy and I sat down across from each other at a small wooden table in the center of the room. We never let go of each other's hand and now they met in the center of the table, her left hand clasped in my right.

"I'm going to leave you now with Kathy." Lucy's voice broke the silence that had begun to build. "While I'm gone I want you to ask her everything you have wanted to ask, and when you are finished, move ahead in your life to the day you die. When I come back we will discuss everything that happened to you."

I agreed to do what she asked, and Lucy left the acupuncture room. I know Randy Rogers' body was on an acupuncturist's table in Los Angeles in 1996, but I was over four hundred years away sitting in a room in England holding my friend's hand, my sister's hand, in as real a setting as I had ever been in. The emotion of the moment had taken a hold of me and my tears began to flow both in England and from my body on the table in Los Angeles.

"It's been such a very, very long time," I said as I looked across the table into my sister's eyes.

"I know, I know it has, and it feels so good to hold you," Kathy said, smiling with such joy it made my tears flow even harder.

"Why are we here at this time?" I asked her.

"You wanted to understand why we are so close so I brought you here to show you this very special time in our lives. We're twin spirits, what you would call soul mates. In this life, we were born from the same egg – identical twins. We couldn't have been any closer physically or spiritually than we were in this life."

"Was this the first time we were together?" I asked her as the tears continued to flow down my cheeks.

"No," she said, shaking her head with a smile that matched the intensity of my emotional release. "We go way back to the beginning of time and all the way forward to where you are today but this was such a special time I wanted to start our journey here first."

My tears had become a torrent as I was now sobbing uncontrollably. "I don't want to go back. I miss being with you so much – I can't go back without you."

"Didn't you get the bracelet I left for you?" Kathy asked.

"I'm wearing it now," I sobbed, realizing that she must know I have it on my wrist back on the acupuncture table.

"You'll never be without me – that bracelet will be a reminder that I'm always around you," Kathy said. The smile on her face helped slow my tears.

"Why can't I just stay here with you?" I asked.

"Oh, you have to go back. You've got a lot of work to do yet," she told me as she started to stand up from the table. "But before we go I've got something that I want you to see."

Kathy led me by the hand from the little one room cottage. As we walked through the door, again I felt my grandmother's presence behind me. I turned just in time to see the woman who was our mother in that life shut the door behind us. Once I was outside I started to think about what Lucy had told me and how I should move forward to the day I died. As I had the thought, I felt the pain of rocks hitting me just as Kathy pulled me back from wherever I was going.

"No, we can't go there now. It isn't time for you to see that. You have to come with me now." So hand in hand we walked back down the lane that led to our house.

Soon I found myself standing in front of a set of wide stone stairs that seemed to lead up to the castle. I climbed the stairs with Kathy and, once at the top, entered a door into a room. There was a long stone table in the center of the room with an arched window to the left side. Sunlight was streaming through the window and casting itself across the table. Also on the left side of the table and near me was a wooden chair pulled out and facing the front of the room. Kathy led me over to the chair and I sat down. I was now holding both her hands in mine as she stood in front of me looking directly into my eyes.

"What did you come here to learn?" she asked.

"I wanted to find out about you, me and L.W. Rogers," I replied. "I wanted to meet L.W. Rogers."

Kathy smiled and nodded her head. "That's what we're here for."

I became very excited and started to look around for the man who was such a mystery. "Where is he?" I asked, not seeing anyone in the room.

At that instant, I felt a vibration unlike any I had felt before. It was so powerful and intense it swept through me like the shockwave of an earthquake, but with the feeling of overwhelming love.

"Oh, no, no, no, it's not time for you to see me yet," replied a powerful, yet gentle voice. "But I will answer any question that you have for me."

I didn't know where he was, as he seemed everywhere at once. I wasn't afraid but this spirit gave me a feeling of humbleness as his power was more than I could ever imagine. My question went out to him but I never remember opening my mouth to speak the words.

"I wanted to know about you, Kathy and me. How are we all connected?" was the thought that escaped from my mind.

"In the beginning, when you and Kathy first became a life force on this physical plane, I was the spirit that was guiding you. When the two of you passed on to the spiritual world, you both guided my journey through the physical world. We leap-frogged like this through time until 1953 when I passed away, just before you both were born. I'm a master spirit now and no longer have to return to this physical plane, but you and Kathy will be back several more times and I will be the spirit that continues to guide you."

L.W.'s explanation left nothing for me to ask. I was digesting everything I had seen and heard.

"It's time for us to leave now," said Kathy, drawing me to my feet. "You'll be able to come back again and even meet him someday but for now it's time to go."

We walked to the door and started down the stone stairs holding on to each other for those last few moments. At the bottom of the stairs, before she could say anything, I told her I had to see how I died so I could tell Lucy.

"I can't let you experience that today," Kathy said to me. "But I will show you where you died."

We took a few more steps and suddenly were standing at the top of a ravine. As I looked over into it, I could see two bodies lying at the bottom. One was mine and the other was my sister's. They looked like they had been savagely beaten, raped and stoned to death. Their clothing torn about them, they were lying together less than fifteen feet below us. I viewed the scene with no emotion. It was like looking at two wrecked automobiles at the bottom of a cliff. I realized the two bodies were not really Kathy and I, only the vehicles we had once used to express our spirits.

As I stood there looking over the scene of our murders, I suddenly understood why Kathy had brought me to this time and place. She and I hadn't just been with each other in a previous life, *we were born together, lived with each other, and died on the same day as well!* How much closer of a physical life could two spirits share?

There was no tearful goodbye as I felt my spirit drifting slowly back into my body on the table in Los Angeles. I grew heavier and heavier just as Lucy returned to the room to guide me back the rest of the way. I felt like I weighed a thousand pounds. I lay there on the table, too weak to lift my arms for several minutes after the session. I spent the next few minutes telling Lucy about all the things I had learned. She was as surprised as I was about the events that had taken place in her office that day. Unknown to us both, this surprise would be mild in comparison to what lay ahead, as the future sessions would soon reveal.

Chapter 14

As the cancer video was nearing completion, I stopped off to see Donna Isman. A baying sound responded to my knock at the door. When Donna opened it, the cutest little Beagle puppy bounced up to greet me.

"This is Bailey, and she's so happy to see you," Donna said.

"I really couldn't tell." We laughed as her dog lathered me with affection.

"How are you doing?" I asked, giving Donna a big hug.

"I'm trying to stay centered and build up my energy. It's low but I'm gonna get through this." Donna had the optimism of a thousand women.

"That's why I stopped by, to see if we can build up that energy of yours." We sat down in her living room to talk.

"Is that the bracelet you've been telling me about?" Donna reached over to hold up my wrist and examine the deer hide band.

"Yes this is it." I replied.

"Can I hold it?"

I untied the double thongs of leather securing it to my wrist and handed it over to Donna. I could feel her level of excitement surge as she grasped the bracelet. She closed her eyes for a moment and held it clasped tightly in her hands.

"I want to hold onto this the whole time you're here. I want to feel its energy inside of me." Donna drew her hands together even tighter.

I was happy to share anything I could with Donna to keep her spirit up and energy flowing.

"You know, you are not going to die Donna." I opened up the topic that I knew weighed heavily on Donna's mind. "Your body may wear out and Donna Isman may be gone, but you… the spirit that drives Donna Isman… will always exist. Nothing can hurt it, stop it, or kill it. You will live on…forever."

"I understand that but I don't want to leave this life just yet... all my friends…" Donna trailed off in thought, closing her eyes and holding onto the only things she could perceive as real; this world, her friends and now the bracelet in her hand.

"None of this is real Donna." I tapped on the coffee table in front of me. "The only thing real is the spirit inside you. These bodies are just a vehicle we use to express ourselves in this world. I have a '53 model and you have a '57. For whatever reasons, some models have problems earlier than others. Poor maintenance, bad conditions, over use, or just a lemon to begin with, they all break down eventually and quit running but the energy that's driving them moves on to a new one. Just like when you buy a new car. The old one is gone but you're back driving a new one."

"I know I should let go of this fear of dying but all I know and can remember is this life." Donna was passionate about her love for living.

"It is the most difficult thing to do… let go of a fear that is buried so deep within you that you can't even find the source. But that is what this cancer feeds on, the fear and anxiety that you will somehow loose all this." I motioned my hands around her room of furnishings. "Kathy told me to 'Feel my spirit, that is what makes us as one.' Once you truly believe and understand that, nothing else will matter and you'll let go of your fear of dying."

"I'm trying Randy, it's just so hard to let go of everything." Donna was resolute in her belief that letting go she would fall and not soar to new heights.

There was very little more I could do for Donna. I sent my love and energy towards her hoping she would eventually be free from her worries.

I felt every ounce of my energy drained when I left her house that day. It made me smile to see it all bouncing around inside Donna. I knew that energy alone wouldn't be enough to see her through what lie ahead. That was something she would have to find on her own. For now, all I could do was give her spiritual support while she fought the battle.

♋ ♋ ♋

My brother Jeff came into Los Angeles on Friday October 4th. He was on his way back to Micronesia where he captained a supply ship around the islands of the Western Pacific.

Jeff had more places that he hung his hat than anyone else in my family. Micronesia was his latest home and it was as far away from civilization as one could possibly get on this planet. I dropped him off at Venice Beach on Saturday morning to spend a few hours shopping for gifts and tee shirts to take home to the islands. He wanted me to pick him up at 1 p.m.

I was about a half-hour early as I drove west on Venice Boulevard on my way back to get him.

As I approached the Los Angeles Public Library, my car started to slow down and something inside me was telling me to turn into the parking lot. I pulled in, parked the car and went inside. I started to walk up to the information counter but walked away when I realized I didn't know what I wanted. I headed straight back into the novel section and ran my hands across a row of books.

"Not on this side," I thought to myself. I turned around and directly behind me I reached for a book and pulled it out. *Psyche* was the name of the book. I didn't spend any time reading it there. I just knew I had to have it and headed straight to the checkout counter.

I felt as if I had just come out of a trance as I drove over to the beach to pick up my brother. I was still a little early when I got to our meeting spot so while I waited in the car for Jeff to arrive, I read the synopsis and the author bio from the cover of the book I had just picked up. It was a fictional story about a young Sigmund Freud using hypnosis to treat a girl suffering from hysteria. I was stunned. This was very similar to the story line in *Many Lives, Many Masters*. The similarity didn't end there. The name of the patient Freud was treating was Lucy, the same name as my acupuncturist! I could see a correlation between the two books. I was also startled to see it was dedicated to Kathleen.

When my brother got into the car he wanted to know where I had gotten the book. I told him I picked it out after spending only a minute in the library, and the only thing I knew for sure was I needed to meet the author, Peter Michalos. I learned he lived in New York City from the brief description on the book jacket. I would have to call him after I read the book.

Ron Siegel stopped by to visit a few minutes after I had returned to my office. I showed him the book and related the strange circumstances of how it came into my possession.

"Wouldn't it be wild if the Lucy in this book was from Russia," Ron said as he picked up the novel and began thumbing through it.

"Yeah, that would be something," I said."

A few minutes later Ron shouted, "Listen to this, *two generations of Lucy's family had settled in the Baltic region of Russia.*"

Ron and I scanned through the book now searching for other parts of the story line that appeared to closely parallel the story of *Many Lives, Many Masters*. I began to view these events as simple signs posted along my path to assure me that everything I had experienced was meant to be.

Later that night I started reading *Psyche*. The story revolved around hypnosis sessions where Lucy was regressed into past lives. She would describe her lives to Freud and, in the process, helped herself get over the hysteria. The entire plot of the story dealt with regression sessions and a woman from Russia named Lucy.

I felt I should call the author, Peter Michalos, and try to meet him the next time I was in New York. Directory assistance had one phone number for a Peter Michalos in Manhattan so I tried it. His message machine was on, and somehow from the sound of his voice, I knew he was the same person that had written the book. I left my number for him to call me back and a few hours later, he returned my call.

"Peter, I just pulled your novel from a library shelf out here in Venice and your story is closely mirroring some events that are happening in my life." There was a slight pause and I held my breath, hoping not to hear a click followed by the dial tone.

"I'm surprised to learn that my book is even in a library," Peter said with half a laugh. "And you say your life has some kind of connection to my story?"

"It does, and I'd like to talk with you about that and how you wrote this story. I'll be in New York in two weeks for a shoot and wanted to see if we could get together then so I could explain it to you."

"I'd love to meet up with you," Peter said, "so give me a call when you get into town and we can arrange something."

"I'll be calling you on October 19th." I thanked Peter for returning my call and hung up the phone. I felt a great sigh of relief that my investigation was moving farther along the path.

♋ ♋ ♋

Sunday morning, October 6th, I went to my office to go through my mail and do some paper work. As I worked my way to the bottom of a pile of mail that arrived Saturday, I found a package from my parents in Pennsylvania. They sent me everything they had on our family history, including a photocopied booklet about my father's side of the family. The cover was entitled *The Goughnour & Bracken Family Tree.* It was a genealogy report created from my great-grandmother's lineage. Her maiden name was Edith Goughnour and her mother's maiden name was Christeann Bracken.

The book's extensive research on both families traced the Bracken lineage to my great-great-great-great grandmother, whose maiden name was Margaret Wakefield. Her father, David Wakefield, escaped to America after implications he, along with his three brothers, had plotted against Catholic rule in Ireland. Two of his brothers didn't fare so well. They arrested and beheaded Robert and imprisoned Gilbert for life. The third brother, Samuel, managed to escape to Scotland. With all this documentation of the Wakefield family history, I quickly immersed myself in their story as it traced them back to the 14th century.

They had come from a place in north central England called Pontefract. The book described in detail what the area was like: *Pontefract castle was built according to the usual plan of a Norman Castle. There was a keep at the western end and a large bailey below it. The towers were set at equal distances in the curtain wall of the enclosure. There was a barbican and drawbridge at the southwest angle and the whole fortress was encircled by a deep fose.*

As I finished reading, a chill crept over me. This description sounded exactly like the castle in my regression session four days earlier! I began to wish I could go to England. If only I had a job over there, I could see if this place looked familiar, but the rest of the year was already booked solid with shooting in Los Angeles and New York. It would take a miracle to get another shoot in London to come along.

Then again, miracles do happen.

V.

QUEST THROUGH TIME

Chapter 15

I drove up to see Lucy for another regression session at noon on Monday, October 7th. I sat outside her office for a few minutes enjoying the warmth of the sun and reading the book *Psyche* while she finished up with a patient inside.

As always, Lucy was smiling when I finally entered. It sometimes made me wonder if she knew more than she was telling me. She would have to have been an accomplished actress to feign the surprise she showed when I told her about the events of the past weekend. After bringing her up to date, I removed my socks and shoes and stretched out on the acupuncture table. As she began placing the needles, a huge shock of electricity shot from my right wrist, the one with Kathy's bracelet on it. It felt as though a capacitor had stored a charge and released it as Lucy made contact with the tip of her needle. Soon, the chi was flowing freely and my body started to relax as Lucy led me to my hall of doors.

As I reached the corridor and started to search for the door to open, I was suddenly joined by Kathy's spirit. She began talking to me as she pulled me along, not letting me stop at any of the doors. "Hurry, hurry! Don't stop yet. Follow me."

We raced down the endless hallway past dozens and dozens of doors. As they flew past us, I began to wonder how many lives we had lived. As if I had spoken the words aloud, her answer came right back to me: "More than you'll ever know. More than you'll ever know."

Suddenly we stopped, but not in front of a door. It was a burgundy curtain trimmed with a gold braid cord. The curtain drew back as Kathy's spirit called me to step through. I ducked under the cloth and felt sand under my feet. I looked up. The panorama spreading out before me was astounding!

I was standing on the ancient sands of Egypt. Before me was an expanse of pyramids, people and buildings that held me speechless. The castle last week was stunningly beautiful, but this was one hundred times the scale of my previous regression. I looked down at my feet and saw I was wearing sandals again, but this time I knew I was a man. I was dressed in a white gown or robe with a cloth over my head, held in place with a band of material that tied around my forehead.

We started to walk forward a few steps and were immediately inside a building. It was a large room with steps down into another room. I stood on the upper part looking at all the beautiful artwork that surrounded me. There was an abundance of gold statues and figurines along the perimeter, and hieroglyphic writing on all the walls. Down below me, in the sunken living room, I could see at least a dozen women sitting, standing and lying around on couches or benches.

I walked down towards the women and thought to myself, "I would like to see what I look like." From the center of the group seated before me, one of them raised a large solid gold plate and held it angled against her head. I stepped forward to look at my reflection in the surface and was shocked by what I saw.

The image staring back at me was not Randy Rogers but another man – young, about 25 years old with very dark skin and black hair. My face was very long and narrow. On my chin was some type of a short stubby beard that didn't appear real to me. Looking into my own eyes, I couldn't take them away from the foreign image. I could feel myself inside this body, but I still had the memories of my present life stored in my head. As I stood staring at myself, the woman lowered the plate into her lap and I found myself looking directly into her eyes.

"It's you, Lucy! It's you," I whispered knowing she was listening to my description of the events around me.

The woman I was looking at was strikingly beautiful. Her face had smooth, dark skin with high rounded cheekbones. Her hair was thick, jet-black and fell to about her shoulders. As I continued gazing into her eyes, there was no mistaking, this was Lucy. She continued smiling at me as I took a few steps back from the women to look at the whole group.

"Who are all these women?" I asked.

"These are all your wives, and this is how you first met Lucy," she said.

We took several more steps and were now standing on a balcony looking over the entire kingdom. There, laid out before me, was an entire city in the desert. Neat buildings of all sizes bordered a central courtyard market area. The view stretched out in all directions to include some pyramids in the distance and a river winding off to the right. It seemed to be a place under massive construction as well with partially finished structures swarming with workers by the hundreds.

"This was all at your command at one time in your life," Kathy said.

"I'm a pharaoh's son! Lucy, I'm a pharaoh's son!"

No name came to me and none was ever asked as I next motioned for Kathy to come with me to have a little talk.

We walked back out to the hall of doors and down the hallway to the first door I originally wanted to open, the one with the peeling paint and rusted knob. I turned the corroded handle, swung open the door on its creaking hinges, and walked through the threshold.

I was standing in my hometown of Johnstown, Pennsylvania. We were in Central Park, just outside the newspaper offices I worked in when I started in the news business. We were young again, I was in my body and Kathy appeared in hers. We sat down on a park bench and I held Kathy's hand as I asked her about her sister Carleen.

"I'm going to visit Sister Carleen again while I'm back in Pennsylvania next week. I don't know what I can say to her to convince her I'm really talking with you Kathy."

"I'll be seeing her soon myself," Kathy replied, her voice filled with joy at the thought of reuniting with Carleen's spirit again.

Sister Carleen was suffering from liver disease. She was on a donor list for a transplant but was far from the top.

"What would you like me to tell her Kathy?"

Kathy paused for a moment before giving me her answer.

"I want you to tell her that my love for her is beyond the earth and sky." Kathy squeezed my hand tightly in hers, radiating the love she wanted me to convey to her sister.

"I'll tell her." We both stood up to walk around.

Instantly, we were in a forest surrounded by beautiful fall foliage. These changes from one location to another, one season to another, swept me away with their intensity. Walking hand in hand with Kathy played out like a dream of something I always wanted to do but never got the chance. Unlike a dream, I was awake – fully conscious – and sensing every sight, sound, smell and feeling of being in a real setting.

"How much did you know about me and you before you left this world, Kathy? Did you know I was a part of you?"

Kathy responded with a nod. "Couldn't you tell from the writings in my diary?" she asked. "I was writing to you from my heart, where the truth lies in each of us. We both had a role to play in this lifetime and yours is not yet finished."

We stood up from the rock we had been resting on and I told Kathy I would like to visit another life and L.W. Rogers again. We had just walked out the door and back into the hall again when Kathy started running down the corridor. I chased after her but she managed to stay ahead of me, running down some stairs to a smaller door with an arched top. She flung open the door and bolted through it as I followed just two steps behind her. We sprinted through a large rolling field of flowers and grass, a spectacularly green place that reminded me of Scotland.

Kathy was now a young woman of maybe 22 with long golden hair braided up around the top of her head. Her eyes were blue and they sparkled in the sunshine of a glorious day. She taunted me as we raced across the field into a stand of trees on the slope. Kathy hid behind one, then another, playing hide-and-seek with me while I chased her to the top of the mountain. Looking over the valley below, I could see many lakes, one leading to the next. We sat on a large rock waiting patiently for L.W. Rogers.

Soon thin clouds began swirling above us, water vapor was building and dissipating as if a summer thunder-head was about to form. I could feel L.W.'s presence surrounding me again. He was nowhere to be seen, only felt, in the billowing force of air, mist and sunlight.

"What am I here to do, what is my purpose?" I asked, looking up into the shafts of light streaming out of the heavens.

"You must gather up the pieces I sent you. When you have them all together then the message shall be clear." He responded gently, but with a power beyond Kathy's or mine.

That was all L.W. said as the clouds fragmented then evaporated from sight. After hearing his message, I left the mountain top with Kathy and she slowly returned me to my body on the acupuncture table.

I was so heavy after the session that I couldn't move for ten minutes after Lucy removed the needles. As we discussed what had transpired, Lucy found it surprising that I discovered her in a previous incarnation revealing a reflection of my past life image. It was very much like our present life circumstances where she's showing me who I used to be through acupuncture regression. I couldn't figure out how she was able to take me to this state of consciousness but I did enjoy how real the events I experienced seemed.

I thanked Lucy and drove home, not knowing that the feeling of reality I was enjoying in my regressions would soon become just a little too real to comprehend and handle.

Chapter 16

Susan was at the house when I got home, so I ran upstairs to tell her about the regression. I knew she wasn't interested and chances were good she would make light of the whole experience, but she was the one person I was determined to have believe in me.

Susan was sitting at her desk in our bedroom when I started to relate the whole story. She was still listening patiently as I got to the part about L.W. Rogers. Suddenly a horn started blowing out in our driveway. It was our son Phil, home from high school, and needing someone to drop him off at work. As Susan ran out of the house, she asked me to finish when she returned.

I sat down at her empty desk and began thinking about what I had just been telling her. I knew it must sound like I was losing my mind, but it all seemed so real. As I sat propping my head in my hand and staring into her computer screen, I found myself literally staring off into space. Susan had a screen saver that gave the illusion of traveling through space. It was very mesmerizing to watch the stars streaming past and I quickly became transfixed in the motion.

My peripheral vision caught sight of a yellow post-it note on the side of her monitor. On it Susan had written the password for logging into her computer system at work. The code consisted of the beginning of our street name, ALTA, and then some other letters or numbers I couldn't make out clearly. I was trying to read the whole thing as one word without taking my eyes off the star field, but it wasn't making any sense to me. As I continued staring into space and struggling with the code, I started saying words I had no idea what they meant.

"*Alten...Amen...Aken...Amen*," I couldn't get the right word to come out of my mouth. It was like trying to pronounce a foreign word that I didn't understand. Something inside my head was telling me I did, and to go to the books for the answer. I got up from Susan's desk and walked out to the built-in bookshelves that comprised our library on our second floor landing.

I was in a trance-like hypnotic state as I reached for the bookcase and pulled out the first book I could place my hand on. It was the "A" encyclopedia, and it opened onto page 252. On the left-hand side was a picture of the Hindenburg disaster under the heading "Airships." I was looking at the picture of the Zeppelin in flames but not knowing what that had to do with me. I went to flip to another section of the book but as my gaze shifted from the left side of the page to the right, my body nearly buckled to the floor in shock. There on page 253, just above my thumb, was a picture of the person I had seen reflected in the gold plate not an hour earlier. I gasped and steadied myself to look at the photograph again. *Akhenaton* was the name under the picture.

"That's what I've been trying to say," I thought as I stood there shaking. I set the book down on one of the banister columns, and ran into the bedroom and then back out. The shock was almost too much for me to handle. I was trying to shake off the goose bumps that had taken over my body.

"Oh my God, it's me. It's me!" I kept repeating as I paced back and forth to the book and then away again. Each time I would walk up to the picture and look again, it was like looking into the golden plate. There was no mistaking the image of the face burned into my memory just a short time ago. I was beside myself with anxiety as I read the first line of text. *Akhenaton ruled ancient Egypt as pharaoh from about 1367 to 1350 B.C.*

I started pacing again and thinking to myself: "That was over 3300 years ago. How can this be true? I've never even heard of this person." I went back to read the next line of information.

He was married to Queen Nefertiti.

I walked back to the bookshelf and pulled out the encyclopedia "N." It fell open to page 168 and there was the picture of the woman who had held the gold dish for me.

"Lucy was Nefertiti!" I cried, as I looked closely at the picture of the beautiful young woman.

My heart was racing so fast I thought it would jump out of my chest. I jumped back to the first book and continued reading.

Akhenaton was a religious reformer. He devoted his life solely to the worship of one god, Aton, the sun god. Early in his reign he was coregent with his father, Amenhotep III.

He was a pharaoh's son just like I said in my regression session and he had become pharaoh himself, one who was steadfast in his belief of only one god, the sun god Aton!

I pulled my eyes from the book and looked around the room. Throughout my fourteen years of marriage to Susan, the one consistent thing I had bought was images of the sun! Our home was full of wall hangings, clocks, candles and plates all with the sun on it.

Chills were now shooting down both my arms. I ran to the bedroom to try to reach Susan on her cell. I knew she regarded these stories I brought back from the acupuncture sessions as something I was creating, but now she would have to see the connection with our lives. I had to try again to get her to understand that this was not a coincidence. As the cell connection went through, I could hear her phone ringing on the desk. I went back to the encyclopedias to read more about Akhenaton and Nefertiti.

I learned how Akhenaton and Nefertiti preached monotheism to Aton the sun god. They changed the way Egypt was ruled which led to a period called the Amarna Revolution. Great changes took place in art, religion and social practices. Their revolution, however, was short lived. Immediately after Akhenaton's death, Egypt reverted to their worship of multiple gods. The country eventually fragmented into smaller states with Rome ultimately taking over and ending the once-great dynasty of the ancient pharaoh kings.

Susan had still not returned home and I was ready to explode if I didn't tell someone what was happening to me. I decided to call Lucy at her office and let her know what was going on. She happened to answer the phone and I quickly blurted out the events of the last hour. When I told her she was Nefertiti, the phone went silent on the other end.

"I can't believe this is happening," Lucy finally said to me. "Ever since I was a young girl in Russia I used to have a picture of Nefertiti hanging above my bed. I felt that she gave me power."

"I can't believe we knew each other over thirty three hundred years ago. How can this be happening to me?" I asked Lucy. "This was no accident. I saw myself when I looked into that plate and my reflection looked the same as this picture of Akhenaton. The girl holding the plate looked exactly like this sculpture of Nefertiti. I've never even heard of this Akhenaton and only know that Nefertiti was some Egyptian queen. Other than that I don't know anything about them."

I had been pacing around the top landing as I talked with Lucy and now found myself stopped at the front balcony door, speechless, as I realized what symbols lay in front of me. Dozens of glass pyramids filled my view and had been since the day I moved in. The Loyola Marymount University building, which was nestled into the bluff directly below and in front of my house, had a skylight structure for the roof. It was comprised of row after row of glass pyramids.

"Lucy, I'm standing on my balcony right now looking out at nothing but glass pyramids, dozens of them have been starring me in the face ever since I moved here. It's one of the things I love about the view… these glass pyramids!"

"I'll see what I can find out about Akhenaton and Nefertiti before you come in on Friday. Just try to relax and remain calm while we discover what this all means." Lucy's voice was very soothing as she reassured me that everything had a meaning.

I had no sooner hung up the phone with Lucy when Susan came pulling into the driveway. I must have sounded like a mad man as I tried to get my story out.

"So now you think you were an Egyptian pharaoh called who?" Susan asked, nearly laughing in my face at the thought of the whole idea.

"Akhenaton…and Lucy was Nefertiti…here I can show you their pictures in the encyclopedia." I bolted to grab the books that were still sitting out on the banister posts.

"I don't see how you can prove that you were this pharaoh. All you have is this story, that doesn't prove anything." Susan was sticking to her hard line defense that this was all a coincidence.

"But look around you… look where we live… pyramids in front of us, images of suns all over the inside of our house and Lucy herself had a portrait of Nefertiti hanging above her bed growing up. She never knew why she was so fascinated with this woman only that she felt that she gave her power."

I tried to make my case, but Susan looked at me like I was talking about little green men from Mars. The fact that these events were all originating from an acupuncture regression session didn't even dawn on me as strange.

"I will agree that we do have a lot of sun images but that hardly makes this story believable."

Susan continued with her reasoning that this was nothing more than a simple series of coincidences and I was just making them all seem interrelated. Since I wasn't getting any support from her, I decided to call Renée and fill her in on the latest.

"Wow, what a session! There's no way that's just a coincidence. Are you going back to see Lucy again soon?" Renée was excited about my discovery.

"I've got an appointment for Friday but I don't know how much more of this I can take. I just about had a heart attack when I opened that book to the picture of Akhenaton."

"I'll bet. I've still got goose bumps on my arm. I can't wait to see Lucy tonight. I'm just going in for a regular session... you know... get the ol' energy flowing. Call me if anything else happens to you."

Renée was now more anxious than ever to see Lucy. Unknown to either one of us at the time, she was about to play a major role in proving my story.

♋ ♋ ♋

Later that evening Renée called me, nearly out of breath with excitement.

"You're not going to believe what happened at Lucy's tonight."

"Now what?" I asked, not sure if I should brace myself for more heart stopping news.

"So I walked into Lucy's office and started joking with her right off the bat. I said, 'I understand you were Nefertiti?' and she said 'I just don't feel that I have the power' then she stopped in mid-sentence and said 'Wait a minute. I just remembered something that I have in my purse.' She walked out of the room and came back with her purse in her hand. Then she opened up a small, zippered, compartment on the inside and pulled out this lapel pin. The minute I saw it I could tell it was something Egyptian, Randy. It was about two inches tall by two inches wide and looked like some kind of cane crossed over another stick type of object. From a distance it looked like an X. There were these decorative bands of vibrant blue alternating with the gold that covered both the cane and the other symbol."

"Where'd she get it?" I asked, cutting into Renée's story.

"That's what I'm about to tell you. So Lucy hands me this broach and says that about two years ago, a patient of hers came in for an appointment. She pulled out this pin and showed it to Lucy, saying that a very close friend of hers from Pittsburgh had given it to her just before she passed away from breast cancer. She told Lucy the night before she had had a dream in which her friend came to her and told her 'Give the pin to Lucy because it's her symbol of power.' She then gave Lucy this pin. Lucy told her she didn't normally accept gifts from patients, but in this case, she'd make an exception. She put the pin inside the compartment of her purse and forgot about it. Then, when Lucy told me she didn't feel she had the power to have been Nefertiti, she remembered the words that patient had told her two years earlier when she gave her the pin."

I was speechless. All I could say was "Wow!" I thanked Renée for filling me in on the events of the evening and told her I'd be in to see Lucy Friday and would keep her up to date on the latest.

I eased back deep into my chair, took a few deep breaths and tried to get a grasp of what had just happened. The story Renée had just relayed to me firmly tied my regression session of a past life in Egypt, to a present day cancer story. Dreams, out-of-body experiences, L.W. Rogers, Lucy Postolov, all these events and people were clearly revolving around my life in a synchronistic way. It was no accident! They were all aligned intentionally somehow and now the puzzle was taking me back in time to show the relationship my past lives had to my present circumstances. My search for the key would continue.

Chapter 17

On Friday October the 11th, I went back to Lucy's office for another regression session. Lucy was very excited to talk to me. She showed me the pin and asked if I knew what it was. I looked it over carefully and could see it was Egyptian, and vaguely familiar.

Lucy pulled out a large book entitled Akhenaton and Nefertiti. I was surprised to see such a large book about this pharaoh. The only one I had seen anything published on was King Tut. No one could've ever accused me of being an Egyptologist! Lucy opened the book and gave me my first lesson in Egyptian antiquities.

"It's called 'The Crook and The Flail,'" Lucy explained pointing out a picture of the same symbol in the book. "They were given to all the pharaoh kings as their symbols of power. Only a pharaoh could possess these symbols and he was buried with them in his sarcophagus. You can see how he held them with his arms crossed over his chest."

Now it was clear where I had seen them, but I had never really paid any attention to what was in a pharaoh's hands or just what the symbolic meaning of the objects were.

"Nefertiti was such a powerful queen though that she was also given these symbols of power," Lucy continued. "It gives me chills to know you saw me as her in your regression session. I've been carrying around this symbol for the past two years. It was given to me by a woman whose friend passed away from breast cancer. This woman also came from your home state area."

The evidence was mounting. I had no prior knowledge of the pin or Lucy having had a picture of Nefertiti over her bed as a child. My original dream led me to discover Kathy's death by ovarian cancer, the same subject of my mini-documentary. Pursuing my investigation further led me to Lucy and her mother's breast cancer connection to the UCLA video. Now my Egyptian past life, which at first seemed an incredible tale, is also linked to a breast cancer story about a woman from Pittsburgh.

These were all very strong indications I was searching in the right direction for an answer to how life worked. All these events were linked by a common theme of breast and ovarian cancer. It was a marker I couldn't miss. It was so prominent in my life with the video project and Kathy's death from it. If it would've been just those two things I could easily say, "Well that was some coincidence!" but it was everything now. All these stories meshing together like the synchronizers of a transmission, shifting smoothly from one gear to the next and driving me forward with incredible speed as I traveled over unfamiliar territory searching for the next clue as to how this all was possible.

I felt the woman relating the dream to Lucy two years earlier, and Renée now triggering her memory was the most startling truth. Symbols left for Lucy years ago now had meaning. A new surge of energy flowed through my body as I rested back to try my fourth regression session.

The session began as all the others and I soon found myself standing in the hall of doors. Kathy's spirit was waiting for me. Lucy left the acupuncture room so I could experience this journey completely on my own. Kathy led me slowly down the hall until I was standing in front of what appeared to be a church door. It was old, and constructed with wood and black hinge plates with a small window centered high in the door. I didn't want to look in. In fact, I didn't want to go anywhere near it.

"Come on, what are you waiting for? You have to see where you've been in order to move forward," Kathy said as she opened the door and motioned for me to follow her.

I hesitated then stepped across the threshold once again. I turned around and looked back through the window at all the other doors I could've chosen.

"Turn around and look. It's not as bad as you think," she pleaded.

I hesitated another few seconds then slowly turned around to face what I had been afraid to confront.

I was standing in the middle of a dusty street in the center of Jerusalem. I could see it was the ancient city by the buildings before me. They were multi-level structures made out of a clay material that had a slight reddish hue in the soft glow of early evening, just after the sun had set. I looked down the dirt street ahead of me and could see a man with a beard and a hooded top walking slowly towards me. He was carrying a cloth sack over his shoulder. It appeared to be a heavy load as he bent over from its weight on his back. He trudged past where I was standing, but I couldn't get a good view of his face. The hood over his head shadowed his face too much for me to see any detail, but my first impression was he was a black man or very dark skinned.

Kathy called out for me to look at her. As I turned back around to face her, a feeling of both total surprise and relief encompassed me at once. She no longer appeared as Kathy, but was now a man with a beard and long hair.

"Jesus," I thought, as I looked at her transformation.

She was definitely Jesus Christ, or at least similar to the impression of what I thought he looked like. My first reaction was one of sheer joy that it was she and not I who had taken on this appearance. Kathy sensed this emotion within me and responded quickly.

"But look at yourself, you are my closest friend Peter."

I glanced down at my clothing and could see I had on garments like hers. I could feel the cloth of a turban on my head and the whiskers of a heavy beard on my face. It was strange to feel Kathy's spirit coming from this figure of a man I had always known as Jesus. I responded quickly to her claim that we were once these two men.

"I know this story already," I blurted back sharply. "I don't want to come here now."

"It's important that you see this. There are answers to be learned here," Kathy said as she gently pulled me along by my hand.

I was hesitant at first because these sessions were taking me into an area I had never fathomed. My Catholic upbringing had branded me into believing that Jesus and Peter were two very spiritual men, iconic symbols of power… *The* founders of the Catholic Church. As Lucy felt about her role as Nefertiti, I now felt the same as Peter. *How could I have ever had that power?* Whatever the answer was, it was sure to be hidden within more cryptic clues and symbols. The fact that we were now religious figures, playing yet another role out of the history books, fell well within my own personal borders of skepticism. My Catholic background was trying to drag me the hell out of there in a hurry. But I was in the play now, and if Shakespeare did have it right, then it was not inconceivable that I, or anyone else for that matter, could've played these roles. My job was still the same, carefully observe everything that would happen and see if any of the events or people I meet re-immerge in my current life, with the same synchronicity as the other regression sessions.

We continued down the dusty street and soon came upon a set of stairs leading to the second story of a building. We climbed the stairs and Kathy opened the door for me to enter. The dim, soft glow of oil lamps supplemented the light of a few candles illuminating a long table in the center of the room. There were chairs on both sides of the table. The person at the far end of the room immediately drew my attention. It was the man laboring with his sack down the street only a few moments ago. His hood was pulled down from his head and I could see he was very dark skinned fellow but I was still uncertain as to his race. I was feeling the presence of a spirit very familiar to me. As I walked up to get a closer look, our eyes made contact.

It was my wife Susan! I could feel her presence. He reached into the sack he had been carrying and began setting its contents on the table. There were plates, glasses, bread, and wine. I didn't try to speak to him, but turned to Kathy and asked who this man was. She told me his name was Thomas and he, too, was one of the disciples. Kathy asked me to look more closely at him. I could see a medallion of some type around his neck. On closer inspection, I could make out the image of a sun with rays of light streaking out from a solid gold center.

"Remember everything you see and do here today. These images will help guide you to the answers you seek in your life," Kathy said.

"Is this the only other lifetime I've known Susan?" I asked.

"No, you've been around her many times before and since."

I wanted to see more people that I knew back then and Kathy, sensing this thought, responded. "They will be arriving very soon."

There was a knock at the solid wooden door and Kathy opened it. Standing on the stairs outside were three more men. As they walked in, Kathy identified each of them for me. The first was a tall man with dark hair and deep-set eyes. Kathy told me I had not met him in my current life yet, but I would soon know him as Peter Michalos, the author from New York. In this life, he was Matthew. The next man had a balding head and appeared older than the first. As he passed by me, the thought of Jane

Semel flashed across my mind. I had just met Jane recently in the meetings for the Fire & Ice Ball, but I somehow knew this man held her spirit. Kathy told me Jane was John in this life. The final man was very short in stature. I recognized him as an old high school friend, David Cooper. David grasped my hand and smiled at me as he entered. Kathy told me that I knew him as Luke in this life.

My friend David had died during our senior year of high school. He had belonged to the East Taylor Rural Fire Dept. and was racing to answer an alarm one day when he lost control of his vehicle. He died in the hospital a week later.

The four men gathered around the table and Kathy asked me to watch closely. They were raising their wineglasses in a toast. I could see a ring on John's finger with some kind of engraved symbol on it. I looked closer to see what it was. It appeared to be a diamond shape with a circle connected to it much like this: ◇○

The toast concluded and Kathy told me to remember the symbols. They would be appearing to me later in my current life.

I then moved forward in time, wanting to experience how I died in this life. I found myself with my head placed on a chopping block. As I watched from outside my body, I saw the executioner lop off my head. I experienced this vision twice, watching as my head rolled onto the ground at the foot of this hooded stranger. As with my previous vision of the twins' deaths, I felt strangely removed from the event itself and experienced no sorrow or remorse because of it.

Leaving this life behind, Kathy and I re-entered the hall of doors. I followed her as she led me down the passageway to an old, simple wooden door. Crossing the threshold, I found myself in a barn with two horses in a stable. Kathy and I mounted up and rode off across the English countryside. I felt so at home galloping through the woods with the wind blowing through my hair. As we rode on, we came upon a field of some type of crop. I could see a woman with a small child, kneeling among the plants. She was gathering up the harvest and as I pulled up closer to her, I could see it was my sister Diane from my current life. The small child with her was Phil, my wife's child in this life. I dismounted and walked up to them to see what they were pulling from the soil.

As my sister handed the plant over to her son, I could see it was a bulb of garlic. I watched for a short while as they continued working, Phil placing the herbs in a basket beside them. I could sense this life was a very hard one, toiling in the fields from sunrise to dusk. I could also feel the garlic they were gathering had some extended meaning beyond a mere harvest. What that was, I didn't know, but was sure it would become clear later in my regressions or current life.

After returning to the hall, I entered a third and final door where I found myself standing on a mountaintop in the middle of a blinding snowstorm. It was so brilliantly white that I couldn't see. I could certainly feel the presence of L.W. Rogers building around me. The wind swirled the snow in a stinging rage. I was immune to the biting cold, protected by the growing warmth of the love generated by the spirit I was there to meet.

I let a question flow from my thoughts. "What role does Lucy have to play in all of this?"

His response was Lucy was here to teach me how to reach my full measure of power. Eventually I wouldn't need Kathy taking me to see him, or going back to visit my past lives. I asked him what my part was in all of this. He told me it would be a healing one, where my touch alone could change a person's life. As he continued speaking, I noticed the weather was no longer a snowstorm but had changed to spring with green and warmth surrounding me. His spirit was also charging me with energy so intense I felt myself lifted from the ground. He told me this is what a person could feel when I touch them after I have become fully aware of the power within me.

I left the mountaintop and floated gently back into my body. I knew this session had many clues in it and it may be sometime until all the pieces fit into the puzzle. I was determined to continue, searching for the answers that would help me put this all into some kind of perspective.

♋ ♋ ♋

The combination of maintaining a good diet, daily meditation, and weekly acupuncture sessions was bringing my spirit and body to a higher level of sensitivity and consciousness. I could now communicate with Kathy's world more easily than my own. My relationship with my wife had deteriorated to the point that if we even tried to discuss anything going on with me there would be an argument. Every new connection that I discovered and shared with her, hoping that this would be the evidence to open her mind, ended with me on the defensive end. I vowed each time, never again, but Susan was still my wife, and so I naively reneged time and again, hoping to eventually convince her.

Monday morning October 14th, Susan was sitting on the edge of our bed getting ready to tie her shoes. "Ow... Oh no...!" Susan cried like she had been shot.

"What happened?" I came running out from the bathroom.

"My back... I just heard a popping sound when I bent over to tie my shoe and I can't straighten up." Susan was grimacing in obvious pain, doubled over on her side.

"Where did you hear the noise?"

"Right here," Susan said as she reached for her lower back.

"Maybe if you just lie down for a while and I massage it a little it will go back into place." I reached over to touch the small of her back.

"Ohh...ow... no don't rub it, it hurts too much." I pulled my hand back quickly.

Looking at Susan writhing on the bed in pain, I wanted to fix the situation; a solution leapt from my mouth.

"I'll call Lucy she can fix this for you!" The enthusiasm was bubbling out of me now. *This had to be fate,* I thought, *what a great time for Susan to meet Lucy and see what a miracle cure, acupuncture could be.*

"I don't know...I don't see how some needles are going to fix this."

"They'll relax you and the muscles in your back. You've just disrupted the flow of energy and Lucy can get it moving again." I then pushed the hard sell on Lucy and her talents. "Come on... your back will be good as new in no time."

It's amazing what a motivator pain can be, even to someone that is in every sense of the word a non-believer in the art of acupuncture.

Susan quickly changed her mind when the next wave of pain pulsated up her spine. "Ow...Okay...Okay...call her and see if she can take me."

I called Lucy and explained the situation. She told me to bring her to the office immediately. I knew Susan was not very receptive to the idea that a few needles, correctly placed, could eliminate her pain and help her to heal. My thinking was if she could only feel what I was experiencing every time I did a session, she might begin to understand there was more to life. Walking around in this body is not our complete being. Yes, this would certainly be the turning point in my battle to win her over.

Less than an hour later I was helping Susan from my car into Lucy Postolov's office.

"Susan, this is Lucy, Lucy this is my wife Susan!" I was beaming, happy that Susan was going to feel the instant relief that acupuncture would bring her.

"I'm so pleased to meet you Susan, I've heard so much about you… come with me so we can get you comfortable." Lucy extended her hand to help Susan hobble into the nearest acupuncture room.

A little over an hour later, the door slowly swung open and Susan emerged, humped over still and looking nearly as crippled as when she went in.

"What happened? Don't you feel a little better?" I was probing now, looking for any sign that she felt a tingling hint of what coursed through my body weekly.

Susan shook her head no. The look on her face told me to shut up and get her back in the car quickly.

"Thanks for getting us in so quickly." I said to Lucy as she opened the door for us to leave.

"I'll call you later to see how you're doing Susan." Lucy's words were met with a weak hand wave from Susan as she put her weight on me to negotiate the single curb to the parking lot.

"What a waste of time that was!" Susan lost no time telling me what she thought of the acupuncture session.

"Maybe you didn't relax enough to let it work for you." My response could've been better.

"I was relaxed!" Susan said, upset that I'd even suggest such a thing.

"But you've got to let your mind relax too!" I was just as emphatic which inflamed Susan even more.

"It obviously doesn't work for everyone and it didn't work for me!" Susan was gritting her teeth and I knew it was best if I dropped the subject of acupuncture.

Why were things going so terribly astray from the way I wanted them to turn out? I pondered this turn of fate as I took Susan back home and put her to bed. There would be no more acupuncture for her. She made that clear. Without a trace of relief, Susan abandoned the idea that this form of medicine had any benefits for her now, or in the future.

♋ ♋ ♋

The visit to Lucy was now having the reverse effect that I had hoped for, making my relationship with Susan even worse. Ever the optimist, I hoped by some miracle that the acupuncture treatment would have a delayed reaction and the problem would fix itself overnight.

The next morning, Susan's back was in no better shape. To make matters worse, she seemed more inclined to fight with me and started another one over the book *Many Lives, Many Masters*.

"This stupid book is a bunch of nonsense." Susan was holding up my copy of *Many Lives, Many Masters*. It had been lying on my night stand next to the bed and she was attacking it like it was the cause of all her troubles now.

"It's not nonsense. These are documented accounts by a trained psychiatrist." I stood my ground defending his story.

"It's a lot of made up B.S. coming out of a psychiatric patient. Anything could've been suggested to her and she would've said it."

Susan wouldn't back off and with her lying in bed it didn't seem like the time and place to carry on this argument.

"I'm going to the bank now." I turned and stormed out of the room leaving Susan to cope in whatever way she felt was best for her back pain and misery.

All the way to the bank I was praying for a miracle that would turn Susan into a believer – not in the spiritual events that were surrounding me – just back into a believer in me.

I made a deposit of the checks for my company and after leaving the bank, stopped and browsed through a book sale they were having on the courtyard in front of the lobby. I was looking at a book on numerology when something else caught my eye. There were three books on herbs set out in a display and I was compelled to open the book in the center. It fell open to a double-page article about garlic. I was immediately taken back because garlic was all I talked about the previous week. I had opened the encyclopedic dictionary at home to an article on how some believed it to be helpful in curing liver disease and cancer.

I purchased the book and on the way home, Kathy came to me saying I would be able to do the same thing in front of Susan and open the book exactly to the article on garlic. Now my faith was going to be tested. Should I dare attempt this feat in front of Susan and risk failure? My faith in Kathy was unwavering. I bounded up the stairs at home and placed the book on the bed in front of Susan.

"You won't believe what just happened to me," I exclaimed proudly.

"Now what?" she asked.

"I came across this book after I left the bank and when I opened it the page was on this," I said as I reached over and promptly opened the book again to the page on garlic.

Susan had already heard me talking about the other garlic incidents and here I had just opened this thick volume to the exact page I had described earlier.

"Give me that book," she said as she grabbed it off the bed.

Susan examined the page to make sure there was no marker or creased pages to help me find the exact spot.

"Let me see you do it again," she said as she closed the book tightly and pressed it together to make sure it was tight.

I could feel Kathy's presence around me now and felt confident that I could do it again. I reached over to where she held the book and again opened it to the garlic page. Susan's jaw dropped at this feat. Even then, she thought there was some trick to it.

"You try it then," I said. "If you think it's so easy."

Susan tried and tried but after half a dozen attempts gave up. I told her I was being given this garlic symbol, but didn't quite know what to make of it yet. Susan didn't say another word. I could see she was angry so I closed the book and walked away. As I slipped into bed that night, the silence was still there like some invisible wall between us. I always wanted to believe she loved me and believed in me, but now I felt my faith in her beginning to slip.

I thought back to my last regression session where I had seen Susan as the disciple Thomas. Thomas, also called Didymus which means "twin," was known as Doubting Thomas. The story was that Thomas earned the nickname because he wouldn't believe the other disciples when they tried to convince him Jesus had risen from the grave and visited them when Thomas was not present. According to the gospel of John, Thomas' response to their claim was, 'Unless I see the nail marks in his hands and put my finger where the nails were, and put my hand into his side, I will not believe it.'

I could see the synchronicity between Thomas and the apostles and Susan in my present day circumstance. Much as before, I was trying to convince her that you do return from the dead. There is no death only continuous life through re-incarnation. And just as before, she wouldn't believe me no matter how hard I tried. *We had been in this adversarial relationship before!*

I turned over in the bed and pulled out my journal from the nightstand. I had to record my thoughts, as the ever widening silence between us grew.

Chapter 18

To lose faith in someone – worse yet, in your self – is much like a cancer. Once the thought is there, it is hard to rid yourself of it completely. The next day, as I drove along Wilshire Boulevard to my acupuncture session, the doubt I had in myself began to surface. The response from Kathy was immediate and harsh.

"Pick it up now and open it," she said, referring to the herb book lying on the floor in the back of my Bronco.

I pulled over to the curb and reached into the back seat to grab the book. Placing it on the console beside me, I had a high level of anxiety running through me. I was anxious to listen to her guidance yet somehow afraid at the same time.

"Open it now," Kathy demanded, as angrily as I had ever heard her.

My hand parted the pages once again directly to the garlic section.

"I won't ever doubt you again," I thought.

L.W. and Kathy were guiding me, at least I could feel confident in that; more so than any faith that my wife would believe in me.

My session was taking place in the same exam room as my first regression. After the usual breathing regimen, I was standing alone in the hall of doors. In front of me was a large white door with black hinges and a black latch. I lifted the latch, swung open the door and stepped inside.

Whiteness surrounded me. It wasn't blinding in any sense, but seamless enough to be disorienting; no visual references to tell what was floor, wall or ceiling. Within a minute, I began to make out the shape of a white marble bench directly in front of me. I sat down on the bench and felt the presence of Kathy's spirit come up behind me. I felt the warmth of her hands touching my shoulders so I rose and turned to face her. She stood bathed in radiance beyond my imagination. She was dressed in a long flowing gown of white. I was clad in a duplicate robe of unworldly material whose brilliance had to be seen to be appreciated.

We walked down a long white hallway until we came to a door at the very end. The door was also white, but smooth as glass. Kathy opened the door and we entered a magnificent office with walls of books surrounding the room. The bookcases were made of beautiful hardwood, finished in a rich, dark, cherry stain. The entire room was trimmed in the wood and a large matching cherry desk sat at one end. Behind the desk was an overstuffed leather wingback chair. I walked up to a smaller one on the opposite side of the desk and sat down. I looked around the office, feeling like I was in an old English study. The walls and ceiling were a deep forest green. I didn't have much time to study the setting. My entire being surged with the familiar presence of L.W. Rogers. I could feel his energy growing with a stronger vibration than ever before.

The brass knob on the door to the left of the desk began to turn just as I thought I might finally get to meet him face to face. The door swung open and through it stepped the spirit filling me with these intense vibrations of love and kindness. He was so small I doubted he reached five feet in height. His hair was full and white as snow, and his face became a broad smile as he walked around the back of the desk and slipped into the wingback chair. In his hand was a thin, cylindrical object about 8 inches in length. It appeared to be some type of smooth, silver metallic rod. His fingers began flipping it end over end on his desk, much like playing with a pencil, as he looked deep into my eyes.

"Well, am I what you expected?" he asked as his smile melted any sense of distance between us.

"I didn't quite know what to expect," I replied, although surprised by his diminutive stature.

Our words flowed smoothly between us even though I never opened my mouth to speak in the physical sense. Kathy was behind me and out of view as L.W. and I sat facing each other.

"I sense many questions flowing through your mind."

"I have many, but don't know where to begin." The image of the garlic clove was foremost on my mind so I asked him, "Why was I shown this sign?"

"Why do you think you were shown this sign?"

"It will either be used in a cure for cancer or it was just a sign to show my wife that I'm not lying," I said.

"And which do you think is the correct answer?" he asked.

"I feel that it will help cure cancer in some way."

"You are on the right path," he whispered.

"What about my friend Donna?" I asked.

"How do you feel about her?"

"I feel good about her."

He nodded in agreement with me.

L.W. could sense more questions but before another could form, he told me he was growing tired of them. He stood up with the metallic rod still in his hand and walked around the front of the desk. As he reached out to grasp my hand, I felt a deep rush of power surge from his spirit through my body.

This energy continued building as he gave me one last piece of advice. "Keep gathering up the pieces and stay on the path." L.W. turned and walked through the door, twirling the silver rod on the way out.

I don't remember the door opening but somehow he went through it. One minute he was there and the next he was gone. It was as though the physical structure of the door didn't really exist at all.

I didn't have time to think about the meeting. Kathy was now leading me back out the other door, down the long white corridor and out into the hall of doors once again.

I entered another door and found myself on a dirt road next to a split rail fence that extended off as far as I could see. The rail posts were crossed pieces bundled together at each joint of the fence. It reminded me of a scene from the rural farming areas of the United States in the 1800s.

I could see a horse and buggy approaching in the distance. It was a black horse pulling a black carriage. The driver was a dark haired woman in her 50s. She pulled up along side me and stopped. I stepped up into her carriage and she continued on, down the road.

I noticed how old and strange my shoes looked. They were brown leather, not fancy in the least, quite worn and scuffed. I looked over at the woman holding the reins. She seemed quite familiar. I searched through my memory and recognized her as Mrs. Ross, an old family friend I visited with my parents as a child. Before she passed away, she left me a picture I had always liked in her house. It was a photo of a small boy and his two dogs sitting on a grassy meadow with the forest in the background. I was always drawn to it, and spent many hours staring at the picture on her wall.

She smiled at me as we drove along the rough country road, but we never spoke a word. It was a hot, dusty summer day and the sky was clear of clouds. I could hear the cicadas humming in the trees as the horse trotted along at a steady pace. Rounding a turn and climbing a slight hill, we pulled up to a rundown old shanty house. I was in the mountains of Virginia in the 1850s.

I had failed to notice I had been holding a bag in my hand. It was an old black leather bag, the type a doctor use to carry when he made a house call. I stepped off the buggy, walked up and opened the door of the shack.

Lying on a bed in the dimly lit room was a frail young woman about 25 years old. She tossed in pain on the crude straw mattress, her long blond hair matted with sweat. I could feel the spirit of my friend Donna emanating from this person. Small pox was ravaging her body and I could tell she was about to die.

"There is nothing I can do to save her," I said to Lucy, who was still listening from beside the acupuncture table.

"What do you have in your bag?" she asked, prodding me to open it.

I set the bag on a counter near the only window in the cabin and opened it. Reaching inside I pulled out a small hammer, then a shiny reflector. The reflector had a leather strap for wearing on your forehead, so I put it on my head. Even though I knew there was nothing I could do for the woman, I looked inside her mouth. Again, I said the disease was too far along for me to be of any help. I reached into the bag again and found a bottle I knew contained castor oil and garlic. Lucy wanted to know what the prescription was.

"There is none, I made it myself," I replied.

Lucy remained interested in the mixture I was holding in my hands. She wanted to know how it was made and asked if I could demonstrate by making some. I told her I had all the ingredients. I reached into the bag, retrieved a small clove of garlic and smashed it with the hammer until I obtained a small amount of juice. I added the juice to two ounces of castor oil in a small smoked glass bottle. There was one more thing that I needed to add to the mixture. I reached into the doctor's bag and pulled out a ginseng root. I explained to Lucy I needed only the tip of the root to cut up and add to the mixture. I diced up the root into fine granules, poured it into the bottle and corked it. The medicine would need to sit in the smoked bottle gathering the radiating energy from sunlight while protecting it from the direct light of the sun. I placed the bottle in the cabin window and sat down in a chair beside the woman lying in the bed.

Even though I was a doctor and had some basic homeopathic remedies, there was nothing I could do or say that would change the outcome. I reached out and grasped the woman's frail hand so she could feel the connection to my spirit and possibly find comfort in her final moments. As I held her hand, I felt the energy leave it and her spirit was free from her body.

The cabin door cracked open and in walked a small girl. She was crying for her mother lying in the bed. As I reached out to hold her hand, Kathy's spirit radiated from the child's body. The young girl led me out the door and down the dusty road from her home. I walked along and soon found myself on a very familiar road. I was back in my hometown on the far side of the Hinkston Run Dam where the stream empties into the reservoir. Holding hands as we walked along, I stopped to talk with Kathy's spirit. The image of the young girl was gone and Kathy was back in her own body, glowing vibrantly in contrast to the shaded forest.

"Meet me back here when you go home to visit your parents next week," Kathy said as she squeezed my hand tight.

"I'll be there," I said, feeling myself slowly slipping back to my body lying on the table.

As we broke contact with each other, Kathy pressed her spirit even closer to mine, charging my soul with the last remnants of our spiritual connection and radiating me with a love that rippled from my head to my toes. I couldn't wait to go back to Pennsylvania next week.

Chapter 19

I called Nancy Williams on Monday October 14th. We were talking about the Fire & Ice Ball coming up Thursday. I asked if her husband Nick would be joining us. She said he would be, but was in Miami on a shoot for the local Fox television station.

"I thought he was supposed to go to Atlanta?" I asked.

"No, I never said he was going to Atlanta. He's in Miami."

"Are you sure he's not in Atlanta? I thought for sure he had to go to Atlanta."

"No, no he's not in Atlanta. He's definitely in Miami."

I don't know what had come over me, but for some reason I had it in my mind that Nick should be in Atlanta. By now Nancy thought I was losing my mind, so I let her have the final word and told her I would call her as soon as I had more details, to coordinate our night at the Fire & Ice Ball.

Early the next morning I received a call from Nancy Willams. "Well, way to go 'Mister Psychic.' Guess where Nick is this morning?"

"Atlanta?" I asked her, only putting half my emphasis in the question.

"Atlanta!" she shouted. "They called him up yesterday and had him fly over from Miami. How did you do that?"

"I don't know. It just came out of my mouth. I don't know why I kept insisting he had to be there."

"Well that blows me away. I've got goose bumps on my arms just thinking about it."

Nancy and I continued talking for a short time, but in the back of my head I was trying to remember exactly what I was thinking of when telling her where I thought Nick should be. After I hung up the phone the day before, I did remember having a strange feeling I could only describe as amnesia like. I felt disoriented, as if I'd been hit on the head. I could not remember why I thought Nick should be in Atlanta.

The Fire & Ice Ball was a massive affair held at Warner Bros. Studio on the back lot. They used a set from the Batman movie in production on the stage adjacent to the party as an entrance to the event. It was a fitting venue, as the set was done up in an ice palace theme for Arnold Schwarzenegger's character, the villain Mr. Freeze. I invited Donna and her companion Suzanne to the ball and they were as excited as two schoolgirls to get to walk down the red carpet, past all the media coverage and into the event.

As far as Hollywood parties go, this was the one you didn't want to miss if you were privileged enough to be part of that circle. We had a good table near the front of the room and enjoyed Bette Midler's singing and comedy routine. As the lights dimmed down for the screening of *Hope on the Horizon,* I could sense the nervousness emanating from Donna. I was confident the video would go over well. It ended, with a rousing round of applause.

Donna became an instant celebrity as the event ended and we exited the soundstage. People recognized her and came up to wish her the best. It was a long evening and she was extremely tired, but the energy of the group surrounding Donna carried her through the long wait for the valet service. This was just the kind of support she needed and I was happy to see the effect it was having on her spirit. If she could just lose the fear buried deep inside her, I felt there was nothing she couldn't overcome.

Buried inside me was a trace of doubt she could ever reach that level of confidence in who she truly was and how life really worked. How could I ask her to believe without a doubt when I myself was searching? All I could do was stand beside Donna and support her, be near her and let my energy flow so she might draw on it now. As a country doctor, I was with Donna, holding her hand as she slipped away. I didn't want her to fade away again, but just as before felt powerless to stop it.

♋ ♋ ♋

Saturday October 19th I was in New York on a Disney junket for the movie "Ransom." It was a Ron Howard film starring Mel Gibson, Rene Russo and Gary Sinese. The shoot was taking place at the Essex House next to Central Park and only a few blocks away from the home of Peter Michalos, the author of *Psyche*. He came to the hotel one afternoon to meet me and discuss the events in my life that had been mirroring his own novel about Freud and hypnotic regressions.

Peter was about six feet, in his early-fifty's with long raven black hair parted on the right. He had dark, deep set eyes and a mellow bass voice that trailed out on certain words making his sentences seem to linger long after he was finished talking.

"This is all just fascinating, your stories of Akhenaton, Nefertiti and Kathy. Did you happen to notice that I dedicated my book to a Kathy as well?"

I nodded my head. "Kathy, Lucy, Russia, the regression sessions, it was all too much of a coincidence to be just a coincidence," I said. "Now I've seen you in one of my recent sessions as the disciple Matthew."

"It's all very heady stuff." Peter replied. "Would you like to visit a book store with me this afternoon? Maybe something else will jump out at you while we're there."

"Let's go! I haven't been to any good bookstores in New York yet." I grabbed my jacket and we headed downstairs.

A few minutes later we were out the front door and walking up West 59th Street when it started to rain. Peter had brought an umbrella with him but the Californian in me said I didn't need one. We were a few blocks from the hotel, trying to cross the myriad of streets and cross traffic at Columbus Circle when the deluge released. Water was flowing like a river in every direction and there was no choice but to wade in and slog across. The wind had picked up, blowing the driving rain horizontal and rendering our one umbrella useless. We ran, jumped and nearly swam across the flooded intersections making our way to the bookstore.

"What a storm, that was intense!" Peter shook off some of the water rolling down his jacket as I swept my sopping hair back from my forehead.

"Yeah, I wasn't expecting that. It really came out of nowhere."

"I can't remember being in anything like that in a long time."

"It never does that in California."

We both laughed and wandered around the store looking for something to draw my attention and give me another piece of the puzzle. I didn't find anything earth shattering. A book called *The Holographic Universe* stood out so I bought it. Back in my hotel room that evening I was lying on the bed thumbing through the new book when the familiar thoughts came into my mind to open the nightstand drawer and pull out the book. I slid open the drawer and looked inside to find a Gideon's Bible.

I ran my hand over the cover searching for any trace of energy that said, 'open it now.' My hand tingled as I opened the book and ran my fingers down the pages with my eyes closed. There was the slightest of vibrations half way down the page so I stopped my finger there and opened my eyes; the gospel of Matthew at Chapter 8 verse 23-27.

And when he was entered into a boat, his disciples followed him. And behold, there arose a great tempest in the sea, insomuch that the boat was covered with the waves: but he was asleep. And they came to him, and awoke him, saying, Save, Lord; we perish. And he saith unto them, Why are ye fearful, O ye of little faith? Then he arose, and rebuked the winds and the sea; and there was a great calm. And the men marveled, saying, What manner of man is this, that even the winds and the sea obey him?

Opening the bible to a chapter by Matthew was an easy sign to spot. I had just identified Peter as the disciple Matthew during my acupuncture session a week earlier. The fact that it was chapter 8 and verse 23 was also not lost on me now with my basic knowledge of numerology.

I was certain Peter and I had known each other for a very long time and our friendship was meant to continue in this life as well. The most important thing Peter did that first day we met was to give me unfailing support; support from a total stranger when I needed it the most.

After my shoot the next day, I returned to my room to find a message from the concierge saying there was a package waiting for me at their desk. I went down to the lobby to pick it up. It was from Peter. Inside were two copies of his book *Psyche* along with a simple note.

"Here's a *Psyche* for you and one for Lucy… What a storm we were out in!"

It was clearly important meeting Peter in my past life as well as this one. I interpreted the synchronicity of the storm and the bible passage by Matthew as a message telling me I could weather any storm with the help of many of the same spirits I had known since the beginning of time.

♋ ♋ ♋

After the junket ended that weekend, I caught a flight to Pittsburgh then rented a car to drive up to Johnstown and visit with my parents again. This was my favorite time of the year in Pennsylvania, with all the leaves changing and that crisp, cold bite to the air that made it feel good to take a breath. I was especially looking forward to escaping to the forest I had hiked in as a youngster and my secret rendezvous with Kathy's spirit. The drive from Pittsburgh to Johnstown didn't disappoint me even though it was dark. I could smell the autumn scent in the air as my headlights caught the bright flashes of gold and red leaves taking flight in the night. If someone banished me to live in just one season, by all means, I would want it to be fall.

I spent most of the next day talking with my parents and making some calls to Kathy's old friends to set up some visits. My mother had invited some of her friends over to the house to hear the story of what had been happening in my life. I felt a little awkward but, not wanting to disappoint my mom, I agreed to the meeting that evening. I had also called Kathy's oldest friend from grade school, Karen Vickroy to come over. She had been in an emotional state ever since I told her about Kathy's passing and in some way I thought I might be able to help her understand that she was not gone.

When the entire gathering of women had arrived, I started from the beginning and told my tale that by now was becoming quite lengthy. Karen was always on the verge of tears throughout my talk and, as I finished, I pulled out some copies of Chris' last photos of Kathy. As Karen thumbed through them, I could see more tears welling up in her eyes but to my surprise, she was not holding a photo of Kathy in her hand.

"Is this your boat?" she asked, holding up a picture of my sailboat that was at the tail end of the stack of photos.

"Yes, that's my boat," I replied, not knowing what was causing her to become so emotional.

"This boat here?" she asked again, this time pointing it out of the center of several boats in the photo.

"Yes, that's my boat," I said. The tears flowed down Karen's cheeks as she began to cry again. "What's wrong?" I asked.

"Déjà vu… that was Kathy's favorite saying," she sobbed. "Every time we went out, she would meet someone and then say to me, 'Don't I know him from somewhere? Oh well, must have been in another life – déjà vu.'"

The fact I had named my boat after Kathy's favorite saying was a jolt to me. I thought back to how the name just came to me in a flash of inspiration. No other name even crossed my mind. Kathy and I were so spiritually one, even though we were seldom physically with each other. The thought weighed heavily on my mind. "Had it always been that way?" I wondered as I tried to console Karen. She was having a hard time composing herself now as the thought of never getting to see her friend again sunk deeper into her consciousness. The pain of that loss was very familiar to me. It becomes a grief that builds on itself and drags your whole spirit into an empty void that collapses upon you, leaving you stranded, all alone, without a single light for direction.

"I wished I'd have stayed in closer touch with Kathy," Karen said. The sorrow was emanating from deep inside her, causing her voice to waver. "I would've liked so much to have spent more time with her before she died."

Karen's wish that night was beyond any power I had within me to grant. "It was never meant to be," I said to Karen. "Everything happened just the way it was supposed to. Kathy isn't gone, she's always around us and you just have to open your heart to feel her presence."

Karen took my words to heart. She still struggled with a question that is the hardest to answer. If I had only done this or done that, somehow, something would've been different or better. I have found that the only consolation is never regretting anything you do. Never look back, always look forward and continue moving along with a confidence that everything you're doing and everything you've done is the way it's supposed to be.

Early in the morning on Wednesday October 23rd I got out of bed and took off down the road for the Hinkston Run Dam. It was the most beautiful fall day you could ever ask for. The carpet of fallen leaves was wet and plastered to the dirt road like a giant mosaic. When I got to the end of the dam, I wandered up along the stream a little ways, just out of sight of the road. The water was flowing along at a gentle pace.

I sat down to rest on a rock along the bank just as the wind began to pick up its tempo. Looking up into the polarized blue sky, I let my mind float away on a single maple leaf that had taken flight from a tree towering over the creek. I watched as the breeze played with it, gently at first, lifting it higher than when attached to its now abandoned parent. Dancing directly above the stream, this invisible force of nature seemed to be giving the leaf one last look at the magnificent scenery of which it had once been a part. There was a pause, for the briefest of moments, just as it reached its pinnacle, then nothing. The energy that had lifted it was gone without a trace. The leaf plummeted straight down, becoming a meteor of red, hurling earthward in a dizzying spin. Just at the last moment, as I expected it to plunge into the creek, a surface wind blew up, catching it again, arresting its fall, and helping the leaf to flare out and make a smooth landing on the pool of water below.

I was somewhere else altogether now. Feeling every sense of Kathy's spirit within me, we were floating on the wind rushing through the pines. We were in the water, the air, the trees and the rocks, feeling the life that emanated from the scenery around us, twisting together in that band of energy to become one again. We didn't speak to each other with words or thoughts, but my spirit was released to experience a love that came from a part of me that had been missing for a very, very long time.

I don't know how long we were together, but when I came back to my body the leaf was gone, swept downstream to decay and become part of the whole cycle of life again. I just sat there watching the leaves fall and breathing in the heavy scent of the death of summer.

"Where do I go from here?" I thought to myself. "Where is this road I've started down going to lead me?"

"Well, you can't stop now," was Kathy's reply. "Just keep searching and see what happens."

I left the forest and my meeting with Kathy fully energized and more determined than ever to continue looking for an answer. I had already found out who Kathy, L.W. Rogers and I were. What I was asking now was how; how does this secret of life work? It was a simple, nagging question and one that's eluded man since the beginning of time. Now I felt that somehow the answer was going to play out in my life's story. Whatever way this life of mine was supposed to go, somehow, some way, I was to be involved in solving this riddle. I was never one to back away from a challenge, especially when I'm told I can't do or be something. Those words would trigger something deep inside me that would set me on a course just to prove that person wrong. I began to wonder if my confidence came in part because of my past lives. After all, I've had so many occupations already.

I couldn't recall details or even a simple recollection of any of those lives in my waking state as Randy Rogers, but I could bring them back easily with the acupuncture regressions. Seeing these connections gave me a new perspective of my current relationships and events. What I really needed now was to move forward to an even higher level of consciousness. There was something else waiting and I felt Lucy would be a great help in unlocking the next level. I decided to continue with the acupuncture treatments and see what developed.

VI.

DÉJÀ VU

Chapter 20

Back in Los Angeles, I received a call from Jane Semel asking me to join her at a dinner for the team that put together the cancer video and fundraiser for the Jonsson Comprehensive Cancer Center. We met at a restaurant in West Los Angeles on the evening of Tuesday October 29th. After we had all taken a seat at the table, a waiter poured the wine and Jane then stood up, holding out her glass in a toast to the entire group's effort.

"I'd like to thank each and every one of you for making this year's Fire and Ice Ball such a wonderful success. More importantly I'd like to dedicate this toast to our continuing quest to find the cure for all cancers in our lifetime."

I raised my glass that evening, not only in a toast to our efforts, but to realizing another image from my regression sessions that was playing out in front of me. We of course were not the Disciples of Christ, but in a way, disciples nonetheless, bound together in this battle against cancer. The image of Jane as John with his glass raised high flashed through my mind. The symbol on his ring still eluded me. I hadn't seen it physically re-immerge in my current life, but the more I thought about it now, at that instant, with our glasses held high, the more the symbol became clear. It was the sign of infinity, a never ending loop with no beginning and no end. I witnessed that it really never ends with my regression sessions of past life events now playing out in eerily similar detail in my life today. I toasted with Jane before in Jerusalem and here I was again in 1996. The message was crystal clear. I was on the right path to answering these questions.

♋ ♋ ♋

Friday November 1st found me in Lucy's office again, deep into another regression session. Lucy had decided to stay in the room with me to hear another first person account of my travels. This time, when I crossed the threshold in the hall of doors, I found myself standing on a mountaintop in Greece.

"I'm a goddess," I said as I stood with the wind blowing through my long flowing hair, "and Kathy is a warrior standing beside me."

Kathy and I were standing on the peak of a mountain overlooking Greece and the Mediterranean Sea below. We walked down from the mountaintop to the shore of the water and looked out to the horizon. As I watched, a ship came into view and sailed up within a short distance from where we stood. A smaller boat was launched from the larger ship and two figures rowed ashore. As the small wooden skiff drew nearer, I could see the two young men. Their hairstyles were identical, curly, short cropped and raven black in color. As their facial features became clearer, I could see they were not only brothers but also identical twins. Hanging from each of their necks was a gold medallion of some type. Each piece was a part of the other. When put together they would form a completed round shape. We greeted each other as old friends and as I looked into their eyes, I could see these twin brothers were my current friends Ron Siegel and Reneé Stauffer.

"We're going on a great adventure, many adventures," I said to Lucy. "We will sail along the Illyrian coast." Standing there as a beautiful goddess, with Kathy a strong and powerful warrior by my side, it was like being in a fairy tale. I didn't know who we were, but I knew at one time we had traveled the ocean together as the closest of friends.

♋ ♋ ♋

Saturday November 2nd I was sitting in my office. On my desk was the D encyclopedia. It had been lying there since Thursday when I had randomly opened it to Dalmatians. I didn't understand the importance of the word Dalmatian but did find it quite coincidental that in a few weeks we would be promoting Disney's *101 Dalmatians* in New York. I reached over and closed the book.

Immediately I could feel Kathy's presence clearly asking me to open it back up. I once again placed my fingers on the closed pages, and this time flipped it open to a short biography on a Civil War era physician named Martin Robinson Delany. As I read the story, I began to see a very strange resemblance to the regression session I had a few weeks earlier in which I described myself as a doctor in Virginia. This person was born in Virginia and, strangely enough, he practiced medicine occasionally in

Pittsburgh. This Western Pennsylvania connection was starting to become a link consistently appearing in everything I did. The other interesting fact about Martin Delany was that he was the first black man to earn the rank of major in the Union Army as a surgeon during the Civil War.

I thought back to my regression session. I never saw myself in that one. I never really looked at myself in any way and I couldn't remember if I was black or not. I only remember my shoes; they were anything but fancy, more of an indication that I was poor or struggling at the time. If I were Martin Delany, I would have to investigate to find out more about him. This short story made him sound like quite an interesting person, a black American army officer, physician, journalist and social reformer, trained at Harvard University. He must have led quite an exciting life. This would certainly explain my interest in the Civil War era, and in particular why I was so drawn to the stories told at Gettysburg about battlefield surgery. When I visited the battlefield as a boy with my parents, I thought it was fascinating to hear how these doctors performed amputation after amputation under the worst conditions imaginable trying to save lives. This curiosity extended to the modern day movie and later television program *M*A*S*H*. It remains one of my favorite shows ever. If past lives had any influence on my present condition, I was beginning to understand a lot more about myself already.

♋ ♋ ♋

Peter Michalos sent me a copy of an essay by Freud called *Delusions and Dreams in Jensen's Gradiva*. *Gradiva* is a novel penned in 1903 by the German author Wilhelm Jensen. The original story is about a young archeologist, Dr. Norbert Hanold, who comes to realize his love for his childhood friend through his infatuation and subsequent investigation of a Roman bas-relief he named *Gradiva,* or "girl who steps." Freud's essay was a psychoanalytical examination of the underlying reasons for Hanold's obsession with Gradiva who had now become a real person to him.

In Freud's essay, he puts out the possibility our imagination might be determined by forces other than its own arbitrary choice.

I found this notion to be particularly interesting. I have long held true to the fact that most of my life, or more correctly all of my life, I seemed driven by a guiding force not directly within me. In other words I could differentiate between my mind reasoning out an answer, as when I calculated a math question or searched my memory for an event I had learned by reading a book, and a feeling or thought that came to me through a connection to some higher power. They all play out in the confines of my mind but there was always a clear difference to me between one and the other. To answer this simple question of why we do things, I felt there were only two answers: outside guidance or my own internal mechanism. To prove this I decided to try an experiment.

I began to reason, think in my mind, if everything I was doing was internally driven, I should be able to know slightly ahead of myself what I was going to do next. I was standing in my bathroom at the time this thought came to me, so I quickly looked around the room for something to focus on. The wallpaper was a pattern of the world map with old-time drawings of the continents and oceans. My eyes quickly locked onto the Arctic Ocean. I quickly walked over to the encyclopedias and pulled out the letter "A."

"If I do have an internal mechanism controlling me I should be able to open this book now to Arctic Ocean," I thought. I flipped open the book. As I looked down to see my results, I found myself reading not an article on the Arctic, but one on the Argonauts. As I read the story, my jaw dropped in amazement – this was describing the regression session I had yesterday! This was definitely not what I was thinking I would do. Something outside of me was clearly controlling what happened next in my life.

In Greek mythology, the Argonauts were companions of Jason, a famous hero. They sailed with him on a voyage to capture the Golden Fleece, the golden wool of a flying ram. About 50 of the greatest Greek heroes took part in the adventure. The goddess Athena helped Jason build his ship, the Argo. They set sail along a route of many adventures following the ancient coast of Illyria. As I finished reading the article on the Argonauts, I could hear Kathy asking me to look again at the Dalmatian story. I opened the other book to the piece on the dogs, but quickly spotted another smaller article just before it on Dalmatia. This place was once part of Illyria and the very same area Jason and the Argonauts sailed though on their adventure in search of the Golden Fleece.

I sat there dumbfounded over my regression session of a tale about a Greek legend. Was this true or was this just a myth? In my session, we were real people; even though I described myself as a goddess, I was still very much a real being and Kathy's spirit of a warrior had to have been Jason. She certainly seemed to be the person in charge of everything. Ron and Reneé were inseparable twins in their past life, and today they are together as well. In our past adventure, we sailed along the ancient coast of Illyria and today we sail along the coast of Southern California. I recalled their names from my Greek session as Dimitrius and Diogenes and today as well they have matching initials for their first and last names.

Session after session I would visit a past event and find the friends I had then were with me today in different bodies. Our situations and relationships were different, but there was enough similarity to easily match settings and events today to experiences of the past. I was viewing them now as highway markers, guiding my way and pushing me onward towards my ultimate quest for The Key of Life.

Chapter 21

I didn't have any concrete proof that we were these people in real life, but now I was beginning to wonder just exactly what "real life" was. My experiment took an unexpected twist, leaving me even more convinced by the theory that some outside force was controlling the story of my life. Even now as I write these words, are they truly mine? Am I guided along this path so completely that nothing is left to chance? I sat back to soak in these thoughts and wonder what strange fate was looming for me on the horizon. I could feel something coming that would bring both sorrow and joy. Whatever it was, I had a more positive understanding that I was powerless to stop it and the best course of action was to just take notes as these synchronicities appeared around me. They were my only source of companionship now as I cut myself loose from the notion that I had any control of my circumstances.

♋ ♋ ♋

Colin Donahue had been a friend of mine from KPNX-TV in Phoenix. He was a fellow photographer who also made the move to Los Angeles after I left and was now freelancing for various clients around Hollywood. He had gone back to a high school reunion in his hometown in Michigan and met an old girlfriend that was looking to change her life. Shortly after the reunion, Kerry Runcie moved out to live with him in Los Angeles.

Several years earlier, I had taken Colin and his new girlfriend out for a day sail on my old sailboat. After the sail was over, Colin asked me what I thought about Kerry. Not one to pull any punches, I told him he should send her back to where she came from, as I had never met a more miserable person in Los Angeles. Everything she had to say about her life and Los Angeles was negative. I wanted to go home, get my gun, and offer it to her as a solution to her problems. Of course, my truthfulness didn't endear me to Colin. We stayed in touch with each other occasionally but the social outings dissipated.

Now several years had passed and Kerry had made a career change to work as an audio person with Colin. She had also taken an interest in astrology and had become a certified astrologer.

Susan had kept in closer contact with both Colin and Kerry and now asked me if we could take them out sailing again.

"Kerry's really changed, she likes it out here now and I think we'd have a good time. Besides she wants to do your astrological chart and I thought that would be something you'd like to have done." Susan was convinced this outing would go better than the last so I decided to give it another try. I knew Colin really loved sailing and I missed getting together with him. We set a date for another day sail on a Sunday afternoon in November.

A few hours before the sail, I was walking through my house when I felt Kathy's presence. She told me that someone named John wanted to talk to me. I sat down on the sofa in our living room and let my mind relax sending her the message that it would be all right for John to talk to me. This was a very new experience for me. Up to this point, the only spirits I had ever communicated with were Kathy and L.W. Rogers. I briefly received from her this person's name was John Walker. I didn't quite understand the second name but knew it started with a W. I didn't know who John was but was ready to listen to him and find out what he wanted.

"I really like sailing," were the first thoughts that crossed over to me when I sensed his thoughts mixed with mine. "I would very much like to go sailing with you today."

His enthusiasm and request took me by surprise, but what really shocked me was the absolutely, positively, overwhelming, without-a-doubt feeling that it was Kerry's father I was talking with. I knew very little about Kerry Runcie, especially whether her dad was alive or had passed away. But the feeling was there all the same that it was her father trying to reach out to me. "Well of course you can go sailing with us," I responded, letting my thoughts drift off into his.

I knew there was something else he was trying to tell me but the only thing I could solidly understand from him was how much he loved sailing and really wanted to be with us when we went out this afternoon. I was sitting on the edge of the sofa now and looked down to see our large encyclopedia dictionary on the coffee table in front of me. My hand reached out for it and opened the book to a section that displayed a picture of a cathode ray tube. I was looking at this television picture tube and trying to understand what he was attempting to tell me but I couldn't feel anything else coming from him. I continued looking at the page but nothing else jumped out at me so I closed the book and started to wonder what I should do about this newfound contact with the spirit world.

My contact with John had been so brief and yet very powerful for the few moments we crossed thoughts. I knew he wanted to be near his daughter and that he had wanted me to convey this to her somehow when I saw her later that afternoon. I didn't say anything to my wife about it as we drove down to the boat a few hours later. I felt avoiding an argument with her today would be accomplishment enough.

Colin and Kerry arrived at the boat in great spirits. I could she was a very different person than the one I met several years earlier. She was smiling and happy, no trace of the old Kerry was left to be found. I usually don't judge someone on my first meeting with them, but when my passion is sailing and I'm out there to have a good time, I'm less tolerant of anyone that's going to ruin it for me. I now felt that I had severely misjudged Kerry earlier and was glad they were aboard *Déjà vu* again.

There was a nice breeze coming out of the northwest and we made good way under a full sail for the entire afternoon cruising up towards Malibu Beach. After tacking around to return home, the boat settled into an easy downwind run with Colin at the helm. I had been looking for the right moment to tell Kerry that I felt her father's spirit earlier that morning but with Susan and Colin within earshot, I didn't want to do anything that would upset a pleasant afternoon. Kerry told me she brought my astrological chart with her and wanted to give me a reading later that evening at dinner. I knew this would be a good time to tell her about her father, but before I did I had to find out if he was even dead. I led our conversation around to talking about my family and then when the opportunity presented itself I brazenly plunged forward with the question that had been on my mind.

"Is your father still alive?" I asked her, waiting with bated breath for the answer.

"No, he passed away a few years ago."

My question didn't raise any alarm, as it seemed to come naturally within the context of our conversation so I expressed my condolences while deep inside I felt the presence of her father surrounding all of us on *Déjà Vu*.

"Your chart is very interesting," Kerry said shortly after we sat down to dinner at the yacht club. I was sitting next to her at the table and she immediately pulled out the printed sheet of paper showing the alignment of the planets on the day I was born.

Susan and Colin were having their own conversation across from us and the noise in the club gave us some bit of privacy, I decided this would be a good time to tell Kerry about her father.

"Was your father named John?" I asked Kerry this question point blank, now sensing her father's spirit around me again.

"Yes he was," she said with a surprise in her voice. "How did you know?"

"Was it John Walker or something with a W?" I continued to ask her for more information before I would answer her question.

"John William," she responded with a more puzzled look now that I had hit even closer to home.

"He came to me this morning," I told Kerry. "He said he loved to sail and wanted to know if he could go sailing with us this afternoon."

Kerry's jaw dropped slightly as she was taken back by my statement. "Oh, he just loved to sail and would take all of us out on Lake Michigan when we were children! I always feel close to him anytime I'm out on a boat."

"Well he was with us this afternoon and is still around us right now," I said, sensing his spirit engulfing me at the table. "He just wants you to know that he's always around you and he had such a wonderful time sailing with you this afternoon. There is just one thing I need to ask you. What did he do for a living?"

"He was a television repair man. He fixed TV picture tubes."

I told Kerry about the events of the morning, how the image of the picture tube made no sense to me then but now was perfectly clear. Kerry was so happy to know that her father was still around her and after some more discussion about her dad, she began to explain my astrological chart that she had printed out.

It was a positive reading and of course, she was on the money with many of the things about my life. I didn't place a lot of stock in anything she had to say about my personality because anyone who knew me could tell me that. She did say two things about my future. One gave me cause to feel secure and the other made me question what was yet to come.

The first thing Kerry told me was I would be very well off financially for years and years to come. I never really worried about it as I had always worked hard and felt secure in my accomplishments. The second prediction, however, concerned my married life, and what she was seeing was a big change coming in the not too distant future.

Kerry tried to put a positive spin on it by telling me that I had to work harder at my relationship with Susan. I didn't want to give it much thought and tried to bury the warning with a cavalier attitude.

"What is going to be is going to be." I said to her.

"But you can make changes and affect the future." Kerry responded.

I shook my head no and could see an immediate concern build up in Kerry's eyes. Whatever she had read in my chart - it was deeply troubling her.

After my sail and dinner with Kerry, we became closer friends. She was very interested in what was happening with my acupuncture treatments and the entire story developing around me. I spent many an hour with Kerry on the phone keeping her updated on the latest regression session or synchronistic event to occur with me. Meanwhile my sessions with Lucy were beginning to take me in directions I never could've imagined existed.

♋ ♋ ♋

During a regression on Wednesday November 7th, 1996, I found myself standing in a large rolling field of tall golden grass. A group of people approached me from the far end of the field. They were dressed in what I would call Mennonite garb; the men with black pants, jackets and brimmed hats, the women wearing long dresses with aprons. The group consisted of three people and one of them was clearly introducing himself to me as Donna Isman's father.

"I'm Donna's father, Joe..." The sound of his words drifted past me like some wafting dream, floating as though they were riding on a breeze.

"His name is Joe…" I repeated the information aloud for the recorder to pick it up. "He just wants to meet me and ask me to say hello to Donna for him." I continued relaying the conversation.

This session was the first one I ever recorded on audio tape, and afterwards when I played it back it had a surreal quality that took me instantly back to what it felt like to be in this other dimension. I couldn't pickup any other sounds on the recording, but my own voice was soft and sedated, with a near drug induced tranquility in the words I spoke. Playing low in the background was the music Lucy had piped into all the acupuncture rooms. After my appointment was over, I rushed home to call Donna.

"Was your father named Joe?" I asked her.

"It was Joel," she responded. "Why do you ask?"

"I met him today in a regression session. I thought he had said Joe but I'm sure I misheard it. It's so ethereal the whole effect of being on this other dimension."

"Another dimension, where was he?" Donna's energy shot up.

"We were in this wheat field, but it felt like I was on some other plane of existence where he was living now. He came walking up to me with two other people. They were all dressed in Mennonite clothing. He had on black pants, a white shirt and black jacket with a brimmed straw hat. Your dad said he just wanted to meet me and to say hello to you."

"I'm so glad he's still there watching over me. Did he say anything else?"

"No, it was a very short meeting. I had never been to this place before so the whole experience was new to me. He seemed very happy with these people that were with him."

I didn't have anything else to pass along but the sheer fact that I had met her dad on this other plane was amazing in itself to me. I seemed to have no control over where I would go on each one of these regression sessions. Meeting him, I would've chalked up to luck before but now I didn't believe in luck. I was definitely on a course, as crazy as it seemed, everything was guiding me to a destiny that remained more opaque the closer I got to it.

♋ ♋ ♋

My work schedule for the remainder of 1996 was easy, with one large junket in Los Angeles for *Evita* starring Madonna and Antonio Banderas. As with everything else, what seemed to be simple was now going to become complex. I received a call from Paul Bloch, Sylvester Stallone's publicist, asking me to accompany Sly around the world to help set up and light the press interviews for his latest film *Daylight*. Universal Pictures was the studio releasing the film and I would be traveling with Thomas Castenada who worked in their publicity department.

After making contact with Thomas, he sent over the travel itinerary for our trip. When I received the paperwork, I quickly looked through the schedule for shooting days. It started with Tokyo for two days, over to Paris for one day, then a day off… in London, England, the one place I needed to have some time off.

I jumped with excitement knowing that some way I would find the time to see the place I had visited in my regression session. What a turn of events! I had wished to see this place and now my wish was about to come true. Something that was not even on the horizon a week ago was now in plain view and within my grasp. The alignment of everything to get me there was no coincidence; I easily recognized the signs in front of me. A few weeks earlier I had been opening books and articles all about Carlos Castaneda, another traveler in the world of the esoteric. Now I would be traveling with someone named Thomas Castaneda around the entire earth. The significance of the sign was clear. It was pointing the way to England and opening a door that could lead me to a confirmation of my first major regression session.

I had to stay aware of all the signs around me. I continued keeping a journal of my daily experiences and looking back at them to refresh my memory in case any of these seemingly innocuous words, symbols or events cropped up again. With time, I may even be able to know a little in advance what was coming in my future.

No one was giving me lessons in this fine art of understanding my feelings. I was aware my emerging psychic abilities were becoming more sensitive every day. The more I tried to keep a lid on the spirits that were beginning to surround me, the harder they pressed to transfer information to me. This daily barrage to my senses finally culminated with a visit from an old friend the day I left on Stallone's around-the-world press tour.

I was rushing around my house, packing my bag and gathering up last minute things I needed for my trip. As I walked out of my bedroom on the second floor with my suitcase in hand, I could sense Kathy calling out to me. She was telling me that someone named David wanted to say hello.

"David," I replied, "David who?"

"Go to the books," I was instructed again as I stood at the top of the stairs only a few feet away from the wall of books on the upper landing.

I walked over to the same encyclopedias that had only weeks earlier shocked me with the Akhenaton revelation. I closed my eyes once again and reached forward for a volume. My hands opened the book and then I opened my eyes. I had opened the encyclopedia N to page 287, and the article was about the New Testament. My finger was pointing specifically to a quote from the gospel of Luke chapter 3 verse *23*. I stood there stunned as the connection immediately rippled through me.

"David? David Cooper? Is that you trying to reach me?" I asked the spirit that seemed so close to me now.

I felt his reply immediately and positively as being my old friend from Conemaugh that I had gone though grade school and high school with. How could I be sure though? How could I positively know that this was David Cooper now talking to me?

"Open another book," was the reply that came through immediately.

I put the book back and reached for another. Eyes closed, I felt again for the vibration, grabbed a volume, then opened it. This time I had opened the letter G to page 277 and my finger was firmly pointing to an article under the word gospel, the *Gospel of Luke* written around *85AD*.

Two separate books and both opened to pages with a quote from the Apostle Luke. I had seen my friend David as the Apostle Luke. Now his spirit was talking to me and providing the proof that he was truly David.

"If this is really David Cooper then I should be able to open one more book so I could positively identify him," I thought to myself as I reached for another volume of the encyclopedias. I didn't want to pick L because that would be too easy, so I kept my eyes open this time and reached for the letter M. I now closed my eyes and felt for the vibration that would tell me where to open the book. It was a feeling that I had become aware of now that I was using this method as a means of communication between the spirits, in their other dimension, and me. As my fingers would feel their way over the exposed page ends, I could sense a tingling as they reached a spot to open the book. It was a subtle clue but now something that I felt easily as my fingers glided over the page ends. My hand stopped at a spot that was producing the most sensation. I pried open the book. As I looked down to see what had opened, my heart skipped a beat to see the heading of *Martyr* staring up at me.

"Luke was a martyr!" I gasped. A very familiar feeling was now sweeping over me in waves. It was as though my friend David had entered the very room I was standing in, not just in spirit but in a physical presence as well. I began to converse with him as though we were standing right next to each other.

"David, how can this be you? It's been so long… and now am I to believe that you were really Luke?" I needed more proof that we could've been the people that I saw in my regressions.

"Get our yearbook down." His reply came quickly.

I reached up to the highest shelf in the library and grabbed hold of the 1971 Conemaugh Valley yearbook that he claimed held the answer to my question.

"Open it," he said. I did, and it fell open to the page dedicated to him. "Look at the day that I died," he said, as I read the memorial looking for a connection to his past. Born July 18th, 1953, Died October 18th, 1970 read the tombstone-like heading underneath his photograph. There was his image frozen forever in time, the smiling face of my friend, taken on a day when he had no clue of the fate that awaited him. As these thoughts rushed through me, I could hear one last message pass over to me.

"Now look up Luke and see that I was him." I felt his presence grow dim around me.

I looked up at the encyclopedia that I hadn't selected yet and intentionally avoided on my last selection. My hands trembled slightly as I pulled the book resting up against the letter K. As it fell open to the page I knew it would find, I spotted the small article on the Apostle Luke.

The article began by saying that very little information was available about the apostle Luke. What was known is that the apostle Paul had described him as a "beloved physician." I reflected back to my friend David Cooper's life and remembered that he was much the same in that respect. I recalled a time he injured himself, a deep cut covered in dirt. David went home, scrubbed it clean with a brush, applied an antiseptic, and then a bandage to hold the cut closed to heal. Any of the rest of my friends would've had to been held down by their parents and forced to endure the agony of the wound's cleaning and treatment, but not David.

A smile came to my face as I thought about my friend and what a strong character he was. He was a short little guy and wiry as they come. What he lacked in height and build he made up for in strength and quickness. I went back to the article to finish reading about Luke. There was nothing else significant except he was believed to have died a martyr proclaiming his faith in Jesus up until the end. The last lines of the article stated that the Catholic Church set aside October 18th as St. Luke's day.

My hands reached for the yearbook again. "Was that the same day David died?" I was sure I had just read it in the yearbook memorial. Yes it was… the exact date, October 18th. I placed the books back on the shelf, grabbed my bag and headed to the airport.

Chapter 22

I arrived in London late in the afternoon of December 11th, 1996. The flight over the English Channel from Paris was aboard a brand new British Airways 777. It was the inaugural flight for the new aircraft and they rewarded me with first class service the likes of which I had never seen before. Individual, isolated seats converted from an office-type setting with desk to a fully reclined bed for sleeping. Exhausted from the constant travel, time changes and work schedule, I was asleep in the bed before the wheels retracted. I didn't even feel the plane touch down less than an hour later at Heathrow and had to be awakened by the flight attendant.

At the hotel in London, I checked in for a good night's sleep so I could spend the next day, my only day off, traveling to see if I could find the castle. I made plans to depart early the next morning for the train station and at 8 a.m. on December 8th, I started out on my quest.

The train station was a bustle of activity when I arrived. It took a few minutes to figure out which train I needed to take north to Pontefract. I determined I would need to change trains at Wakefield and then head east for the Pontefract area. I had just missed the 7 a.m. train, and the next train didn't depart for an hour. I decided to go to a small newsstand and find something to read on the way. I was perusing the aisles looking for a special book, but I didn't know exactly what kind. I just knew when I did find it, it would definitely be different. I was scanning my eyes over the non-fiction area when I spotted it among the novels just below. The book was reaching out to me somehow. I could feel the title jump off the shelf, standing out from the numerous other choices.

Sophie's World. I had to read this book today. My mind locked onto these thoughts as I pulled the title toward me and quickly headed for the cashier so I could begin reading it. The jacket was a nondescript, muted red with the title in gold lettering. The brief description laid out a story of a young girl, Sophie, who begins a correspondence with a mysterious person who leaves letters in her mailbox. They appear magically every day, and contain questions about philosophy and life that take Sophie down a road of intrigue and learning as she tries to understand how mankind's thought process has evolved over the eons of time.

I calculated the trip north would take me approximately three hours, including the train change at Wakefield. I was already hooked on the storyline by the time I boarded the passenger car. I didn't really know where I was headed but had a good idea that something would feel right when I got there. The book was mesmerizing, especially since I never went to college. I was learning as much as Sophie about the great philosophers' different thought processes. Descartes and Aristotle were the names of people I had known very little about. "You think, therefore you exist," was pretty much the extent of my philosophy education.

As I neared the Wakefield station, the story took a sudden personal twist in the plot line. It turns out that all this mystery surrounding the stranger's identity and why he sends Sophie questions daily will culminate on her birthday, June 23rd. To make matters even more interesting, she was born on a very special date, midsummer's night eve. It was a magical time, held in special esteem to be the day when night and day were equal and all the world was in perfect balance.

I knew there was something special awaiting me in this book and now it stuck out like a sore thumb. The number was clearly there for me to see and, even though this was a work of fiction, I had a feeling the story was closer to the truth than many accounts published as non-fiction. I had to stop reading to disembark the train at Wakefield station but the story had me hooked now and the 544 pages would keep me busy for the entire flight home and beyond.

The train departed Wakefield station, leaving me feeling temporarily stranded while I waited for another one to come along and take me to my destination. I was beginning to feel apprehensive now, anxious to see what, if anything, existed from my regression experience. As the second train appeared on the horizon, a wave of support washed over me with the familiar closeness of Kathy's spirit promising to guide me when I had any questions about which direction to turn. Her guidance was needed nearly as soon as I boarded the second train. Looking up at the rail map I faced the added confusion that Pontefract has two train stops. Which one should I take and how far away was this castle – if anything even remained? These questions were now beginning to elevate my anxiety level. Kathy wrapped herself closer, and I could feel her energy telling me to trust in myself. "You will know when the time is right to get off the train." Her thoughts flowed clearly in my head.

I watched the first stop appear and then disappear behind me without moving from my seat. A few miles down the track, I exited the train at the last station for Pontefract. As the train rolled out of sight, I felt a strange calm wash over me, as though I was going home, but nothing looked familiar as I surveyed the surrounding countryside. In the distance, I could see the twin stacks of a power generating station, indicating that the landscape had changed drastically since the days I had experienced in my regression session. I stepped down off the elevated train platform – alone, but feeling completely confident what I was seeking was not far down the road in front of me.

As I walked along the lane towards the town, it dropped me out onto a highway that wound its way around a small hill. There was no signage saying "This way to Ye Olde Castle." In fact, there was not even a sign announcing the town of Pontefract, but I was beginning to feel something familiar as I approached a church tower I spotted from the train platform a few minutes earlier. I could see from its crumbling old stonework and gravestones surrounding the facility that the church was ancient. I entered the property and began to walk among the final epitaphs of the past citizenry of Pontefract. The tombstones were so old many of the messages had faded into unreadable oblivion. The ones I could read dated from the late 1600s onward. I felt as though I was slowly drifting back in time, but still had another hundred plus years to descend to find the layer I was looking for.

I walked out of the courtyard and started back on the road snaking its way around the hill. As I started to climb up the grade away from the church, I passed a gas station on my left. Then to my right appeared a set of wide stone steps leading up the hillside, the same ones I had seen in my regression session. I still couldn't see any signs to indicate a castle was near, but these steps I knew. I had walked up these very steps last month in Lucy's office, and they led me to the castle. I had shot most of my film in Paris the day before so I quickly backtracked to the small convenience mart-gas station, and bought another roll to document my discovery. I fired off a couple shots of the stone stairs and then, taking a breath to slow my excitement, walked up them again, this time as a man in the 20th century. As I reached the top, I found myself on another narrow roadway lacking signs, but now I didn't need them anymore. I knew where I was and, if correct, the castle would be just up around the bend to the right.

As I rounded the turn, there in front of me stood the ruins of what had once been a massive castle, *the* castle from my acupuncture session. Directly in front of me and slightly to my left was a large rounded stone structure, part of the main tower or the keep I was assuming. It was lopped off approximately twenty-five feet up from the base, and the appearance of everything that remained standing was that of a large continuous series of massive stone walls that had collapsed and been ground down over the centuries by the erosion of weather, people and time. The stones themselves, once brilliant and white were now stained with a patina of pollution and dirt, black in many areas but generally smoggy brown overall.

Closing off the roadway was a padlocked double-gate, mounted between two stone columns. A second smaller side gate connected to a third matching column continued on into a stone and wrought iron fence. A medium sized, beautiful stone cottage with a red pitched roof made out of flat tiles stood behind the fence on my right. The relatively modern day structure was built in the same stonework as the castle, giving it the appearance it had been there nearly as long as the ancient ruins. A small plaque explained this was the historical site of what had once been Pontefract Castle.

I walked around the asphalt driveway that led to the fence. I was trying to get my bearings but something wasn't the same. I remembered a deep ravine surrounding this place with a drawbridge leading across to the entrance. All that was standing now was a portion of the keep and a base of what I could only guess was one of the towers I had described. Everything else was paved with asphalt up to the path that led onto the site. To my right and just inside the gate was the entrance to the tourist shop-cottage. It was strangely quiet here without any cars or people milling about, just myself as far as I could see. There was no one to take admissions and, as far as I could tell, none to be charged so I let myself in the gate and walked around the paved area still trying to figure out where I was in relation to my regression. I finally gave up and headed over to the store, hoping there would be someone inside who could answer my questions.

The shop door was locked so I decided to walk around the grounds and see if anything else felt familiar. The area was meticulously landscaped. The grass was a vibrant, lush green and growing beautifully all around the inner grounds of what I guessed was once the outer yard. As I followed along the pathway, I found some more plaques explaining what area I was looking at, and ended up walking the entire grounds along what was once the perimeter of the outer castle walls.

From what I could see, this place had been as massive as I had described. From the little I could learn from the plaques, the castle had been built up over the centuries starting in the 1200s and reached its peak in the 1650s when the civil war began to reduce it to ruins. I photographed every angle and view that seemed interesting to me and as I made my way back to the entrance, I could begin to see how this place must have stood out as the prominent geographical feature, seen from miles around.

The small hill I had been circling from below now hid from view any signs of what once was. Even from a distance, the trees now concealed any remains of the foundation when I approached from the train station. Now, from up on top, I could see a panorama of the countryside below and could only imagine what a view it must have once been from the top of the towers. This had definitely been a commanding fortress in its day. I climbed down from the ruins and walked out onto the paved area in front of the shop, still trying to picture where I had stood in my regression session. I looked over at the tourist shop and could now see someone was inside.

"Hello!" I called out, greeting the person inside behind the counter. He was younger than I expected, working in a place like this. Of course after seeing everything in England of such an ancient stature, I was expecting that its citizenry, or at least people in charge of ancient things, should be ancient themselves.

"Good day," he replied, with a heavy Yorkshire accent.

"I was wondering if you could help me?" I asked, not thinking about how to phrase my next question. "Wasn't there a drawbridge that used to lead over a ravine to the castle out there?" I asked, pointing out the window to the ruins.

"Indeed there was, in fact, it was straight out there in the asphalt area, directly where I saw you walking around a few moments ago. Come here with me and I'll show you." He motioned for me to follow him into the rear half of the store.

The back section displayed the historical timeline of the whole region, including the castle. On the walls were drawings, paintings and detailed information about the various rulers that had once reigned over the area. As I got to the very back of the room, there was a print of the most beautiful painting of the castle and the surrounding English countryside.

"See… here." He pointed with his finger to a small part of the painting that showed the drawbridge clearly, with a person painted standing in the exact spot I had stood holding onto the stone wall. "This is where you were standing in the parking area outside. They've filled in and paved over the ravine now but this is what it used to look like."

I was standing there listening to him but only half his words were getting through to me. For all I knew my mouth was hanging wide open in utter disbelief as I looked at this frozen moment in time, the time I described so thoroughly in my acupuncture-induced regression. There, in front of my eyes, was a time and a place I had seen, felt, breathed and touched not a month earlier in Lucy's office. The painting even depicted the life I described in the grass-roofed house in the country complete with the crooked stick fence that surrounded the place and a person chopping firewood to the right of the house. I couldn't take my eyes off the painting. Every detail was a mirror of the image I had burned into my mind at the regression session that day.

"I must have a copy of this," I said to him. He responded by pointing out the rolled up tubes of prints to the right of the one I was viewing on the wall. I picked one up in addition to a sketch of the castle that dated from the 1560s – the exact time that I believed I was standing on that drawbridge.

Before I left the shop, the young man told me that in the town's museum I could see the original of the 1650 painting. He started to give me directions, but I was already halfway out the door and called back to him, "I know where I am now and how to get there!"

I took one last look at the castle and turned to walk down the familiar road. The lane would take me to the marketplace, the same marketplace I had met Kathy, my sister of long ago.

The walk into the village was a short one. As I strolled along, I could clearly remember what it used to look like nearly 450 years ago. Back then there weren't any buildings along the simple country lane, but trees and fields of grass instead. Now the street was lined with homes, many of them old stone and brick, and by my estimation, built in the 19th and 20th centuries.

As I approached the area that marked the beginning of the square, I was amazed to see that it was still an open-air marketplace, but now with buildings along both sides of the lane leading up to it. It was now called Market Place. What really floored me was the accuracy of my other identifying marker in the acupuncture session. On my right-hand side, just where I had seen my Uncle Bob in his previous life as a butcher holding a goose in his hand, was now a shop. The sign on the front in big bold red letters read: Butcher Shop. I could still feel that moment, his presence standing there, helping me to get a bearing of where I was, where he was, and who we once had been.

This was no dream. I was here once in a different time. I looked directly ahead of me at the market square, now paved with cobblestones and lined with dozens of shops, but still crowded with the open-air peddlers selling their wares from modern carts in the center.

I found my way over to the museum and had a good look at the original painting of the castle, which was as large and impressive, as the castle once had been. Before I left I found several books on the Pontefract Castle and people of that time. The day was getting late so I hurried outside to grab a few pictures of the marketplace and the butcher shop before the short winter day ran out of daylight. I really wanted to head in one more direction to find the cottage in which my meeting with Kathy had taken place. Looking at my watch, I realized I wouldn't have time to continue searching and still get something to eat, or at least drink, before I had to catch the last train to London.

I had been running all day now, on just my adrenaline and could use a rest. I found the mighty fortress of an impregnable castle reduced to near rubble. Surely the frail, tiny cottage with its thatched roof and crooked stick fence would've suffered the same fate as time marched on. Even the lonely country lane I had walked down with my twin sister was built over with businesses now and unrecognizable. I had seen enough during this trip and it was more important not to get stuck three hours north of London with no way to get back in time for tomorrow's shoot with Stallone.

I stopped in a pub near the train station and had a pint while I reflected on the day's revelations. They had been an absolute confirmation for me, proof that my previous lives were real and not just tall tales spun from regression sessions as Susan believed. I was standing in an actual place and seeing remnants of things that were exactly where and how I remembered them nearly 450 years ago. As I sat sipping my beer and watching the locals arrive for their afternoon gathering with friends, I couldn't help but feel at home here. Maybe some of them were even my old acquaintances, reincarnated into the same setting here in current day Pontefract.

As they smiled and nodded a friendly hello to a stranger, I wondered. *"Were we really strangers after all?"*

♋ ♋ ♋

I finally had the answer to my first question, who am I? It was a tricky little subject that required a trip to England and a confirmation first hand that my regression session was right. I can now say without a doubt that we are all a life force of energy, re-incarnating into a new role, time after time. The characters we play, in the lives we've chosen, build and shape each spirit through birth, life and death. Yet underneath it all we're identical, you and I, an indestructible force of power, who's limits I had yet to explore.

This Key of Life was still hidden, scattered across the eons and buried in clues that were yet to arrive. Whatever I found, I knew it would make me feel complete again, like putting the final piece of a jigsaw puzzle in place. I would be connected on all sides. As

Déjà Vu

I prepared to travel this cryptic path through other dimensions
I made a promise to myself to stick with it and stay the course.
Wherever it would lead, I would follow and find enlightenment
across the sands of time.

VII.

ALONG THE PATH

Chapter 23

I was back in Los Angeles again and things were not any better with Susan. Sure, I had photos of the place that I claimed I was in back in "merry ole England" and stories of how everything was exactly where I said it would be but that didn't seem to matter to her. She was still playing her "Doubting Thomas" role.

What upset me most about our relationship was how she withheld any affection as a means to bend me into her way of thinking. I tried to separate my quest for an answer to all that had happened to me from my relationship with her, but she didn't want to play that way. At night, she would bait me into a conversation about my experiences and I would bite believing she was interested.

"I like those prints of the castle you brought back from England. I'm going to take them in to get framed this week," Susan said as we got into bed for the evening.

"What I find amazing is how incredibly accurate the detail is. They even painted a person standing on the draw bridge exactly where I was standing when I entered that door in my regression session."

"It's just a coincidence I'm sure," Susan said. "Don't you think that a lot of these things are just you creating them because you want them to happen?"

"No, they're not! There's more than just that person on the painting. Every detail I remember is turning out to be true, including the butcher I saw on the right side of the road as I walked up into the market place. I found out all the butchers setup shop along that right side of the lane as you entered the market place. How could I be creating this when the history of the place is telling me it's true?"

"I'm sure I could see things the way I want to see them if I looked hard enough at something. It's like when you buy a new car, you begin to notice all the other people with the same car."

"This is not the same thing as noticing something because I happen to have one! I experienced this place in a regression session, then 'coincidentally,' as you put it, got a free trip over there to see first-hand that every detail I spoke of was in the exact place and looked the same as I had described it on an acupuncturist table in Santa Monica." I tried as hard as I could to get Susan to see it from my point of view, but she reached over and turned off her night light. I tried to put my arm around her but she gave a shake of her body indicating she had no interest in my touching her, let alone making love tonight.

I turned over to pull out my journal from the nightstand drawer. I was getting tired of writing the same old phrases of how Susan was shutting me off sexually to try to shut me off spiritually. Occasionally she wouldn't let the subject of my psychic experiences get between us and we would still have some spark of romance left to explore, but those days were few and far between. I was too busy with my job and my quest to concern myself with it though. As we went to sleep that night with our backs to each other, I naively thought someday it would return to normal.

♋ ♋ ♋

It was almost Christmas again. It seemed like the years just flew by. Dana and Phil were getting older too and the holidays weren't as much fun as when they were younger. Even back then, now that I think about it, they were far from the ones I knew as a child. Almost every Christmas we would rush through the gift opening and quickly whisk them off to their dad's house in Arizona so he could spend his winter week visitation with them. Susan and I would sometimes take the opportunity to have a week's vacation, but now even that wasn't happening.

Susan wanted to see her relatives in Arizona and I didn't really care to go. We always got into some kind of argument there. Susan and I used to do best away from all relatives, but I guess now she didn't really want to spend time with just me. This holiday was going to be even more unusual because Susan was on jury duty and impaneled on a trial that was running right up to Christmas. I didn't mind because it kept her off my back and out of the house; anything that did that was all right in my book.

I really enjoy just sitting around with a good book to read when no one is there. I was still working on *Sophie's World*, entranced as ever, wondering what was going to happen on June 23rd. I often felt something would happen to me on June 23rd. I did tell everyone that I would probably die on the 5th, 14th or 23rd

of whatever month that would happen in. I deduced this from the fact Kathy had been born on a 5 – June 23rd – and died on February 26th – an 8, my number. The least I could do was to die on her number, and that gave me three options every month. But waiting for my death to happen was not exactly the final piece of the puzzle I had envisioned. More messages were now beginning to surface and they were not pointing toward death.

♋ ♋ ♋

I was reading *Sophie's World* one morning when I felt a compulsion to go to my library of books and pull one out and see what the message would be today. I stood in front of the shelves, eyes closed and just reached for whatever my hand would pull back.

When I opened my eyes, I was holding a copy of *The Secret Garden*. The book was one of Susan's and I had never read it. I closed my eyes again and split the book open on whatever section it fell to, then ran my fingers over the pages until I felt that familiar vibration telling me to stop. I opened my eyes again. My fingers were underlining the sentence, 'I will cum bak.' I stopped and read the sentence again. It was intentionally misspelled and isolated into its own paragraph with single quotation marks surrounding it. I could clearly see that someone was talking to me, but who? Who was coming back?

I went about my work back up in my office but about mid-day I came over to the house to get some soup for lunch. I decided to open another book to see if anything else would help me. I sat down on the couch and placed the large encyclopedic dictionary on the coffee table in front of me. Again closing my eyes, I pried it apart and opened my eyes to find my finger on the words *come again*. It was an example of the use of the word *come* and many of the phrases associated with it. I sat there mesmerized. I had now opened two separate books to the same phrase.

I was startled out of my mini-trance by the ringing of the house line. On the other end, sounding very excited, was Nancy Lipscomb, Susan's half sister. I could feel the enthusiasm coming from her voice. I told her Susan was on jury duty, asked her how she was doing and if I could pass on any message. She wouldn't give up her secret and no amount of prying was going to get it out of her. She wanted to share it with Susan first.

"Just tell her to call me as soon as she gets home," Nancy said.

I started to wonder about Nancy's call just as I was looking at the words *come again* in the dictionary. I started to think about the fact that Nancy was pregnant with her first child, due sometime this coming May. I figured the call probably had something to do with that. Was whomever it was coming back arriving by way of Nancy's baby? I had no idea, but it was a starting place and I already knew there are no coincidences. Nancy called at exactly the right time to drive home some kind of message to me. I went back to work in my office.

About 5:30 I was back over in the house again and the phone was ringing just as I heard the garage door open. It was Nancy again and she sounded disappointed to hear my voice on the end of the line.

"She's just pulling into the garage now, Nancy, if you'll wait she'll be upstairs in a minute," I put the phone on hold.

When Susan got to the top of the stairs, I handed her the phone. "It's your sister and she's pretty excited about something."

Susan grabbed the phone. From the side of the conversation I could hear, I knew it was news about Nancy's first baby. When Susan hung up the phone she told me Nancy had just found out she's going to have a baby girl. I wondered just who this new girl was.

The next day I awoke to a song playing in my head. I was humming it in the shower and couldn't get the tune out of my mind. "Here you come again, just when I thought that I was getting over…" I couldn't get this Dolly Parton tune out of my head. I got dressed and went down to read the paper before work.

I was on the last page of the paper, still humming the song in my head when I flipped over to the daily TV listings. There, right at my thumb, was Dolly Parton. *How am I doing this?* I thought to myself. I read the listing for the new TV movie on that evening, *Unlikely Angel.* "Dolly plays a small town country singer that dies in a car crash and comes back to earth as an angel to help a family at Christmas time," the caption read.

Okay, so now what, was someone coming back to help me? I was fairly sure that was the case, but who is it? My friend Kathy or my friend David? I'd spoken to both of them recently, getting no hint as to who was coming back to see me. The only person I knew expecting a baby was Susan's sister so this spirit must be arriving through her. Why would someone come into a person I would have little hope of having a close relationship with? It was not as if I would be living with them or taking care of her in any way. What else could be happening here? I pondered the possibilities.

Her sister Nancy's unborn child could possibly be an old friend of mine, reincarnating back into this life to be with me. I knew this was a concept I would have an extremely hard time selling to Susan. I decided to bide my time. When I finally met her in person, I would know if she were an old friend back for another lifetime. I knew I could count on my feelings to sort out who was who. These questions and more would be racing through my head for the next five months.

Chapter 24

January 1st 1997 - this is the year - something big is on the horizon. I could feel it growing closer with each passing day. I made a resolution to stick this out. I would keep a good record of the events around me and soon it would all become clear as I struggled to find these last few pieces of my puzzle.

As Father Kelly preached many a time from the pulpit during Sunday mass at Sacred Heart Church, "The road to hell is paved with good intentions." These words rang in my head every time I failed to include Susan in my journey. I surely thought at times I was marching through hell, trying to bridge the ever-widening chasm developing between us. We couldn't even broach the subject of my spiritual quest without ending up in a bitter fight. I avoided talking with her about it at all costs but that just strained our relationship further. I couldn't pretend I had given up on it, but I also couldn't talk about it. I just stayed away as much as possible, burying myself deeper in my work and regression sessions. My only comment to her would be, "Just wait and see what's going to happen." That infuriated her even more.

♋ ♋ ♋

January 8th 1997, I was back at the Drake Hotel in New York. I was in town to setup two Disney movie press junkets, *Metro,* starring Eddie Murphy and *Grosse Pointe Blank* with John Cusack, Minnie Driver and Alan Arkin. It was going to be a big setup day tomorrow with twelve cameras running for the two movies. I went to bed at 11 p.m. to try to get as much sleep as possible before my early call. I was awakened from my sleep at 1 a.m. with another journal entry flowing in my mind:

Once upon a dimension, many, many dimensions ago, we were as one spirit. Before there was time, before there was space, an energy existed that was part of all of us. In order to grow the spirit gave of itself in a tremendous burst of energy, creating more dimensions, the beginning of time, the beginning of space. All of the energy that was given from the one spirit became many smaller spirits existing on a level above the physical dimensions but in the same space and time.

It may be hard to understand how more than one object can occupy the same space but you have to free your mind of this dimension and imagine many levels layered over each other. It is the same as how many radio waves fill the air but only hearing the one your tuner is set for. So many things are misunderstood in this world. We search too hard for answers when they are right in front of us. We are looking in space for other life but the search should be here in our own dimension. We only need to build a receiver to search these other wavelengths and see these other worlds.

Just as we are all part of one original spirit, we all are individually part of each other, and just like a puzzle is made up of many pieces, so is the life force that exists in this time and space. Imagine those many pieces, and within each piece, another cut in the same shape as the original. That is the best way to describe the spirit that is closest to each of us. We are all inter-connected to become as one but the pieces that join to form one are soul mates. This puzzle is larger than you can ever imagine and when you spread it out over many dimensions, time becomes irrelevant in our quest to grow back into one energy, one spirit, in one dimension and no time.

♋ ♋ ♋

My sessions at Lucy's were continuing on a weekly basis for the most part. If I was out of town on a shoot or busy in town I missed a session now and then, but with each session, my spiritual friends were pulling me to a new level of awareness. One particular regression became a turning point, showing me there was no limit to the powers I was dealing with.

I had just gotten to the hall of doors when Kathy led me into an auditorium. I was sitting in a front row seat all alone when the room began to fill with hundreds, if not thousands of people. I could recognize many of them as friends that had passed on, in particular my grandmother, Donna's dad and a good friend of mine I had worked with in Phoenix, Steve Pacente. Steve died in an auto accident in Washington D.C. while he was covering a football game for KPNX-TV. Steve was one of the sports anchors in Phoenix I had worked with on many stories over the years.

As the throng of spirits grew around me, I remember telling Lucy that there were so many of them and they were all there to show me they were supporting me and giving me great power. As I relayed this information, I told her they were taking me to higher and higher levels. I felt them surrounding me. My spiritual presence in their world seemed to be floating higher and higher right through the heavens themselves. It was not strange for me to experience this lifting sensation of my spirit. I had felt it many times before starting with the dream that first night with Kathy beside me. This time the sensation was even more intense.

"They're taking me higher and higher," I said to Lucy as the energy emanating from all those souls surged through my spirit and through my body lying on the table. I was soaring up so smoothly and powerfully that I barely noticed Lucy was not speaking to me any longer. Her silence was welcomed because I didn't want to let go of the connection I had established.

"I'm going so high," I said to Lucy. On the spiritual plane, the energy was so intense I can only describe it as magnetic. The combined force of all those spirits was engulfing me with a radiation of love and power that felt like some kind of magnetic field, holding me in place while gently pushing me up physically from underneath. I was also aware that I could feel the weight of my clothes, my pants in particular, as they pulled down on me back in the physical world. At first I thought Lucy was tugging at my pants, but I couldn't sense her presence near me. My eyes were closed as I hovered in the heavens with my spiritual friends. I stayed there for a few minutes until they brought me down again and back to my seat in the auditorium.

"I'm back," I whispered to Lucy, waiting for her to ask me where I had been.

"Are you sure you're back?" was the reply that now seemed to come from the corner of the room.

"Yes, I'm back and my friends are all leaving now."

"Okay, now just stay there," she said "and I'll count backwards from five to one and when I get to one you will be back here with me, understand?" Lucy's voice seemed a little nervous now as she counted down and I opened my eyes to see a visibly shaken acupuncturist.

"You scared the hell out of me," were the first words out of her mouth as she removed the needles from my wrists and feet.

"Why, what happened?" I asked. I expected her to say that she had seen a bright blue or purple glow emanating from my body because that's what I had seen while my spirit was soaring in the other dimension.

"You came completely off the table," she said shakily in her heavy Russian accent. "I started to reach over to grab you but was afraid to touch you in case you fell. Instead, I moved away from you to the corner and stayed quiet to watch. I was afraid you would fly out of the window." Lucy was so visibly upset I knew I had to do something to calm her fears.

"If I ever do leave out the window, call my wife and tell her I'm flying home because I've never done that before and I may not make it all the way!" My joking seemed to ease her tension but she couldn't get over the fact I had physically levitated off the table in front of her.

"Didn't you feel yourself lifting off the surface?" she asked me.

"I told you they were taking me higher, but I didn't know I was actually floating off the table in this world. I could feel someone tugging down on my pants at one point," I added.

"Those were your clothes settling down on your body as you rose into the air."

It made sense now. That is what the feeling felt like, my clothes settling against my skin. I sat there for a minute, almost not believing her, but she was too upset to be making it up. It was hard for me to fathom that the energy from one world could transfer into this one and physically lift my body off a table. I didn't deny that I had experienced the most powerful energy transfer to date in the session, and if anyone could lift my two hundred-pound body and hold it in suspension, my friends on the other side could.

♋ ♋ ♋

When I got home that evening, I didn't even want to tell Susan what had happened in the latest regression. She had belittled me so much already I knew this would just provide more fuel for her fire. I also knew I had turned another corner in my search and what I was going to learn now was not in the past, but somewhere in the future. These spirits didn't take me to new heights just for the fun of it. They were trying to show me something. I felt it had to do with building me up on a spiritual level. To do what, I didn't know, but they wouldn't energize me like that without a reason. I personally felt it was to help me physically get through what was to come. I did notice I had reached an amazing physical and spiritual peak and never felt better in my life. This helped me hold off the criticism Susan leveled at me. Even that would eventually grow old, but how long would I hold out, another year? Something big was going to happen and I knew it was going to be this year.

♋ ♋ ♋

My job became very hectic, juggling a constant stream of movies flowing from Disney and Warner Bros. If I was not working on a shoot in LA, then I was in New York, or any of a hundred other locations they could send us. One job for Disney this spring would take me to Orlando. I felt strange that I would now get a shoot where Kathy used to live. At least I could make this trip worthwhile and maybe see Kathy's old friend Tammy and talk about what Kathy had been like in those years living in Florida. I would have to call Chris to get Tammy's number.

Chris had been such a help to me during all this. She was the only connection to Kathy's life I seemed to have left. I would call her weekly to talk about my investigation and fill her in on the latest regression session or synchronistic event that would always follow. What I really enjoyed most were the times I was able to go see her in Palm Springs. The entire place had an energy about it that made me feel closer to Kathy.

The irony was that I was really closer to Kathy now more than anytime when she was alive. When I began to feel like I was just stumbling through a series of endless regression sessions looking for clues, one call to Chris would give me a real world connection to a person with first hand knowledge about Kathy's life on this plane.

I made the call to Chris for Tammy's phone number in Florida.

"I know I've got it in one of these phone books somewhere… Hold on… I've got three of them to look through now." There was a pause as she went to get her address books. "Well that was too easy. Here it is in the first one." Chris read off the phone number to me.

"I hope Tammy will be able to tell me some stories about the years Kathy spent living in Florida. It's the one big hole in her life that I haven't heard anything about." I said.

"I'm sure Tammy is the one to talk to. Give her a call and let me know what you find out."

I hung up the phone and dialed the number. Tammy Maier was a co-worker at the insurance company where Kathy had worked. When she answered the phone I introduced myself and asked her if she had time to hear my story about Kathy when I came to Orlando in a few weeks. She said she had time right now if I would care to tell her over the phone. As succinctly as possible I brought her up to date with everything that had happened. Tammy was very surprised to hear my story and then in true synchronistic fashion, passed along some news to me that was even more startling.

"I believe Kathy had an affair with a co-worker named Randy," she said. Her words bounced around in my head for a minute before the second round went off like a shot. "He was married to a woman named Susan. Kathy always felt ashamed that it happened and never talked much about it." Tammy's last jolting round left me stunned in disbelief.

After telling Tammy that my wife's name was also Susan, she seemed quite amazed at the synchronicity with my life. I promised to call her when I got to Orlando to set up a meeting in person if our schedules would permit.

What odds made it possible a girl so close to my heart and so far away from me physically could meet a person with my first name married to a woman with my wife's name? What forces were at work to have Kathy develop feelings of attraction overwhelming enough for her to throw her moral values out the window and give in to her physical urges? I felt sure her affair was sub-conscious in origin, driven by our spiritual past and present circumstances.

♋ ♋ ♋

A few days after my latest news from Florida, Chris called to ask me a question. She wanted to know if I would take Kathy's remaining ashes and scatter them in Florida at their parents' grave. I told her I would have to think about it and would call her back with an answer soon. It wasn't that I didn't want to do it, I just wasn't sure it was what Kathy wanted or even something that I should do, as opposed to a family member. As was my usual custom now, I took off on my sailboat for some time alone to let the answer come. I was barely clear of the breakwater at Marina del Rey when my cell phone rang.

"Randy, this is going to seem like a strange request," the voice on the other end started. It was Ron Malvin my friend from the editing facility. "I need a boat to scatter some ashes for a friend and was wondering if you could help me?"

"You what?" I responded in disbelief at his question.

"I know it seems strange, but I have a friend who recently passed away and they want to scatter his ashes at sea and we need a boat for them to perform the ceremony on. I know you have a sail boat, but we need a large power boat to handle all the guests. Do you know where we could charter something like that? We just need to scatter some ashes."

I was absolutely stunned by the timing of his call.

"Ron, you aren't going to believe this but I'm out on my boat right now just debating the same issue. Kathy's sister Chris asked me to scatter Kathy's ashes for her when I go down to Orlando. I just asked Kathy to give me some kind of sign that she wanted me to do it and you called at that very moment."

"Well, I'm glad we're on the same wavelength," Ron said with a laugh. "Now can you help me out with my problem?"

I gave Ron the number of a good friend who worked in the boating industry in Marina del Rey. I knew he would have no problem setting him up with what he needed.

If I had any doubts before, I didn't now. I immediately called Chris to tell her what had just happened. I made a date to pick up the ashes before I left for Florida. I was still wondering how I would feel when it came time to hold the last remains of Kathy in my hands.

♋ ♋ ♋

By this point I had lost track of how many regression sessions I had done. They ran the gamut from a Russian peasant in Siberia with my brother Jeff as my young child, to being part of a Pueblo Indian tribe in the Four Corners region of the Southwest with my sister Rosemary. I even saw scenes of my future in this life. It was all very interesting to say the least, and mixed within these brief glimpses of past lives were more visits with the spirit of L.W. Rogers.

One of the simplest meetings with him occurred at a lake. I walked into the scene as soon as I entered the regression. A few deep breaths and I was walking up a country road to a tranquil lake setting. No doors to enter, just instant access to as serene a setting as you could imagine. As I approached the shoreline, I could see L.W. sitting there resting on an old log. A rod was in front of him with the line cast out in the water. When I approached he motioned for me to take a seat on the log.

"I spend a lot of time out here, just getting my line wet mostly," he said. "But it never gets old no matter how many times I come."

I smiled but didn't say anything because I knew exactly what he meant.

"Every meeting we have together is another step closer to understanding who you really are." That was all L.W. said before he stood up and reeled in his line. At least I think he reeled it in, because the next thing I actually remember seeing was him walking off down the road, the whole scene surreal and extremely tranquilizing. L.W.'s energy wafted away leaving me with the fading image of him carrying his rod in one hand and I swear a stringer of fish in the other. This simple meeting leveled my energy to the same calmness and composure he exhibited that day.

In my next session, I found myself traveling with L.W. away from this world, feeling my true spirit as Kathy had tried to describe to me in her first visit. The session started out like the last one, no doors to enter and this time L.W. met me and guided me to a gate I can only describe as being at the top of the world. It was a white column structure with an arch across it, and I needed his guidance to enter.

"Beyond this gate is the sum of all man's knowledge," L.W. said as he took my hand to cross over.

I turned to look back at myself on the table for a moment then began floating quickly out of the room, rising up through the building, above the clutter of Los Angeles, higher and higher through the air. As the city disappeared, California's outline emerged, then shrunk away, revealing the United States and quickly the entire world. Everything reduced in size as I pulled away. I could feel myself growing, not physically but spiritually, to a point in space where we hung there for the briefest time, experiencing how truly small the world really was. Then earth disappeared, past the moon and into a cluster of stars, our Milky Way Galaxy. Then our galaxy shrunk further until I could no longer tell it from the thousands of others. It was much like a child's snow globe now, rapidly continuing to diminish in size until all creation condensed into the tiniest speck of light, so small that it was barely visible at all.

I felt disconnected from whatever I had once been a part of. More than that, it didn't matter at all that I had been a part of something. My spirit and L.W.'s were all that existed now, surrounding this point of light. I reached out and held it, the entire universe, in the palm of my hand. It was barely discernable as anything at all.

"It is but a speck in a gnat's eye," his thoughts transcended into mine.

The feeling of true power was indescribable. Nothing else mattered, nothing at all. I could feel a surge as my spirit enveloped this microcosm of light, surrounding it now from all directions and saturating it like water into a sponge. I was experiencing exactly what Kathy had described it was like to become part of the spiritual world!

The sum of all man's knowledge, past, present and future, was now in my hand. It was nothing more than a pin prick of light, insignificant in comparison to what I had become, yet an essential element to the growth I had experienced. I couldn't discard it because it was all I knew of this universe, but in relation to the spiritual world its power and knowledge would never approach what I was experiencing now.

"How will I ever find my way back?" I asked L.W. The planet that seemed so large when I was standing on it was now dissolved into a speck that was once an entire universe!

I had no sooner asked the question when everything began to expand and my spirit contracted right back down through the galaxies, rushing at the speed of light. The earth loomed larger and larger until I entered its atmosphere and was back on the table again. I could hear Lucy's voice asking me if I was ready to come back now.

"I'm back," I replied as she began to remove the needles.

I was back all right, but I knew at that moment my life was heading down a path where spiritual force overrides anything logical. Thinking about anything was now out of the question. I would know when I had the solution to my enigma. It would be a feeling so strong that no force on earth could stop it.

VIII.

A GATHERING STORM

Chapter 25

If I were to choose a single word to describe my life in the spring of 1997, it would be "incomplete." I could feel Kathy's spirit around me all the time but it was not enough. I know many people feel as if something is missing in their lives even though they may appear to have everything they could possibly want. This void had always been in my life, but now Kathy's spiritual absence from this dimension had isolated and magnified it at the same time.

Like the archaeologist Hanold in Jensen's *Gradiva*, I was fixated with finding a solution to my dilemma. Just feeling the presence of Kathy's energy surrounding me was not enough to stop my search. I needed to touch her again on this plane, if only for a moment.

Maybe what happened next was just an illusion, or it may have been real, but the end effect was the same. I was in Lucy's office on April 2nd 1997, deep into an acupuncture session, when I found myself standing with Kathy's spirit at the Gates of Knowledge. This time, Kathy and I entered the gate and again I found myself with her at the top of the universe. L.W. Rogers was there to meet us, this time holding the same metallic rod I had noticed in our first meeting in his office.

I was having an extremely intense session in this alternate state of existence. My spirit and Kathy's began pulsating around about each other, much like the first time she visited me during my out of body experience. But this time we were melting completely into one spirit, one boundless piece of energy with no separation of where her spirit began and mine let off.

We soared in low flight over mountains and fields of beautiful natural scenery. It was such an exhilarating escape of physical boundaries that to be in my body would've left me breathless. The sensation of being in a combined spiritual state left me floating high from my physical presence. The seamless transition from hollowness to complete satisfaction was astounding. The void I had been experiencing was gone and replaced with a feeling of balance. I now felt complete.

"We've only done this once before," Kathy said to me. It must have been a long time ago because I couldn't remember it.

"All the things I have learned in this life and all my other lives are within you now. You need to let my spirit grow with you for a while and allow its knowledge expression through your actions."

I didn't understand how this happened, but the session was now over. I found myself back with Lucy and a new feeling that made me want to jump for joy. I hadn't felt this way in a very long time. As I left Lucy's office, I wondered what to make of my new condition. How long would this feeling last; through the day, the week or the rest of my life? Only time would tell. For the moment this feeling of being one in spirit again was a phenomenal energy boost. The balance of male and female would also help me to understand what was to come.

It was very strange not to have to call out to Kathy for answers. For the past nine months, we seemed so close yet completely separate. Now I felt very good but didn't want to overpower her spirit within me. Just the thought caused me to smile and question that maybe it was her spirit overtaking mine. I was just so glad to be one for however long it lasted. I had no concerns over who was driving.

A few weeks later on April 14th, I was standing alone in a desolate Florida cemetery, looking down at the sand blowing over the graves of Kathy's parents. My thoughts were focused on the small bag of ashes I held in my left hand. How could this tiny amount of dust ever have been my friend Kathy? She was such a beautiful, loving soul and closer to me than I had ever realized. She was right here inside me now and closer than we ever could have been physically. I still missed seeing her face, but exactly whose face was that now - my twin sister, my brother, perhaps a parent from long ago? I was sure we had played all these roles and many more.

I lifted the bag of Kathy's ashes and turned it over, raising both hands in the air. The ashes spilled out and started blowing in the wind. As I watched the last specks of dust fall back to the earth, I longed to have Kathy's spirit back in anybody that I could touch and know, without a doubt, that a part of me was very definitely a part of them.

♋ ♋ ♋

April 30th, 1997 and I was at Lucy's once again. I relayed all these stories to her while she placed the acupuncture needles. I began the familiar slow rhythmic breaths as I quickly relaxed into the regression. At the hall of doors, I found my hand on a very familiar old wooden door.

"I'm at Sacred Heart Elementary School," I said to Lucy, stepping through the old doorway and into the entryway of the small schoolhouse.

Once inside, I walked into my old classroom on the left side of the hallway. The scene was so vivid and real, I thought I would hear the hand bell ringing at any moment. As I walked into the classroom, L.W. Rogers was standing at the blackboard with the metallic rod in his hand. I took a seat in one of the school desks lined up in neat rows. The smell, the feelings and the sights around me made my senses tingle. I hadn't felt this kind of apprehension in a long time, the same apprehension I felt daily as a student wondering what was going to happen next. Now I was sitting here, merged with Kathy's spirit, and still nervous about what was to come.

L.W. motioned for me to come to the front of the room. I could tell my combined spiritual days were coming to an end. He held the rod over my head producing a spinning sensation that separated our two entities. I was now beginning to understand Kathy's words that night nearly a year ago when she asked me to "Feel my spirit, that is what makes us as one." Standing there now, with her and L.W. Rogers, I could feel that we were all one soul. We were three individual entities, but our pieces fit together like the finest parts of a Swiss watch.

Kathy took my hand, leading me from the classroom. Before we parted ways, I sensed a new stronger spirit in both Kathy and myself. Our time together made me realize one day we would never be separate again.

♋ ♋ ♋

The highs during my regression sessions couldn't make up for the new lows I was experiencing on my home front. Susan and I were having intense arguments daily over anything and nothing in particular. It was all centering on my research in the occult, but I had no idea why such a chasm was opening up between us in every aspect of our lives together.

Dana was graduating from high school on May 30th. It was a small graduation ceremony held at Le Lycée Français School on Overland Avenue in Los Angeles. Emotions were naturally running high with Susan. Her daughter would be venturing out into the real world in a few months, far away at Whitman College in Walla Walla Washington. I imagine the combination of those thoughts along with our battles about life were just too much for Susan to handle. We only had to drive a few miles over to The Stinking Rose Restaurant for lunch with Susan's family, but the arguing hit a fevered pitch immediately after leaving the parking lot.

Susan's brother-in-law, Paul Lipscomb, was the catalyst for our latest round of fighting. He was married to Susan's sister Nancy who had just given birth two weeks earlier to Annie. Paul Lipscomb was certainly not one of my favorite brother-in-laws. I had had many of them over the years, but none quite like him. The time I spent around him left me wanting to be anywhere else. Expressing my dislike for Paul ignited an emotional response in Susan. She could reach a venomous rage in her arguing that scared me at times, especially the way her words rang with hatred towards me. This was one of those times, and one of those arguments I could feel quickly escalating out of control.

"I don't care what you think he is, Susan, he's trouble waiting to happen for Nancy and Annie," I blurted out. "Just wait and see. I can feel it coming."

"What is going to happen?" She always wanted an exact answer to every statement I made now.

"I don't know exactly, but it's not going to be good, you can mark my words on that."

"Stop the car and pull over now!" Susan screamed in as nasty a tone as she could muster.

I pulled the car over to the curb on La Cienega, two miles down the road from the restaurant. Susan jumped out, slamming the door behind her.

"I'll get my own ride from here!" she yelled. I rolled down the passenger window to begin pleading with her to get back in, but stopped before I said anything. In Susan's book, Paul's job as a Secret Service agent made him several notches above me in class. She made that clear many times, and for her to put her faith in him and not me left me angry and hurt. I put the car in gear and just drove off. It wasn't a horrible neighborhood and a walk might calm her down. I arrived at the restaurant and told the rest of the family that Susan would be along shortly. It was no secret we were having running battles, and this was just one of many.

I was most anxious to meet Annie and see if she could possibly be anyone that I had been in contact with in my regression sessions. I hadn't felt that Annie's body held Kathy's spirit, as Kathy's energy still seemed to be surrounding me. The last time I had actually seen Kathy was in my April 30th regression session so it was not impossible that Kathy could've reincarnated on May 14th, the day Annie was born.

"So this is the Annie I've been hearing so much about." I peered down into the baby carrier sitting on the floor next to Nancy's chair. Annie was sleeping soundly, wrapped up in her blankets with just her face peeking out. Upon first sight, I had no feeling of what spirit she held. I had a firm belief that Kathy's energy would be so overwhelming to me that no matter what body she came back in, I would recognize her immediately. I had no such feelings coming from Annie. I began to think maybe she was too young to exude that kind of aura, but then came back to my original belief that if it were Kathy, nothing on earth would stop me from sensing my connection to her spirit.

There was some meaning I was missing in Nancy Lipscomb's call back in December while I was being shown the message "I will come again." Annie's birth was clearly not the vehicle my friend Kathy was going to use to return. I was sure Annie was a spirit I had, in all probability, known in a previous life, but she was not *the* spirit, my soul mate and the missing part of me who I wanted to return so desperately and become a part of my life again. I had been open to the possibility that Kathy would return as Annie. Now my first attempt at trying to understand the messages surrounding me had clearly failed. I hadn't read the signs correctly, yet I still believed the original message to be correct. I was still developing a skill that when accurate was unnerving and flowed from my heart. I would have to open my heart wider now and let Kathy's spirit and love guide me through this maze of emotions, as she made her way back to me.

Chapter 26

On June 23, 1997, Kathy's forty-fourth birthday, I went to see Lucy for another regression. I entered the hall of doors and my grandmother was there to meet me. She took me by the hand and led me to her home back in Johnstown. She and I sat down on her couch in the living room to have a talk.

"You and Kathy mean so much to me," she began in a soft voice. "We are all so very close." She touched my hand and instantly transported me back to the inside of a church in England.

I felt removed from this scene, unlike the others in which I was part of the action. Before me, I saw a funeral for the twin girls Kathy and I had been so long ago. The caskets were there with our bodies inside, and a church filled with people mourning. I didn't have time to see who was there or any other details as the scene before me changed to another period, not of a past life but an historical event. It was as though all of history fast forwarded right in front of me.

Highlights of different eras and events unfolded at a rapid pace in three-dimensional reality. The speed at which time was moving seemed blinding, yet I somehow was able to take it all in, even breaking some events down to feel the effect of what it was like to have been Lincoln assassinated by Booth *and* be Booth assassinating Lincoln. The sensation was so thorough that I also became the bullet and the gun!

I was being shown that I was not just a part of this physical place called Earth, but all time and events taking place were also connected and a part of me. The sum of all man's knowledge, that speck of light I had viewed in the palm of my hand was accessible within me and always had been. When I freed my spirit from its physical constraints I could access anything - all events, people, places and things.

I felt someone touching me and suddenly awoke from this time transportation to find myself in a bedroom at my parents' house in Pennsylvania. It was Kathy touching my face, gently, bringing me back from my rapid romp though history. I arose from my bed and she led me out of the house and up the road to the Hinkston Run Dam.

We walked to the far side of the dam near the bridge that crosses over the Hinkston Run, the small stream that feeds water into the dam. Kathy and I stood there in the forest talking for a few minutes. I was telling her about what I had learned and the sensations I had felt.

"I have loved you for eternity and now I understand what eternity means." My love for Kathy's spirit radiated out from my soul and shimmered in the dappled light that filtered down through the trees.

"When you opened up your heart, your perception of reality slipped away and let our true world come in. Do you understand how the illusion of time drives all souls through past, present and yet to come?" Kathy wanted to know if I grasped the lesson at the Gates of Knowledge.

"The sum of all man's knowledge is frozen before me, neither moving forward nor receding, yet it is all these things at once. The lifetimes we've lived are still playing there and all souls share the experience. Our interaction as individual entities enlarges and unifies the consciousness of all." Kathy smiled now as she could see I had imbedded an awareness of universal consciousness.

Her smile was so captivating that I stopped talking just to feel the love radiating from her core.

"Today is going to be a very special day for you," she said, holding both my hands and looking right into my soul. She was wearing a long white gown and the aura that surrounded her seemed to be glowing brighter as she spoke.

The vibrations emanating from Kathy suddenly doubled, and then tripled in strength and magnitude, like an earthquake building to its maximum level. L.W. Rogers now appeared and stood beside her in the forest wearing the same beautiful white gown. The fabric of this garment was so unworldly it appeared to be made from stardust itself. It was such a surreal scene to behold. They stood there enveloped in the brilliant green foliage and dark rich soil of the Pennsylvania landscape. The aura of their being enhanced the entire image in a seamless blend of natural energy. The sheer vibrancy of life that pulsated from their combined presence took my meeting with them to a new level.

"You have been searching for something," L.W. said.

I moved closer to the two of them standing along the side of the road. "I have gathered up many of the pieces of the puzzle but still have no solution," I replied as we began to walk through the forest.

"Life has many paths to lead you to the same destination," he said.

"I'm searching for the Key of Life," I said, hoping for an answer to my quest today. We stopped for a moment and I turned to face them directly.

I watched as L.W. held out his hand. In it was the cylindrical object I had seen many times before. It looked like a simple silver metallic rod about eight inches long and three eighths of an inch in diameter, but the power it possessed was unlimited. He was holding the same rod in our first meeting as he sat in his study, flipping it end over end through his fingers against the desk. Now he was holding it out for me to take. I reached out, grasping it with my right hand and the sensation of pure love began to course through my body.

"This is *The Key of Life*," he said, releasing his hold on the cylinder.

I held the rod in the palm of my hand. My body on the table seemed to warm with a glow that can only be described as an inner radiance of love pouring from every molecule of my body. As I stood in the forest feeling as one with it and the entire universe, a pulsating, radiation of pure love replaced my very soul, who I was, what I was. There was no denying the feeling that the Key of Life is pure love.

"Hold this key within your own heart now," L.W. said as he placed his hand upon my chest.

I responded by taking the object now with both of my hands and clasping it over my heart. Waves of energy intensified with each second I held the rod. It seemed as though I was lying in a warm bath rocking from head to toe with the water replaced by waves of saturating love. The power it possessed immersed my soul with love and a complete understanding that it was always as simple as that. When I took my hands away from my chest, the cylinder had vanished.

"You will always have the key with you," he said as I looked over at L.W. and Kathy, who was now beginning to fade from my sight.

"Where is she going?" I asked L.W.

"All questions will be answered from within," he replied.

These thoughts stayed with me as I melted away from the scene in the forest and back to the table in Lucy's office once again.

♋ ♋ ♋

I now had the answer to life's biggest question. Through the use of a simple metallic rod, L.W. Rogers unlocked the limitations of my heart and directed all the love of our universal consciousness into my very being. This symbol, *The Key of Life* as he called it, was always with him and had been with me as well. Week after week I had been lying on a table, with metal pins placed in my wrists and feet to help me open up my chakras and let the energy flow smoothly through my body. L.W. wanted to use something that I could easily recognize and relate to as he showed me how our spiritual life also "flowed" with the energy of love. What better key could he use than a silver metal rod?

The acupuncture sessions had taken me to a level beyond anything I could ever have imagined. The knowledge I now held of what we are and who we were, combined with the charging effect of holding *The Key of Life* made me feel renewed and reinvigorated. It was as though life for me was starting anew. I had brought the key with me onto this level of existence. It was part of me, or I was part of it. Whichever way I looked at it, *The Key of Life* – pure love – was within my very being.

♋ ♋ ♋

July 8th, 1997 I was at the Drake Hotel in New York, lying in bed watching the last eight minutes of my forty-fourth birthday slip away to midnight. I couldn't believe I was still here on this earthly plane. I guess it must be for the long haul. Kathy was so close to me spirituality now, but physically as far away as ever. Something was building and the clues were everywhere in plain sight. I had become so keenly aware that to try to explain it to anyone else made me sound like a mad man.

The next morning, July 9th, Paul McCartney became my latest puzzle piece. He was all I talked about yesterday with Ron Siegel and the rest of the crew. His new song, *The World Tonight*, kept playing in my head after I listened to it on the plane to New York. Now I'd been awakened by an early phone call from one of the New York crew. I decided to flip on the television and Paul McCartney was staring me in the face. He was on the Today Show talking about his wife Linda's breast cancer and his mother's death from the disease. I knew some key part of what was to come had something to do with him now, but what, will only become apparent with time.

♋ ♋ ♋

During the return trip to Los Angeles July 11th I was very restless. I was feeling some kind of loss again during the entire flight. When I got back to my house, I sat down on the couch in the family room and actually felt sick. It was nothing I could put my finger on but my whole energy was drawing down and I was emotionally uncomfortable. If I were not around Susan and the kids, I felt I would be crying now for no apparent reason.

At 3 p.m., I decided to force myself to get up and work a little on the video I had in post-production. Susan had made plans for a group of us to go to Hollywood Park at 6 o'clock for a night at the horse races. I figured I could get a little more editing done on the umbilical cord blood video before then. The project had come to me through Lucy's service on the board of a company called The California Cryobank. Their main business was preserving donor sperm and eggs, but they were now branching out into the stem cell business and offering long-term storage of a child's umbilical cord blood. I had just finished spending weeks on call, rushing out at the last minute to shoot footage of babies coming into this world and their umbilical cord blood being harvested and preserved. It was the ultimate personal insurance protection for a new life. Your own stem cells captured at birth and stored for any future need that may arise. The research on the promising therapies and uses derived from them was just scratching the surface.

I had only been working for an hour or so when the phone rang in my office. It was John Dreyfuss calling from UCLA's Cancer Center.

"I've got bad news Randy," he said. "I just found out that Donna Isman has passed away."

"When? Where?" I asked. A queasy feeling returned to my stomach.

"I'm still trying to find all that out," John said. "I just heard from her doctor that she's gone." Donna had been such a symbol for other cancer patients. I could feel his sadness of her passing weighing heavily upon him.

"I'll try calling her partner Suzanne. If I hear anything, I'll let you know." I finished my call with John and sat in stunned silence thinking about Donna.

I had just spoken to Donna a few days before I went to New York. We had been trying desperately to get together before my trip but our schedules wouldn't allow it, so we made a promise to see each other as soon as I returned to Los Angeles.

I picked up the phone again and called Donna's home. I figured Suzanne wouldn't be there. I was certain Donna had just passed away that morning. It explained my feelings earlier in the day. Donna's passing had impacted me severely. I left a message for Suzanne to call me and then walked over to the house to give my wife the news. When I walked in, Susan was sitting at the kitchen counter going through the day's mail.

"Donna Isman passed away today. That was John Dreyfuss calling to let me know." She stopped what she was reading and looked up at me.

"I'm sorry to hear that. I know you had become good friends with her. Do you still want to go out tonight or shall I cancel it for this evening?" Susan was genuinely sad to hear the news.

"I don't feel really great right now but I think we should still go," I said. "Besides, almost everyone that's coming knew Donna so it will be good for us to get together tonight so I can tell them."

♋ ♋ ♋

Nancy Williams and Nick Hankocy were the first to arrive at the racetrack. She was shocked to hear about Donna, but what came next was even more astounding.

"Nick just told me he felt like someone had died today. Tell him the story Nick." Nancy prodded Nick to replay what had happened with him a few hours earlier.

"I was driving back to the television station this afternoon when I smelled this overwhelming odor of formaldehyde. I told the reporter I was with that it smelled like death. I hate that sickening odor. You know the smell Randy, like you're in the morgue or a hospital with the chemicals they use to preserve the bodies. The reporter smelled it too but we didn't know where it was coming from."

Having been around morgues and hospitals, I knew the odor Nick was describing. It was a nauseating chemical smell. To be around it for even the shortest time made me physically ill.

Nancy and Nick finished telling their story when Ron Siegel and Renée Stauffer arrived. After telling them about Donna passing away and Nick's scent of formaldehyde in his news car story, Renée piped in with one of her own.

"You guys won't believe this. Ron and I were downstairs working this afternoon when this sickeningly powerful smell overcame both of us. It was so bad we had to run outside to get away from the fumes. It made me physically nauseous. It turned out that the guys refinishing our hardwood floors upstairs were using a formaldehyde-based finish for the process. One of the workers came out to tell us 'Yeah, it's the same stuff they use to preserve bodies.'"

The three of us having these strange experiences on the day of Donna's passing didn't elude me. Nancy had written the cancer video and Ron did the audio for it. But the trump card was yet to come into play.

I called my voice mail from the racetrack to check for any possible messages from Suzanne Coffman, Donna's girlfriend. There was only one recording on the machine, about thirty seconds of lyrics from a song were left without any message. I had heard the song before but was not sure the name of it. I saved it to listen to more clearly at home. The song remained on the machine through the weekend and into the following week.

♋ ♋ ♋

"Look at all those crows," I shouted to Ron Siegel, pointing out the dozens of noisy, large black scavengers covering my yard and driveway. "There's so many I can't count them!"

It was early Tuesday morning, July 15th. Ron and I were headed up to Big Bear for a shoot with Shirley Jones for American Movie Classics. Shirley had us up to her house at least once a year to do her host segments for the family movies they played. I really hit it off with her, and of course was not too surprised to find out Shirley was from just outside Pittsburgh. As we neared the top of the mountain, we came across another large flock of crows covering both sides of the road.

"I don't know what kind of sign this is." I threw the question out to Ron. "That's the second time I've seen so many of them today."

I returned from Big Bear that evening and remembered the mysterious clip left on our answering machine. I asked our daughter Dana to listen to it hoping she could identify the artist for me.

"It's The Counting Crows," she said after humming along with the tune over the phone.

"The smell of hospitals in winter…" The words Dana was singing were clearly a message from Donna. How could I possibly get this song into my voice-mail? I had another hunch. I played the clip back again and timed it with my stopwatch. With out even looking I could feel the answer: twenty-three seconds. Twenty-three seconds of a clip of music from The Counting Crows recorded on my answering machine, less than an hour after Donna passed away. Twenty-three seconds of a track dealing with "the smell of hospitals," while we were experiencing the odor and nausea ourselves. Donna had left me a message from the other side, a message that she was there and life does go on.

At Donna's wake, Suzanne Coffman gave us one more story of her final hours. Suzanne was standing by Donna's bedside holding her hand and talking to her. Donna was slipping in and out of consciousness. After one of her sleeping spells, she opened her eyes and said to Suzanne, "I was just out in the hall by the vending machine and they have those frosted animal cookies you really like in there. You know, those Mother's brand ones that you can never find. You should go out there and get some."

"That's great," Suzanne replied, trying to pacify Donna's dreams of having just walked down the hallway.

Suzanne stayed with Donna as she slipped off one final time and her breathing finally stopped.

"You know, I left the hospital that day," Suzanne said, "and as I was walking down the hall I passed a vending machine set back in a corner off to the side. Something told me to walk back just to see what was in there. Can you believe those Mother's Circus Animal Cookies were right where she said they would be? Donna had never been on that floor or down the hall of that hospital. She had never even left the bed from the time she was wheeled into her room and I know she didn't see it from the hallway because I had to step out of the hall to see what was in the machine."

"It was her spirit taking little side trips during her cat naps," I replied.

It was just like Donna to be looking for something for her friend, even on her deathbed. Her spirit was free now to combine with the universe and move on to her next level of growth and adventure. I was sure now, that someday, we would all meet up together again.

♋ ♋ ♋

I was working on the cord blood video and trying to make the piece really stand out. I decided to use my Adobe® After Effects program to design a custom animated company logo for The California Cryobank. I had harp music playing in my head for some reason and had to have it for the logo. After an extensive search, I purchased several clips from a stock music house. I was working with the music late on a Saturday night in my edit suite when the phone rang. It was Susan calling from over in the house. She wanted to know if I was going to go to the christening for Annie the next day. Even though we had been battling intensely, I still wanted to get to see this child and try to understand my connection to her. I told her I would be going.

"Nancy would like to play some music she has on CD at the baptism and I told her you could bring your portable stereo to the church. Is that OK?"

"Sure." I packed up the boom box to take with me the next day.

The next afternoon I walked into their church carrying the stereo and asked Nancy if she had the music she wanted to play. She reached out and handed me two CD's of harp music. I didn't need to be hit over the head to see this connection to my umbilical cord blood video so I just smiled and put in the music she wanted. After the service, we all went over to the party at Nancy's place. As I walked into the backyard, you could have knocked me over with a feather. There was a large harp setup on the lawn with a harpist in a beautiful gown sitting there playing a lovely melody for all the guests.

"What is happening here?" I thought to myself. "Is this child somehow connected to me?"

As the party got underway, I eventually got a few minutes of time to hold Annie, talk to her, and look deeply into her eyes trying desperately to find some connection. She was a beautiful little girl but I could feel nothing other than the joy of holding a new baby in my arms. Whatever this harp sign meant, I knew it was important. I had now seen it three times in a row. I didn't feel that Annie was the connection, but I knew that the symbols were a new baby and a harp.

I had become used to collecting these enigmatic pieces of the puzzle. Yes it was something important, but as with everything else, why it was important would become apparent when it was time. My job was merely to gather up the pieces.

Chapter 27

On the evening of July 30th, Susan and I were getting ready for bed and having another strained discussion over harps, crows, lyrics to songs, you name it. The list was endless now. She was also leaving the next morning for a weekend in Phoenix visiting her parents and attending their 40th wedding anniversary party. I wasn't going with her due to all the work, the kids and everything else needing my attention in Los Angeles. I also didn't want to be in an atmosphere where my presence could set Susan off and ruin her parents' party.

I don't know what came over me next. Out of nowhere, I blurted a final remark before turning over to go to sleep. "There's going to be a big plane crash tomorrow," I said, quite calmly.

This of course got her attention immediately and she demanded to know more information about what plane would crash. I honestly wasn't even thinking about the fact that she was flying the next morning when the thought came into my head and slipped out of my mouth.

"It's going to be a big plane," I said, "but no one is going to get hurt. We'll know about it when we wake up."

My last statement, of course, did very little to pacify her curiosity. I imagine she was lying there, wide-awake, wondering if it was going to be her flight. Even though I clearly told her we would know about it when we woke up, she wouldn't put the slightest bit of trust into what I had said. It would've been great for Susan to turn over to me and say, "I'm not worried honey, I believe you." Neither those words nor any others like them ever came from her mouth that evening, or anytime since.

The next morning I awoke at exactly one minute to seven. I quickly sat up and grabbed the remote. As the screen came to life, The Today Show's Matt Lauer announced Newark Airport is closed this morning following the crash of a Fed Ex jet on the runway. They had a live helicopter shot playing full screen while Matt continued with the report that the crew had escaped with no one injured seriously in the crash. Susan sat straight up in the bed and looked over at me.

"How did you do that? How did you know that would happen?"

"It just came into my head and I said it."

Even though it was quite amazing how accurate my prediction had been, I knew my little demonstration would do nothing to settle down the conflict between us. Susan wanted hard-facts to explain it all. I only knew that the information came into my head as a pure thought. I would then verbalize that thought to whoever happened to be around. It was as easy as that.

Susan was not buying it. She wanted to believe there was some logical explanation for the things she saw me do. Susan's only problem was that the logic she was applying went out the window when my answers were coming from information stored in another dimension. I couldn't get her to see the simplicity of it all, and nagging at me now was my gut feeling she may not be with me when she finally figured it all out.

♋ ♋ ♋

In August we decided to move my production company out of the back building on my Altavan property. In only two years Telefilm had outgrown the small structure so it became an immediate priority to find bigger quarters. We finally settled on a 4,500 square foot open warehouse space just over the hill from our home. It fit our needs perfectly and would make an excellent soundstage facility with the addition of soundproofing, a light grid and more electrical power. We moved in on September 1st and spent the next few months putting in all the upgrades.

♋ ♋ ♋

On October 12th 1997 I was back in Pennsylvania for my annual fall visit. Kathy's friend, Bernie Punako, and I got together and spent the day hiking in the woods talking about Kathy and everything that had been happening. Bernie wanted to go by Kathy's old house about a mile and a half away from mine. I drove us up the steep grade out of Parkhill to the top of Dormer Street where it connected with Kenwood Avenue and stopped in front of what used to be the Lynch's mailbox. Kathy's house sat back off the main road but Bernie could see it clearly. She vaguely remembered visiting Kathy there over twenty years earlier.

I decided to give Bernie a quick tour of the rest of the area and as I was driving out the back way along Jackson Street, I did a double take upon seeing an airplane parked on someone's front lawn. It was a white, Long EZ, experimental category aircraft, manufactured from a kit that was created and sold by Burt Rutan. Burt is the brother of Dick Rutan, one of the pilots that had flown the Voyager around the world nonstop. The plane was a tiny canard winged design, made out of composites and just a little over fifteen feet in length with a 26 foot wingspan. I pointed it out to Bernie and told her in all my years living here I had never seen an airplane in a yard like that.

Back at my parent's house, several relatives had stopped by so we all sat on the back porch chatting. I asked if anyone had seen the plane sitting in the yard. Apparently, we were the first to discover it. Someone else started to talk about the big air show held up in Wisconsin every year.

"That's the Oshkosh show," I said. "It's a big event for the experimental builders like the one I saw over in the neighbor's yard."

As soon as I started to talk about experimental aircraft, I could feel that familiar nausea overcoming me again. It was the same feeling I had on my flight back the day Donna passed away. Now I could sense it again and I didn't know what to do. It took all I could to stay out on the porch talking but within an hour everyone had gone and I immediately went into the house to lie down on the couch. I stayed there for six hours shaking with cold and a sadness that made no sense at all.

"Someone close to me has passed away," I told my mom. "I feel like I'm freezing now and the sadness is unbearable. We'll know tomorrow morning who it is."

The next morning I awoke and got up feeling much better. My mom was in the kitchen making a pot of coffee and watching the Today Show.

"How are you feeling this morning?" she asked as I sat down at the dining room table.

"I'm 100% better now," I replied.

"Well, they just had a news story on about John Denver. He died in a plane crash yesterday out in California."

I sat there, stunned by the report. John Denver had been one of Kathy's favorite singers. Her sister had given me John Denver music cassette tapes that belonged to Kathy. She also had given me tapes of Kathy playing the guitar and singing Denver songs. This had to explain the sickness that came over me along with the cold chills. I would need more details to see if his death coincided with the beginning of my experiences.

I began asking my mother for more information about the accident, but all she knew was that he was in some kind of experimental plane. My mind immediately flashed back to the conversation on the back porch about Oshkosh and the experimental fly-in and the discovery earlier of an experimental plane in a neighbor's back yard. I could see the events were meshing together in perfect synchronicity. My sense of his passing had to have been pulled from the universal consciousness within me and everyone around me. I didn't know it would be John Denver, but the signs I had seen all pointed to an event occurring that had something to do with an experimental aircraft.

A few days later, when I finally got all the details of the crash, I found out that the beginning of my feelings of someone close passing over and John Denver's death in the water off Northern California locked in perfect time. His plane, a homebuilt Long EZ, just like the one I had seen in a neighbor's yard, plunged into the frigid waters of the Pacific at 5:28 p.m. on the West Coast, 8:28 p.m. in Pennsylvania, the same time I was lying on the couch, shaking with cold and telling my mother that someone close to me has passed away.

♋ ♋ ♋

On November 23rd, Disney studios called with details on the upcoming junket for their next movie. The film was *Kundun*, a beautifully artistic production written by Melissa Mathison and directed by Martin Scorsese. The scope of the set design and costuming was a mammoth undertaking beautifully crafted by Dante Ferretti. Because of all the expense of period costumes and ornate sets, Disney wanted a massive effort on our part to use all this pageantry as background for the press junket. I knew re-assembling all these costumes and set pieces would be beyond anything I had ever done with my current crew. I began feeling a little intimidated by the size of the project and felt I had to find an art director that could step in and handle this part of the job.

I suddenly remembered someone sending me a resume looking for just this kind of work. I ran over to my filing cabinet and in a few minutes found the file folder.

Michele Kohse, read the name at the top of the resume. I didn't know if any of the numbers listed were still good, it was over a year old. I decided to give her a call. I tossed the resume on my desk and picked up the phone.

Michele's answering machine was on at her home so I left a message and also put out a call to her pager. A few minutes later, the phone rang. It was Michele Kohse returning my call. I quickly explained the situation to her. As usual we had very little time to pull it all together. I would need to get rolling on it right after Thanksgiving, seeing the movie and then looking through all the costumes in storage and figuring out how to get them to New York.

On top of all the organizing involved, we also had the burden of taking the whole show to New York. This complicated the entire project and increased the cost tremendously. The good news was Disney was the client and they always promoted their movies with the utmost flair and polish. We would have access to whatever it took to do the job right.

Michele checked her schedule, said she was clear for those dates and agreed to take me up on the offer. I told her I would be in touch as soon as I could arrange a look at the costumes. It would be shortly after the Thanksgiving weekend.

♋ ♋ ♋

Susan and I were as far apart as ever as the holiday approached. She wanted to go over to Phoenix for Thanksgiving and I wanted nothing to do with it. I planned to spend the day sailing and relaxing in Los Angeles, which is exactly what I did. Our relationship separated to greater distances and the closeness I had once felt for her grew into a widening void as I searched for the next clue to my puzzle.

I met Michele Kohse a few days after Thanksgiving. It was my first time seeing her, in this lifetime anyway. She had a quality about her that was different than other people I had worked with. She was an artist, but not a kooky one like some others I had met. She knew a lot about art history. Knowing what belonged in the scene would come in handy when we had to re-assemble all these pieces in New York. I wrapped up the meeting with her and went back to the office to plan the rest of the junket strategy with our New York people.

It was going to be a five-room junket meaning there would be five stars of the movie to interview in separate hotel rooms. In addition, we would need seven print rooms for the newspaper and radio people to get their interviews. All of these rooms required set decorating. This meant a crew of thirty people, a dozen cameras and a truckload of sound, lighting and grip equipment. The set decorating alone would fill two trucks. More trucks, more people, more everything – this was going to be one big event.

♋ ♋ ♋

Michele and I left for New York on Monday December 8th 1997, a day in advance of the rest of the crew. She had to find mannequins to display the costumes and go to several prop houses for various other background pieces, mainly the chairs to sit on for the interviews. These are the type of things most people don't think about when I tell them what I do for a living. Making sure we have everything is a big part of my job.

On the flight to JFK, I talked with Michele about the movie we screened at Disney before we left. *Kundun* was a story about the Dalai Lama. It began with how they came to find him and decide he was the reincarnated soul of a previous Buddhist monk, then followed him through his life to eventual exile from Tibet.

In discussing the movie, I found that Michele believed in reincarnation and many of the principals in the movie. This common bond of belief in life after death and Michele's artistic personality sparked an attraction in me. I had been searching so long for a kindred spirit, someone to help me in my quest. Perhaps she was someone I was supposed to meet. After all, I was now working on a movie dealing directly with what was happening in my life.

If I believed in fate, then this was something I should pursue with no thoughts about repercussions or residual effects. If it was going to happen, it was going to happen.

On the plane to New York, I began to open my heart to another woman. A woman that I truly believed could hold a very important piece of my puzzle, a link that could take me to the next level in my search for the meaning of life.

I believed in the synchronicity of events in my life. The one thing I could look back on and clearly recognize was that everything flowed together as I walked through life. If I just kept my eyes open I could see the relationship of why something happened, or catch a glimpse of what was to come.

All types of signs were now appearing around Michele. To begin with, Michele had an uncanny resemblance to the facial characteristics of Kathy and me during our first regression reunion. There was something very familiar about her and I could only think and feel it had something to do with England. Talking to her, I found out her mother was from England, the place where Kathy had decided to start my journey. It was chosen intentionally, as a sign post of what was to come.

The *Kundun* press junket was a complete success. It was the toughest production we had ever done in terms of grueling hours, set decorating and the shear amount of camera props, costumes and set pieces that all needed to be moved into and out of the hotel. The entire crew worked until the wee hours of the morning getting everything in place and the Disney people loved the results. All that remained now was another long evening of wrapping out.

After the last truck was packed and most of the New York crew had gone home, a small group of us gathered on the roof of the Parker Meridien Hotel to have a drink and enjoy the night lights of New York City.

Things were moving along on a cosmic level between Michele and me. I could feel an attraction to her that extended beyond our mutual belief in reincarnation and the universal consciousness of mankind. As I said goodnight to her I knew I was close to shedding the ball and chain of Catholic guilt I had been dragging with me all my life. I was just waiting for one more sign.

♋ ♋ ♋

After we arrived in Los Angeles, I asked Michele if she would like me to give her a ride back to her place in Glendale. It would give us more time to discuss the things I liked to talk about without getting in a shouting match with my wife. We arrived at Michele's place and I helped her carry her bags up to the second story apartment. She asked me to come inside for a minute because she had something for me.

Michele walked over to her library shelves and pulled out a book. "*Zen in the Art of Archery*, this is the one I think you should read." Michele handed me a small paperback book with a calligraphy designed cover. "It's by Eugen Herrigel and I think you'll really get something out of it."

The minute I grabbed the book, a question popped into my mind.

"I wonder if they have a book like this about golf?"

"I don't know. Why do you ask?" Michele said.

"I was going to get my wife golf lessons for Christmas and I just had the thought that this is the kind of book she needs to read to understand what I'm trying to tell her. I have this weird feeling that there's a book out there called *Zen in the Art of Golf*. It would be perfect to go with the lessons."

Michele had never heard of *Zen in the Art of Golf* but in my mind I could already visualize the cover. Holding this book now and feeling its vibrations, I knew my next stop would be a bookstore. I clearly remember standing there on the sidewalk saying goodbye to Michele and thinking: *You can stop this whole insanity now, just shut it off and walk away.* But there was something much greater pulling me the other way, and it was saying: *Let go, let go. Just jump off this cliff and you will not die, but fly!*

I promised Michele I'd get her book back to her soon and then drove to the Burbank mall to find a bookstore. When I got there, I went straight to the shelves in the very back of the store and found the book I had envisioned in my mind. I hadn't even read *Zen in the Art of Archery* yet and now I had *Zen in the Art of Golf*, by Joseph D. McLaughlin in my hands.

I was locked onto the path now and certain that what I was about to do was the right choice to make. I had created this story long before I came into this life and now it was time for me to follow it through to the end, no matter how hard it was to let go of my previous values and ideas.

IX.

FALLING AND FLYING

Chapter 28

For Christmas, I received an introductory flying lesson from Susan and she received golf lessons from me. It was a strange exchange. It was the first time I had ever received lessons for anything and I had only bought lessons once before as a gift. Sixteen years earlier on my first Christmas with Susan, I bought her scuba lessons. What had begun our relationship was now signaling the end as well. What I was hoping to do by getting Susan the golf lessons and the book was to raise her consciousness to a new level. Susan's message was crystal clear to me. She was giving me the sign it was time to spread my wings and fly, both literally and spiritually. I was going to take her up on both.

With the gift giving out of the way, Susan took off for a week in Phoenix. I wanted to do something else together, anything else, but she insisted on going over to her parents place. I stayed back in Los Angeles alone. I didn't want to spend my one week off getting into arguments with her. The kids were in Phoenix as well visiting their dad for the holidays.

It's hard to talk about an affair, how it starts, what drove me to do it or even where it all took place. I do remember taking the book, *Zen in the Art of Archery*, back over to Michele's after Susan left town. It started innocently enough with a cup of tea and some small talk, but we both knew what we were doing. It was no accident we had found each other. We both believed fate had thrown us together at this time and in this place for a reason. So who were we not to explore what that reason was?

The affair had the biggest effect on my outlook on life. I felt invincible and daring in ways I could only express through personal adventures. I had been a sailor for over ten years but I had always wanted to be a pilot. I hadn't even thought about it since I left the news business. I figured my flying days were pretty much over except for commercial trips. Now, two weeks after Christmas, I took my medical exam and jumped right into the lessons at Santa Monica Airport. I was hooked the minute we were cleared by the tower to roll out onto runway 21. The instructor let me take the controls and a thousand feet down the centerline I was rotating to make my first takeoff. I was flying and the thrill of soaring beyond the limitations of anything on earth matched my outlook in my personal life as well.

On New Year's Eve, I went out to dinner with Susan and a few friends at the California Yacht Club. It was a nice time but the love was draining out of our relationship. We pulled into our driveway after the festivities when I told her how I felt.

"Susan, I can just feel us slipping away from each other, can't you?" I asked.

"I don't know what you think I have to do with it. You're the one who insists on acting the way you do." Susan was cold and distancing herself from me further.

"I don't know why we can't fix this problem we have. Is that the way you want us to end up? I can see myself without you someday."

I was met with silence. Tears were welling on my face. I felt hopeless about our future together and there was nothing I could do to change Susan's beliefs or attitude.

I continued on with my daredevil lifestyle.

♋ ♋ ♋

Later in January, Ron Siegel called and asked if I'd like to try skydiving. He had done a jump the year before and was eager to get a group of us out to try it. I immediately signed on. I had no reason to fear dying and jumping out of a perfectly good airplane was a great way to test my faith.

On January 18th, a group of six friends drove out to Perris Valley Skydiving to take our lives in our hands. The training session took a few hours, and by the time it was over they pronounced us ready to go. We boarded the twin-engine aircraft for the half hour climb to eleven thousand feet. On the way up there was plenty of joking about what it was going to feel like. You could see the apprehension in a few of the faces, but for the most part everyone was smiling and anxious to step out the door.

I was near the back of the plane with only one other set of jumpers behind me. As we reached altitude and the plane made the first pass over the jump zone, it was surreal to watch the people disappear out the cargo door. In my mind, I thought they would float off away from the plane, but in reality it was zip, they were gone. It happened so fast I couldn't see them falling.

We were jumping in tandem, which meant I would be attached to the jump instructor. He had the parachute on his back and he was strapped to mine. I was to pull the ripcord at five thousand feet and if I didn't, he would do it for me – at least, that was the plan. I had an experienced skydiving photographer freefalling alongside of us to get some photos of the occasion, so he had to step out in front of us to get in position. The pilot circled back around after the first group cleared out, lining up for a second pass over the zone. The plan was to jump on three.

I'll never forget the feeling of the wind rushing madly past the open door as we hunched in it, hanging onto the hatch, counting up in unison.

"One...Two...Three!"

My heart was racing with adrenaline when we flung ourselves out into the cold January air. Within three seconds, we were at terminal velocity, hurling at a violent rate towards the ground below us. I flared into the position they had taught us with my knees slightly bent and angled out behind me. I had been looking down initially and now looked out to see the photographer falling in perfect synchronization in front of us. We waved for the camera as he maneuvered around us getting all the angles. The view from a freefall is incredible. It was a beautifully clear day. The snow covered mountains in the distance contrasted sharply against the crystal blue sky, standing out from everything else. I know we were in freefall for nearly a minute but the time went by so quickly that the instructor began pointing at the altimeter. It was time to release the chute. A strange feeling came over me as I settled into that freefall zone. I wanted to see how long we could ride this out. Of course, my instructor would have none of that on my first jump and sternly motioned for me to pull the cord.

My hand firmly grasped the large D ring handle of the ripcord and pulled straight out with a hard tug. Instantly we seemed to jerk back as our forward momentum reduced to a crawl. I was now dangling under a full canopy less than five thousand feet above the earth. The rest of the ride was sedate compared to the freefall. It didn't get exciting again until we swept in, across the grass landing area and flared our chute for a perfect walk-in touchdown.

The experience left me feeling more alive than ever. It was a lot of work for a one-minute ride, so I knew I would not take it up as a hobby.

I began spending more and more time at Michele's apartment, working on the brochure for our new stage facility and continuing our affair. It was inevitable this was going to end my marriage, but I had no idea how or when that was going to come about. The dreams were continuing. As I look back now they couldn't have been more prophetic.

On February 27th I awoke from a dream vividly lodged in my mind. I wondered if things I planned to do influenced where or what my dreams were about. In this instance, parts of my dream had taken place in Palm Springs again. I knew I was going out to see Chris in Palm Springs on the 28th so I began to wonder what bearing that had on this dream.

I was in a hospital waiting for Ron's wife Renée to have a baby. Ron was with her. At 7 o'clock, she was in labor and dilated two centimeters. It would be a while yet so I took a nap in a room at the hospital. I awoke from the nap and Renée had given birth to a healthy baby boy. I decided to go outside for a swim.

As in all my dreams, I seamlessly moved from one scene to another and never thought about the strangeness or lack of time and distance.

Before I left the hospital, a group of Cub Scouts came into the room. They were going to stay there while I was gone.

The surreal quality of what I'm relaying now never occurred to me while it was happening. To look back at it, I would say it was very "Twin Peaks" in composition. David Lynch couldn't have done a better job of mixing strange images together.

I was now in a lagoon with other people swimming around me. It was very secluded and romantic in a way but I just enjoyed their company and finally swam up to some stairs and climbed out.

I now found myself walking along some storefronts in Palm Springs with Susan along side me. We looked into several of the windows and the one that held my attention was a shoe store with sheepskin slippers on sale. We next stopped at a bakery to purchase a plum pastry for Renée at the hospital. A few more steps and we walked into a deli for a sandwich.

The dream was such a bizarre mixture of seemingly unrelated scenes, and yet I knew they held some kind of meaning as I repeated them to Renée later on the phone. I told her that I somehow felt we were living on multiple levels of existence and maybe this was actually bits of different realities. All the images seemed very familiar to me. I knew they would re-appear in this lifetime, I just didn't know when or how.

I was driving in my car less than two hours later when I heard a commercial begin with the sounds of someone giving birth. "Push… push! It's almost out… almost… keep pushing… congratulations! It's a healthy baby boy," said the woman's voice. The only thing is, it was the dad giving birth and the mom was coaching the delivery!

An announcer's voice came in saying, "There are those that believe that we exist on many planes at once, perhaps thousands of levels at the same time. If you are one of them, then tune into Sliders" Sliders was a TV show about time travelers moving about on different planes of existence. Many modern physicists believe this is an entirely plausible theory and it actually would explain many of the basic principles of modern quantum physics. I have an easy time understanding exactly how this principle works. It is something most people do not grasp quickly and even fewer believe in. After all my dreams and acupuncture sessions, and studying exactly what happened after those dreams and sessions, I have come to the belief that some form of this principal is at play in our existence here.

When we go to sleep at night, we're slipping the bonds of attachment to our conscious reality, this life we are living. Like changing the channels on a television set, we skip and hop through the various airwaves picking up pieces of other channels, other lives we are experiencing. We're even jumping ahead to see parts of this life we are in now or going back to previous ones. To be concise, we're everywhere, anywhere and anybody because time and space does not exist outside the reality we have created. I may have very well been L. W. Rogers and he may very well have been me, two separate spirits each experiencing the same life on different levels of existence, simultaneously. Two spirits, but in reality one entity that had divested itself to grow on many levels. It is a concept that has so many variables that anything is possible.

Not only possible, but actually occurring on a continuous basis like a master computer running all variations of a program.

It is a never-ending, *infinite* life cycle. We can stay locked into this life for the duration of the program, then onto another birth and another experience. Forwards or backwards, the only linear time that exists is on the plane you chose. Washington is still crossing the Delaware, Lincoln is still president, and you are still being born somewhere else out there. Untold numbers of individual spirits but part of a greater whole are experiencing these events repeatedly. The transfer of your spirit to these multiple dimensions occurs during the births and deaths in the program. That is the only time you are between dimensions other than when you are asleep.

The spiritual level of existence with no time and space is a perfect explanation to our dreams. On this level, the laws of physics do not allow us to travel any faster than the speed of light, so it would fall to reason that we have to be on another plane of existence to move faster. That place cannot have the limitations of time and space, and without those limitations, any and all things must exist. When you visit a place like that during the brief moments we rest, we return with a jumble of thoughts and stories to tell as farfetched as you can imagine. Yet while we were experiencing them, they are as real as can be. That is because on some other level, all things are happening.

As far as my relationship with Susan was concerned, nothing was happening and I had to do something about that.

Chapter 29

Saint Patrick's Day of 1998 was approaching and that had always been a special time for us. It was on that night back in 1982 Susan and I became intimate for the first time. We had been dating for nearly two months, and that particular night we did quite a bit of celebrating with some Bailey's. I ended up staying the night with her and from that point on we spent as much time together as two people could.

I had bid on and won a weekend getaway for two during a charity event Susan and I attended over the Christmas holidays. It was for a spa resort called "Two Bunch Palms" in Desert Hot Springs. The Saint Patrick's Day holiday seemed like the perfect time to use it.

Susan and I drove out to Desert Hot Springs early on Tuesday March 17 to meet up with Kathy's sister Chris for breakfast. She had heard about the resort but had never been there. It was a secluded little spot; an oasis marked by two bunches of palm trees and placed on the map by a U.S. Army Camel Corps survey team in 1907. Legend has it that Al Capone's gang built the first structures there in the late 1920s. After settling into his armed fortress, Capone's gangster associates and movie moguls alike were reputed to have made it the place to hide out. With illegal gambling and liquor during the prohibition era, it truly was a resort "hideaway."

Susan and I checked into our quiet bungalow for the evening. Things were not going smoothly. We weren't arguing, but we weren't doing anything else either. She picked up a book and said she wanted to stay in the room and read, so I headed out to the spa for the evening.

The spa was a naturally fed, man-made lagoon with lush vegetation that blended into the desert surroundings. A clear night sky hung above me, lit with billions of stars as I made my way down the stairs into the pool. It was not too crowded, but I did find myself swimming among other people who were out enjoying the evening. I found a quiet spot to lie back and empty my thoughts while the energy of the universe filled me with peace and contentment. Kathy seemed close to me now, surrounded by the same sky she used to look up at from her last home not far from here. I sat in the quiet solitude of the desert thinking about her and feeling somehow, someway we would be together again. Time was irrelevant. Just let it all go and before I knew it, our paths would cross again. I could clearly see the signs as I climbed up the steps and out of the lagoon.

When I returned to the room, Susan was not in a romantic mood and I didn't want to push the point. The next day we took a mud bath together with a complete spa massage treatment. That was a first for both of us and, quite an enjoyable experience. We spent the rest of the day in the lagoon reading. It was a pleasant experience but nothing was occurring on a spiritual level that would bridge the ever-widening distance I felt.

That evening we went into Palm Springs for dinner. Afterwards we were walking along the storefronts looking in the windows. As I got halfway up the block, I did a double take on the window in front of me. It was a shoe store with a sale on sheepskin slippers. The red sale sign was exactly like the one in my dream two weeks earlier, as was the lagoon where I took my evening swim. I was on the path for sure and this was just a preview of something to come. The remaining events of my dream were yet to play out in our dimension but they were coming. It was only a matter of time.

♋ ♋ ♋

My flying lessons were progressing quite rapidly. I was going up to the Santa Monica Airport every spare moment I had, flying at least three times a week as weather permitted. Five days after Saint Patrick's Day, March 22, 1998, I was ready to solo. I had accumulated just over twenty-four hours of flight time and was itching to go up alone. The funny thing about learning to fly is you never know when the instructor is going to feel it is time to set you free. That morning he had me prep the plane as usual for our lesson. After I finished the preflight, he walked out to the plane with me as usual, but this time he didn't get in.

"You're taking it up by yourself today," he said after I climbed into the left seat.

That was all I needed to hear! I was not nervous in the least and actually quite anxious to see what the plane performed like without the added weight of another passenger. After giving me explicit instructions on what to do, three take offs and landings to a complete stop then return to the school, he shut the door and walked up to the observation deck by the restaurant. From there he could watch the flight and listen in on the public address speakers as I communicated with the tower. I taxied to the run up area to finish the checklist. After a thorough check of all the systems, I moved up to the hold short line and called the tower for clearance to take off and remain in the pattern.

As the little Cessna 172 throttled up, it quickly built up speed down the runway. I felt in complete control. The first thing I noticed was how much faster I got into the air without an instructor sitting next to me. With a light aircraft like the Cessna, every pound makes a difference. I reached pattern altitude before my usual point as well, so I was careful to stay at thirteen hundred feet. Everything was happening faster now, or at least it seemed to. Before I knew it, I was on my down wind leg, abeam the tower and calling for final landing clearances. I'm sure the guys in the tower were told I was a student pilot on his first solo. They didn't say anything to me about it, but I noticed they didn't jerk me around either by sending me on extended down winds or short approaches. I was cleared for the landing immediately and did my final GUMPS check. Gas on the fullest tank, Undercarriage down, Mixture at full rich, Prop set and Seatbelts securely fastened. These things had been imbedded into my head from the fifty-seven landings I had done so far. This was going to be number 58, if I didn't screw it up. The way I looked at it was, one way or another, this plane was going to end up on the ground sometime today.

The first landing was a smooth one and gave me more confidence to do it again. The second one I bounced, not hard enough to count as two landings, but it wasn't smooth. The third was about the same as the first: uneventful, no panic, no missed approaches, just getting the plane down safely and maintaining control on roll out. I taxied back to the flight school and the instructor climbed in for the rest of my lesson. After another hour and a half of flying, we returned to Santa Monica where he signed me off in the logbook.

It was a day of feelings I will never forget as long as I live, the exhilarating feeling of freedom, all alone and in the air, in total control of my life – a life that on the ground seemed very much out of control.

After "cheating death," as some would call it, with my solo flight, I really began to take a devil-may-care attitude about what I did next. I was not reckless by any means and, if anything, quite the opposite as far as my flying went. I listened to my instructors and made quick strides towards my final checkout ride.

Where I was becoming reckless was with my marriage and the affair I was having with Michele. It was now May and any hope of recovering my relationship with Susan had been thrown out the window. I was firmly in the mind-set that fate would show me my next turn in the road. Wherever that would lead me, I would follow. I still had nagging pangs of guilt trying to confuse me and drag me back to some kind of imaginary bliss. The guilt wanted me to let go of my search for something that may not exist and be happy with the life I was living. Although these thoughts were still popping into my head, they would fade out quickly, overpowered by my own guiding spirits telling me to never give up, be patient, a change was coming soon.

As I look back now, I realize that Susan had given me the tools to fight off the guilt. Her constant ridiculing of my education and upbringing brought out anger in me that I had repressed since Catholic grade school. I thought about how she was making light of what I was experiencing and how all through our years together she made jokes about the guilt imbedded in me.

"Maybe she's right, get rid of this guilt, don't listen to it, it's only trying to hold me back." That's what I heard now, and as I listened to my thoughts the guilt just disappeared. By May 18th 1998, I had thrown caution completely to the wind.

On May 28th I took my checkout ride for my private pilot's license. I passed the test easily. Susan came to the airport to watch. She had taken out a large insurance policy on me so I wasn't sure about the smile she was beaming my way. As I took the celebratory photos with my examiner, I knew nothing was going to stop me now. I was flying, and if I fell… well, hell, I wasn't going to fall! Fate had something bigger in mind for me. I had made up my mind to push my life to full throttle and see where the flight would take me.

♋ ♋ ♋

Synchronicity was still a big part of my life and after I had my pilot license, I relied on it heavily to guide me to a plane I could purchase. Everyone I talked to would ask me if I was going to buy a Cessna now that I had my license. I would tell them that I wasn't looking for a Cessna but another type of plane. Cessnas were nice planes and everyone had one but that was exactly the problem, everyone had one. I wanted something different, like my boat; an aircraft I would know when I saw it, but couldn't describe now.

Our daughter Dana had been hanging out with her friends at a local coffee shop. She came home one day and told me one of her friends had a grandfather who was selling a plane. She brought pictures to show me, and when I saw them I knew this was the plane for me. I wasn't even sure what it was. I started an Internet search to determine the model. In the meantime, Dana was working on getting the phone number of the owner.

I had just pulled up the image of a Stinson AT-19 on the computer when the phone rang. It was Dana with the number. I immediately called the guy and to my dismay found that he had sold it several months earlier. This started me on an Internet search to find another one like it and resulted in a tale of synchronicity that is still incredible today.

I first located a database of all the Stinson owners in the country. There were hundreds of names on the list. I went down it carefully and looked for anyone who had a Stinson AT-19, or Gullwing, as they were known in the flying community. I found plenty of people that owned them but circled just two names on the list. A fellow named Paul Shacklette down in San Angelo, Texas and another one named Rick McMarlin up in Albuquerque, New Mexico.

My first call was to Paul Shacklette. His answering machine picked up after a few rings so I just hung up and figured I'd call him back later. I intentionally left no message because I wanted to talk to him for a while about the planes and figured I should do that on my dime. About three hours later the phone rang in my office and it was Paul Shacklette.

"Is someone there that is looking for a plane?" were the words first out of Paul's mouth.

"I'm looking for one," I said, "but a special model, a Stinson AT-19."

"Well I'm standing here looking at hull number 32 right now," he said, "It's for sale." I didn't have to go any further. The number thirty-two jumped out at me like a beacon in the night.

"I'll be down to see it tomorrow." I made plans with him to get out to his dusty little town of San Angelo in West Texas.

I had found the needle in the haystack on my first call. Paul explained he had restored several of the same model over the years and now he had this one sitting in his shop, just beginning the restoration process. He had seen my number come up on his caller ID when he returned home and thought he should give me a call back. He had a feeling I was looking for a plane. So far, I liked the guy a lot. He was using his feelings to guide him through his daily life. I was sure that this and the serial number thirty-two were signs to move forward on it.

The next day was my birthday, July 8th. I boarded a plane at LAX for Dallas then switched to a commuter to take me into San Angelo. Paul picked me up at the airport and we drove miles over desert terrain to get to the Ducote Airpark. Paul was a great character, someone you would find in central casting if you were looking for an airplane mechanic who had been everywhere and done everything.

He was an old geezer, about five and a half feet tall with a large girth. He was wearing a khaki shirt pulled out over his khaki pants giving one the impression it was some kind of uniform. He had on a tan cowboy hat with a low, flat peak. His snow white sideburns and heavy mustache along with the Coke bottle thick glasses set in horn rim frames gave the illusion he was Wilford Brimley. His voice was a dead ringer for him as well. He spoke in short bursts of a half dozen words at a time.

"So how was the flight? Did you run into any weather?" Paul could've held up a box of oatmeal just then and I'd have bought if from him.

"Nothing really, we skirted a bunch of stuff coming into the airport here but managed to stay clear of the rain. It was pretty turbulent though for the last fifteen minutes."

"Yeah, we get that everyday. You just missed it by a half hour." Paul continued driving west from the airport, heading out to his hangar home in the desert.

He told me how he had gotten interested in the Stinson AT-19 down in Panama where he worked as a hydrologist on the Panama Canal. He re-built one with a friend down there, but crashed landed it into a lake after using bad auto gas in the engine. The plane was intact after the water landing so they pulled it ashore and years later they re-built it again. Paul told me it was now in the Slaton Air Museum up near Lubbock, Texas.

When we arrived at his place, I was expecting to see something that looked like a plane but instead he showed me the stripped down fuselage of what would become a large high wing aircraft when he was finished. He walked me into his office to show me a wall covered with photos of the other planes he had restored over the years.

They were beautiful military birds, used by the British Royal Navy during WWII. Built by the Stinson Aircraft Corporation in the United States beginning in 1942, the one he was restoring now had been in service down in Trinidad patrolling for German submarines off the coast and training British pilots. They were a large, tail dragger, aircraft with a forty-two foot wing span and nearly thirty feet overall in length. At the tallest point they were over nine feet high. With the large Lycoming radial engine sticking out front, they struck an imposing presence.

They were nicknamed "The Gullwing" because of the arched curve and shape of the massive wings. Only five hundred of the aircraft were made and most of them had been shipped out to the British as part of the lend-lease program during the war. It was essentially an AWAC plane of the 1940s. They communicated long range with a telegraph key and trailing antenna. An aerial camera for reconnaissance work was another piece of equipment that was carried on the plane.

The one Paul was working on now even had the original radios and wooden float bombs used to mark the target. He had the pieces of the Stinson scattered all over his shop now but Paul assured me when he was done it would look just like the others he had shown me in the photos.

I really hit it off with Paul as he invited me into his kitchen to have a glass of iced tea and talk. I asked him where he was from and to my surprise, he responded Pennsylvania.

"I'm from Pennsylvania too. What part are you from?" I asked him.

"I'm from State College," he replied.

"Why I'm from right down the road in Johnstown," I said. "You know, I only circled two names on that list of Stinson owners to call."

"No kidding. Who was the other guy?"

"It was some fellow up in New Mexico named Rick McMarlin," I replied.

"Rick McMarlin, well I restored his AT-19," Paul said, "and you want to hear something really strange?"

"What's that?" I asked.

"Rick's from Johnstown," he replied.

Out of hundreds of names in the database, I had circled the two people from my boyhood home. I struck up a deal with Paul to begin restoration on hull number thirty-two with plans to come back and help during the time it would take to complete the project.

When I got back to Los Angeles, I called my mother to relay all that had happened in Texas, mentioning that both Paul and Rick, whom I hadn't met yet, were from Pennsylvania.

"Why that's Lotte McMarlin's son," she replied.

I said, "Mom, you must be mistaken, this guy has got to be somebody else."

"No, no. I'm sure that's him," she said. "He's an airline pilot for U.S. Airways."

It turned out that my mother was best friends with Rick's mom. They both belonged to the same quilting guild, which my mom joined years after I left Johnstown. Rick was younger than I was and had gone to Westmont High School. I had never met him, and yet I had circled his name along with Paul Shacklette out of hundreds of names.

I contacted Rick and told him the story. We made plans to get together when my plane was close to finished so I could get some time in his Stinson and a feel for what I could expect from mine. I now felt more secure than ever that things were progressing smoothly along the flight path I was following. Of course, even the clearest air can hide some wicked turbulence.

Chapter 30

I returned from Catalina on Monday August 10th 1998 to continue my search for more information on L. W. Rogers. I discovered he last worked with the Theosophical Society in Ojai and they still had an extensive library and school. Michele gladly agreed to join me on my drive up to Ojai, so on August 11th, Michele's birthday, I picked her up in my Bronco to continue my investigation.

The Krotona School was just a short drive off the main highway into Ojai. Ojai was a small rural community just south of Santa Barbara in the desert mountains. It had a reputation as a spiritual center, with quite a few of the population believing in the karmic philosophies of life. I didn't know what to expect from the people at the Krotona facility but as we wandered into the library we were greeted by one of its Theosophical members. We explained that we were doing research on L. W. Rogers.

"Did you know his son still lives up here in Ojai?" replied the librarian.

"No we didn't, but we would sure love to talk with him."

The librarian brought out another member to give me some details on how to get to Grayson's place. Both these people seemed quite agile and in remarkably good health for someone I was guessing to be in their seventies. They seemed to have a wealth of knowledge about the entire Theosophical movement. Some of the information they were relating happened so long ago I finally came out and asked them their age.

"Why, I'm 98," the man said without batting an eye.

I was in total shock. I had never met a person that old in that good a physical condition, and with all their faculties. I came to find out that not only was he in his nineties, so were several of the other people we talked with that day. He was a vegetarian and had strictly followed the doctrines of the Theosophical Society most of his life. They all were shining examples of great health in old age. I began to get the feeling that there may be something to this Theosophical philosophy.

With directions in hand, Michele and I left the Krotona School library and headed out into the avocado orchards to find Grayson Rogers. By my calculations he had to be somewhere in his late 80s by now, but if the last two people were any indication, he was probably out jogging somewhere. We had a phone number for his home but there was no answer. The people at the society told us to go out anyway because most of the time he was outside working in his avocado orchard.

We found his place hidden deep in the avocado orchards that surround the community of Ojai. I parked out on the main road and walked down the dirt driveway up to his house. After knocking on the door and waiting for a few minutes, it was apparent no one was home. Michele and I were walking back down to the main road when I spotted a small pickup truck coming towards us. As the vehicle drew near, I became quite excited to see the occupant. "That's him!"

"How do you know that?" she asked.

"He looks exactly like his father did when I met him in my regression."

As the pickup rolled up to a stop beside me, I reached out my hand to introduce myself.

"Grayson Rogers, I'm Randy Rogers, no direct relation to you that I know of, but I'd love to talk to you about your father."

"I'd be glad to do that," said Grayson. "Just head on back over to the house and I'll meet you there."

Michele and I walked back down the drive leading to his house. When we got there, he was just about to exit his truck inside the garage. I could see he had quite a few packages with him in the bed so the first words out of my mouth were, "Do you need a hand?" He jumped out and turned to face me, I could immediately see that he was missing his left hand. It was an awkward moment to say the least, but Grayson moved right past it, handing me a couple of bags of groceries to carry into the house. The gaffe hadn't slipped by Michele however, and as we followed him into the house, Michele was behind me hitting me repeatedly in the back.

Grayson was extremely short. Like his father, I doubt he even reached five feet in height, but he stood erect, not hunched over in the least despite his advanced age. He was 87 years old but looked and acted much younger. His demeanor was friendly, and he smiled a lot displaying a full set of teeth. He had white hair that was close cropped in a crew cut leaving his ears to stand out a bit more than normal, especially his left ear which had part of it missing. His facial expressions and mannerisms reminded me of Anthony Hopkins. Grayson's voice was higher pitched than Hopkins, yet like the actor, he was deliberate with the words he chose to use.

Grayson was anxious to find out what stories I might have about his father. I began telling him about my acupuncture sessions and how they eventually led to meeting his father face to face.

"How did he appear to you… I mean, what was his physical appearance when you saw him?" Grayson asked.

"He looked exactly like you," I replied. "He was extremely short and wearing this brilliant white gown. The minute I saw you today I knew you were his son. Your faces look exactly alike."

Grayson smiled. "I just wondered if he appeared in a physical form or if he would look like something else."

"At first he didn't appear to me physically. His thoughts came into mine and he appeared to come from all around like an energy that permeated my spirit. But he eventually revealed himself in this physical body that was just like yours. I don't know if he did that so I would recognize you later but I do know that our physical bodies are only needed in this dimension so we can express ourselves. In fact L.W. later took me to a level where we had no bodies, only these spiraling bands of energy"

I could see Grayson believed me and understood the things I was telling him. I still didn't know a thing about him and his relationship to his father so I asked him about that next.

"My father wasn't around much during my childhood. He was out on the lecture circuit most of the time so we were left at home with my mother. The biggest two trips he took us along on were to Australia in 1918 and then India in 1925. The Theosophy movement was really my father's calling. He never talked about it with us because he felt we were born into it and didn't need any further instructions." Grayson laughed a little as he reminisced about life with his father.

"So you didn't follow in his footsteps and join the Theosophy movement?" I asked, wondering just what Grayson did believe in.

"I believe in the same principal views as the Theosophists, reincarnation and a universal consciousness, but listen to the teachings of Krishnamurti who used to be part of their movement. He broke away from them back in 1929. Krishnamurti once said 'The moment you follow someone you cease to follow Truth.' I don't believe in any organized religion or movement, only in the truth. Krishnamurti once told a story of how the devil and a friend of his were walking down the street one day when they saw a man ahead of them stoop down, pick up something from the ground, look at it, and put it away in his pocket. The friend said to the devil, 'What did that man pick up?' 'He picked up a piece of the truth,' said the devil. 'That is a very bad business for you, then,' said his friend. 'Oh, not at all,' the devil replied, 'I'm going to help him organize it.'"

Grayson's stories were fascinating. He told me that Krishnamurti lived his final years in Ojai, passing away at the age of ninety back in 1986.

"What about your father, where did he spend his last years?" I asked, wanting to get back to the story of L.W.

"He was here in Ojai as well. He had his own place and was living there unassisted when I went up to check on him one day. When he didn't answer the door I let myself in and found him lying on the floor, unable to move. He had suffered a stroke so I had to put him into a nursing home up in Santa Barbara. He finally passed away up there in 1953, just a month before his 94th birthday."

I don't imagine anyone ever told Grayson a story quite like the one he heard from me that day. He didn't seem shocked to hear any of it though, and said what I was telling him fell in line with his father's beliefs and teachings. Grayson also told me his brother Stanley was still alive and living near San Diego. This Rogers family definitely had the longevity gene bestowed upon them.

With all this new information in hand, Michele and I thanked him for taking the time to talk with us. After driving off, we decided to make our way up to Santa Barbara and have some dinner to celebrate her birthday and our success in finding L.W. Rogers' son. On the drive up the coast, our discussion centered on the fact that most of the people we had met that day were octogenarians and older. We wondered if it was more the vegetarian lifestyle or following the doctrines of Theosophy that produced the remarkable results displayed in their longevity. We came to the conclusion that it was a combination of both and that these people had a grand blueprint for living life to its fullest.

♋ ♋ ♋

I took off for Chicago on Thursday, September 24th. The shoot was an Oprah Winfrey project for Disney called *Beloved.* It is a movie about a woman, played by Oprah, who escapes from slavery and is visited by the spirit of her deceased daughter. Of course the supernatural theme didn't slip past me unnoticed. Everything went smoothly on the junket and we planned to leave Chicago early on the morning of September 27th.

I had become quite adept at recognizing delays and changes as manipulations to put you in the right place at just the right time. Those types of events started to take place as soon as we left the hotel in Chicago. I ordered two vans to handle all our crew and equipment but only one showed up to get us. This of course threw our schedule off for a half hour while they brought us another one. We eventually got under way, though, and started talking about the previous evening.

Keith Sherins and I began relating a story about our cab driver from hell who picked us up and drove us around the city at breakneck speeds with total disregard for pedestrians, other traffic and especially his own cab. The conversation led to all the guys telling stories about destroying vehicles in their youth. I told a story I had shared many times before about the day a friend of mine, Randy Leidy, and I traveled up to Erie, Pennsylvania to pick up my sister Rosemary and her college roommate at Edinboro State. We had just dropped off her friend Gretchen at her home in Butler, Pennsylvania and were only ten miles down the road when my car wouldn't shift into the next gear. I babied my '69 Javelin into the next gas station, and after putting it up on the rack determined that something had jammed inside the clutch housing.

Rosemary called her friend Gretchen's place to see if we could spend the night there. Gretchen's parents not only said we could spend the night, but we could also have the car towed back to their garage so I could work on it. We did just that and after removing the transmission, the clutch came falling out in pieces. The pilot bushing had disintegrated causing the clutch to explode. Randy Leidy volunteered to call his parents to come pick us up and drive us back to Johnstown.

The next day Randy, my sister and I were riding in the back seat of his parent's car when the following exchange took place:

"Guess Who's playing at Slippery Rock Mom," Randy said to his mother.

"I don't know, who is playing at Slippery Rock, Randy?" replied his mom.

"No, Mom. Guess Who's playing at Slippery Rock."

"I said I don't know, Randy. Who is playing at Slippery Rock?" His mother asked again, getting testy with what seemed to be a persistent line of questioning.

"Mom, I said Guess Who's playing at Slippery Rock," Randy tried one last time to get his mother to understand that he was making a statement.

By now, his mother had lost all patience and interest in the game and refused to respond to his statements. I had to cut in and explain that the Guess Who was the name of a band and they were indeed playing at Slippery Rock, a college in Western Pennsylvania.

Remember this story. It'll come back soon.

We arrived at Chicago O'Hare airport and of course the flight to Los Angeles was delayed. We went up to the American Airlines Admiral's Club to wait for the new departure time. I pulled out my laptop and began to work on transcribing all the audio tapes of my conversations with Kathy's sister Chris. As I listened to her stories again about Kathy and her battle with ovarian cancer, I stopped the machine for a moment and asked L.W. to send me some kind of sign that I was still on the right path. Anything to bolster my confidence at this point would help me to continue moving forward when the easiest path was clearly to just give up. I didn't have to wait long for an answer to my request.

They announced the arrival of our aircraft so the crew and I started to leave the club. As we made our way towards the elevators, I could clearly feel the thought come across my mind to get ready to meet someone special. I was just ready to go into the elevator when a woman stepped ahead of me wearing a Revlon

Walk-A-Thon tee shirt. It didn't take a brain surgeon to see this was the sign I had been looking for so I struck up a conversation with her by asking if she walked in the cancer fund raiser.

"Oh yes, I'm very involved in it," she replied, and then asked, "Are you?"

I told her that I produced the videos for the Fire & Ice Ball and the UCLA Jonsson Cancer Center. She motioned towards her husband who had been standing at the front of the elevator directly behind me. As I turned to meet him, I was shocked to find Dennis Slamon, one of the doctors I had profiled in the cancer documentary. His team at UCLA had discovered the HER-2/Neu gene therapy program.

"Jesus Christ, Dennis! What are you doing here?"

"We just came over to Chicago to get away for a few days," he said. "I do that once in a while." He smiled a big, boyish grin.

I congratulated him on the recent national news that had just come out on Friday September 25th. The Herceptin drug, developed as part of his research, had been approved by the FDA for administering to patients.

When we got to the gate we had another 15 minutes until the plane boarded, so I mentioned to his wife that I was organizing my notes I had collected about my friend that had passed away from ovarian cancer. Dennis' wife wanted to hear the details so I gave her a brief synopsis and then told her that a few minutes ago, while I was working on the transcript, I had asked for a sign that I was still on the right path. I told her running into them was no coincidence. She seemed floored that we had met under this condition. Dennis had walked away to check on the flight and I realized I hadn't gotten her name. I introduced myself and asked her for hers.

"My name is Donna," she replied.

I didn't know how many more surprises I could stand, but this wasn't the last one. Dennis walked back up and asked me if I lived in Los Angeles. I told him I did but I grew up in Pennsylvania. I could see a big smile come across Donna's face.

"Don't tell me you're from Pennsylvania too?" I asked.

"Dennis is from New Castle and I'm from Butler," she answered.

"Oh my God!" I exclaimed. "I was just talking about Butler, Pennsylvania a few hours ago with my friends."

I then retold the Butler story for her and when I was through, she had one last shocker to add to my list.

"I went to Slippery Rock College!" Donna exclaimed, putting the final synchronistic connection to a story that had followed me for 26 years now.

I now knew one thing for sure. The synchronicity in my life was not an accident. It was not a coincidence, fluke, chance meeting or stroke of luck. I was certain I was following a script set in motion long before I took up my role here, and the hidden clues were actually in plain view all along. They simply pointed the way forward for all of us to follow. As long as you opened your eyes, they would be there every time. The path before me had never been clearer. I would finish gathering this story together so others could see how easily it worked.

Chapter 31

After the Chicago job, we moved on to New York on October 8th. We had two junkets going at the same time in two different hotels. By the end of the weekend of work I was ready to get away. I headed straight from New York to Pennsylvania for a weeklong visit with my parents and my yearly fix of the fall foliage. I met up with a few of my old friends and had a very relaxing time taking in the fall colors. The leaves were changing everywhere, and as I think about it now, what more appropriate time was there for things to change in my life as well. The change occurred for me with a simple phone call to Michele on Friday October 16th.

"I think I'm pregnant," were the words she greeted me with on the day before I was to return home.

"Don't worry," I said. I was startled by the news but surprisingly calm after hearing it. "I'll be back tomorrow and we can find out for sure."

There was nothing else I could do now, but I reassured her everything would be all right. After I hung up the phone, a feeling of peacefulness swept over me. This was it, the change I knew was on the horizon. Instead of panic or anxiety, I felt very much at peace now that something was going to happen at last. I was going to be a father, a real father. For the first time in my life, there would be no question that I was responsible for another person's well being and upbringing. Someone was coming into my life to share and be a part of it with me. I was so excited, but also knew I had to contain my excitement until I knew for sure it was really going to happen.

I departed Pennsylvania the next day, happy to be going home and finally move on with the changes that awaited me. All I focused on was the amazing fact that this was actually happening to me at this late stage of life. I was forty-five years old and Michele was forty-two. I had given up on the idea of ever becoming a father a long time ago. Susan and I had tried shortly after we were married, but her tubes had been tied and the damage done to them so severe that the in-vitro fertilization we attempted failed. I could clearly see her heart was not in it for a second try. She had her two children, and that was all she really needed.

As I look back now, I remember how I felt left out in the cold as far as feeling part of a real family. I was just a guy that was working and paying for everything they needed.

During my long flight home, I thought about the fact that this was not an ideal situation to be in by a long shot, but I couldn't let that bother me now. This is my life story playing out. With everything I had experienced, it was not that strange of a twist when I thought about it. Everything happened for a reason and Susan and I didn't have kids together because that was never in the plan from the beginning. She was right in many respects, and the biggest lesson I had learned from her was to do what was right for me. She did that and it worked out fine for her, now it would work out fine for me too. We would both get what we wanted out of life.

Once in Los Angeles, I called Michele to find out when we could get together to do this test. She told me it had to be in the morning, just after she woke up. I told her I would come over early the next day to bring the testing kit and see what life was going to bring us. The next morning I waited outside her bathroom as she ran the test. Two minutes later, I was staring at the solid blue line indicating positive for pregnancy. I held her and told her everything was going to be just fine now. I knew I was married and some people may look at this situation as the worst, but I viewed it as an escape from my old life and the start of a brand new one for me. In the strangest way, I was looking forward to telling Susan and ending the secrecy and deception. It was time for us to move on and see what was around the next bend.

Michele was nervous about the whole situation she now found herself in. She loved me very much, but she also had to trust me to do the right thing and leave my wife to stand beside her from here on out. Michele didn't appear to be overly stressed from worry, but I knew I would have to move quickly and break the news to Susan, then try to get all three of our lives moving in their new directions.

On the Sunday evening of November 1st 1998, I went to a dinner party in Malibu with Susan. Diana Johnson was a friend of mine who had just gotten married and was now pregnant. Her baby was due the following May and she planned the dinner party to gather some of her closest friends together to celebrate. It was such irony that I planned to tell Susan about the affair after a party for another friend who would be having her baby just before mine. As the dinner wore on, it was the hardest thing to stop myself from blurting it out at the table in front of everyone. I had several Walter Mitty moments where my mind wandered off into another world and the entire scene played out to the stone silence of the guests complete with Susan dropping her wine glass onto the table. The only thing that kept me from doing it then was that Diana was pregnant and this was her dinner party.

I sat at the table listening to all these little conversations going on, unusually quiet for someone who always had a lot to say. No one seemed to notice. Before I knew it, we were out the door and driving back to our house in Westchester.

"I've got a little announcement I'd like to make," I said, surprised at my own words.

"Oh, what's that?" Susan replied.

"Michele's pregnant and I'm the father."

There was a moment of silence after my last word came out that seemed to hang longer than it actually did. Susan was reeling from the news. I can only imagine the feeling inside of her at that moment as she saw her world crumble before her. She unleashed all her rage in one furious assault.

"Of all the rotten, God damn things you've done, this takes the cake... I've had that woman over to my house...we've gone sailing with her... and her friend. How long has this been going on?"

"Why does that matter?" I asked.

"I'll tell you why it matters. I want to know how long I've been made a fool of by you and your rotten morals." Susan was sobbing uncontrollably but continued questioning me. "I thought you were a stand up guy Randy...you always talked about your Catholic upbringing...How could you do this to us?" Susan started thrashing out at me at this point and screaming, "Let me out...pull over and let me out here, now!"

"I can't do that. We're on the Pacific Coast Highway and there's no room to pull over safely." I pleaded with her to settle down and I'd pull over as soon as I could get off the main highway.

A minute later I came upon a small gas station-convenience store. I pulled into the parking lot and she stormed out of the car, into the store and bought a pack of cigarettes. She stood outside the car smoking, a habit she had quit after she met me. Now I guess I was the reason she was going to take it up again. I kept trying to convince her to get back into the car so I could drive her home. She was so confused by everything she didn't know what to do next. She finally got back in. It was one bitter ride the rest of the way. Her wrath was so volatile I actually thought she might become physically violent, to the point of harming me while I drove.

"I thought you loved me? I thought we'd grow old together. What happened to all that?" Susan was sobbing again and slamming her fists into the seat next to my head. "All the times I could've done something like this to you but I didn't…" Susan stopped short of explaining what she was talking about.

"Susan, when I met you, you were having an affair with a married man. You told me you had to break it off when you started dating me. Don't preach to me about morals or any kind of guilt. I'm over that now. You taught me that."

My last statement cleared the air and we drove the rest of the way home in silence.

We made it to the house where more bad news came in a phone call just after we walked in the door. Her son Phil had fallen through a glass patio door after stumbling down some stairs at a friend's house. He was now heading to the emergency room for stitches. Susan bolted out the door to meet him at the hospital. She was gone for a couple of hours before she returned with Phil. Other than a few stitches in his arm, he was okay.

Susan sat out on the front steps half the night, smoking and rehashing what went wrong. I sat out there with her some, trying to tell her things would be better for both of us now because she never liked this house or neighborhood to begin with, and now she could live by and associate with the kinds of people she wanted in her life. I realized she was not crying so much about losing me but losing the lifestyle that gave her everything she wanted. My intuition was right. This would become very apparent once the divorce proceedings began.

When I figured that out, I went back inside. I actually thought that in the days and weeks to come, we would get over this fighting and work things out between us – but hell hath no fury. The first thing she did early the next morning was to call my parents before I had a chance to tell them. She told my mom and dad that she should've listened to her own mother. She had told Susan she could do better than marry someone like me.

My parents politely listened to her rage and when it was over, called me at my office. The phone was ringing as I sat down at my desk.

"I'm sorry you had to hear about it this way. I was going to call you as soon as I got here. She shouldn't have done that to you."

"It's not the first time she's called me to complain about you," my mother replied. "In fact, the last time she was here, Susan told me how she had been discussing divorce with Dana. I thought that was something she should be discussing with you, not her daughter. Susan would always say to me, 'Randy could've been so much more if he had only gone to college.' Well, that hurt me Randy, and I didn't say anything to you because I knew you loved her and I didn't want to start something up."

I could feel the hurt coming through my mom's voice. She had treated Susan's two children as though they were her own biological family, making custom stockings for our first Christmas together and always sending cards and gifts out for the smallest of holidays and occasions.

The one good thing about Susan was she didn't procrastinate. I had told her she could live down in Manhattan Beach where she always wanted, so she got a realtor and found a place by November. I helped her move into it and for a while, it seemed things might work out between us. Susan planned to stay on as a partial partner in my production business, helping with the office work, bookkeeping and year end tax preparation. Most of all I hoped we could see our way through this turbulent time in our lives and remain friends in the end.

♋ ♋ ♋

November proved to be a time of many changes. I received a call from Chris Russell just before the middle of the month. Sister Carleen had passed away on November 10th from a simple fall down some basement stairs at her sister Lynda's home in West Virginia. She was carrying a grandchild with her when she fell. The baby wasn't hurt. She had protected him by taking the brunt of the impact on herself.

I recalled Kathy's statement during a regression session that she would be seeing her sister soon. With all the medical problems Sister Carleen had, it was fortunate she passed as quickly as she did without having to suffer through a slow death from liver failure.

Michele had moved into my house on Altavan just before Christmas in 1998. It was an adjustment for us, since most of the furniture went to Susan's new place. Learning to live with a new person, who was also pregnant, was the biggest adjustment. Hormones were raging and nine months seemed to stretch into nine years at times.

Michele was insistent on attending every child birth, baby care, baby safety, breast feeding, pain management in child birth and basically anything with the word child, baby, breast or pain in it, class that was currently being held in the greater Los Angeles area. This kept me running from one end of town to the other with a pregnant woman that constantly had to stop to pee.

"Do we really need to do this class on how to child-proof your home?" I asked one day as we headed up to Santa Monica for her latest discovery.

"Yes, it's important. What if we miss something in the house and the baby gets hurt?" she asked.

"What can we miss?" I asked. "I've got child locks on every cupboard and electrical outlet blocks stuck in every plug in the place. They didn't even have those when I was a kid. I remember once I stuck a fork into a wall outlet. The shock alone taught me never to do that again."

Michele looked over at me with a glare. I kept on driving.

Michele was also a prolific reader and the area around her side of the bed was under constant danger of becoming buried under an avalanche of books and magazines on anything to do with having a baby. She started out with one called *What to Expect When You're Expecting*. The title sounded harmless enough but the inside of this 479 page monster held dozens of articles just waiting to crank up the paranoia level on any child bearing woman that dared to cross paths with it. Depending on what your fear was, this book had something for everybody. There wasn't a syndrome, defect, disorder, symptom or possible problem you or your baby could encounter that wasn't spelled out in graphic detail. As if that wasn't enough, she bought the companion book, *What to Expect the First Year*, as well. This gave Michele an additional 671 pages of continuing diseases and calamity's waiting to befall your little one if, by some miracle, you both made it through the delivery in the first place. Whoever said "ignorance is bliss" was definitely referring to having children. I was extremely happy when Michele eventually moved on to *The Best Baby Name Book in the Whole World*.

In between the books and classes, Michele and I were making regular trips to see her doctor and during one of them, they did an ultra sound to check the baby. The image on the scan turned out to be a good enough one to see the sex. We were originally going to let it be a surprise but when the nurse asked if we wanted to know, we both said yes.

"It looks like you're going to have a boy," the nurse said. A few seconds later, I was holding the first photograph of our son in my hands.

I continued to watch for signs and any type of dream or premonition as to what spirit was coming back into this life. Nothing seemed to be happening now. I was on the path and what was to come would come. I did know one thing. His birthday was going to fall in June sometime and very close to my friend Kathy's.

♋ ♋ ♋

On the evening of June 17th 1999, I ran over to Paco's to get some take out Mexican food for dinner. Michele was on bed rest for the last two weeks because of swelling in her legs. I returned with our food and ate dinner with her up in the bedroom. It was shortly after 8 p.m. when the contractions started to come. Being new to pregnancy symptoms, it took us a while to figure out that these were indeed the contractions we were waiting for. Neither of us slept much that night and by morning, they were occurring at one-hour intervals so we called the doctor's office. The doctor told us to get to the hospital as soon as we could and he would see us there.

We packed up the few things Michele would need and headed out the door for Cedars Sinai hospital in Los Angeles. The drive there was calm and stress free. I pulled up to the emergency room to drop off Michele. By the time I parked and got up stairs, they had her in an examination room on the delivery floor. The staff began by taking measurements of her cervix that confirmed she was in labor. The nurses transferred her to a labor room where we waited it out through the day and into the early evening.

Dr. Brusch decided Michele was naturally dilated enough to start the delivery. He wouldn't have to induce labor.

All our months of training and reading were now going to pay off. We were instructed to begin the breathing exercises along with all the other techniques to help get the baby to come into the world. Michele was pushing as hard as she could through the ordeal, but she was not able to get his head through the birth canal and by 7:30 p.m., her energy was nearly gone. Dr. Brusch told her to rest a moment and then he would make one more attempt to deliver him naturally before performing a caesarean section.

With plenty of encouragement from all of us, and the doctor's expert help, we all focused our love and energy towards Michele as she began to push again for the very last time.

X.

THE KEY OF LIFE

Chapter 32

On Friday June 18th 1999 at 8:12 p.m., Kyle Michael Rogers finally emerged from his dark, but secure and comfortable, hiding place. Bursting out into the bright glare of the hospital delivery lights, he let out a little cry just after the doctor suctioned his lungs but a quick checkup pronounced him extremely healthy and they handed Kyle over to me for the very first time.

His eyes locked onto mine immediately and I became swept away, back to a time imbedded deep in my memory. I was not in an acupuncture session now. This was a real experience. A flood of emotions swept over me. All I could do was continue to stare deeply into his piercing blue eyes. I was in a complete *déjà vu* moment, and for once I didn't have to strain to remember where I had felt it before. It was all very familiar, this feeling of overwhelming love and deep connection.

I was on a schoolyard at Sacred Heart Grade School in Conemaugh, Pennsylvania. It was September of 1961. There were kids playing outside on the playground next to the schoolhouse, tons of kids, with the girls, dressed in their green and white uniforms, standing out from the boys. I found myself gazing at one particularly tall girl that stood out from all the others. She didn't stand out because of her height or her hair, which was shining a golden brown in the sunlight and bouncing from her shoulders as she ran. It was because of her eyes and the feelings they evoked as they met mine. It was the same feeling that was now drowning my entire body as my eyes remained fixed on hers for what seemed like a very long time. This memory poured out of Kyle's eyes and deep into my soul as I held him so close in my arms. We became transfixed in a gaze that confirmed who he was and who we both were. My friend and soul mate had returned to me.

It was Kathy's spirit for sure. I would know her energy anywhere. However Kyle was *not* Kathy and that was something I understood from the very start. The energy giving Kyle his life was the very same energy that had given Kathy hers. It had grown tremendously and was now going to take on this new role as my son. I couldn't have been more excited about this radical turn of events. It was going to take some getting used to. I was back together in the physical world with another part of my spirit.

Kyle's bright blue eyes staring up at me said everything I needed to hear. I would be able to watch over him and guide him along his new path with more wisdom than we ever could've had if he had stayed in Kathy's incarnation. There was a definite plan to all this reincarnation. I was going to learn from him as he was going to learn from me. At that one moment in time, I felt there was nothing the universe could throw at us that we couldn't handle. Our life together may not always be easy but at least now it had a purpose that made sense and that alone made all the difference in the world to me.

Epilogue

As I look back now at all the pieces of life's puzzle thrown in front of me, I marvel at how many clues I missed or couldn't interpret correctly when I first received them. One of the easiest, that you may have caught on to as you read this story, is the recurring use of the same first name on many of my friends. It was one of the first things my editor, Alan Rinzler pointed out after his first pass over the book. His comments were "Any problem changing the name on this guy. You have too many Pauls, Rons, Nancys & Donnas. It's too confusing." Alan wanted to cut out something that I hope all *The Key of Life* readers understand. I hope you'll realize that it's no accident when you see, hear, smell or taste the same thing over and over, coming at you from all directions. All the Pauls, Rons, Nancys and Donnas in my life were there to point the way, and when you have the same thing going on in your life you should sit up and take notice.

Of course, the biggest mystery was the birth of my own son and Kathy's reincarnation into a new life. I knew someone was returning but if I had just opened my eyes I would've seen the connection a lot sooner. As fate would have it, a key piece of the puzzle that was always there was pointed out to me in dramatic fashion just after the birth of my son. Some people would say it was just a wrong turn, but you can decide for yourself.

I was working with Nancy Williams on another cancer piece, shortly after Kyle was born. It was October of 1999 and we were driving out to Glendale to shoot a story on breast cancer screenings with a UCLA mobile screening unit. October is Breast Cancer Awareness Month and the Cancer Center at UCLA had us doing the story to help spread the word that all women should get regular checkups. They were going to send out the piece to all the local news organizations.

I didn't have precise directions to the shoot and as I exited the 134 freeway on Glendale Avenue, I asked Nancy if I should turn left or right. She couldn't find the directions quickly enough so, feeling that it was probably to the left, I made a left and immediately realized, after traveling a short distance up the street, that we were going the wrong way. Nancy, who I've had to have known in some previous life, was chattering away a mile a minute about everything under the sun while I was desperately trying to find the right way to go. I had pretty much tuned her out when I realized I was on the street leading up to the apartment Michele lived in when I met her.

"Oh, look, that's where Michele used to live," I said pointing over to the right as I started to find a place to turn around.

Nancy had been talking non-stop, but she became even more excited about something on the left side of the road.

"Look, a harp shop, a harp shop!" She pointed excitedly to a small building just down the street from Michele's old apartment. "When was the last time you ever saw a harp shop?"

Everything seemed to shift into slow motion. Her words were finally registering in my brain. I looked over to the shop she was pointing out. Sure enough, there was a harp shop, an honest to God harp shop, and within spitting distance of Michele's old apartment. All the times I had driven up there, I never saw it. All this time it was right in front of me. A piece of the puzzle handed out four months before I ever met Michele was now revealing itself.

Just as Susan's sister Nancy Lipscomb had handed me the harp music and had the harpist playing at her baby's christening party, I now had another Nancy shouting out the final clue. Nancy had no idea what she had just done. I, however, realized it immediately.

A smile crept over my face as the entire sequence of events started to fall into place. They were all there, all the signs in one convenient package. I was on a cancer shoot with a Nancy pointing out the harp sign to me. What started out as a simple wrong turn became the crowning example of how synchronistic events would play out to show all my premonitions had been correct. What forces were so perfectly at work here to bring all these elements together? Is there really any such thing as a wrong turn or an accident?

When I returned home, I began to wonder about another clue that never made sense to me, the Paul McCartney connection that occurred also in July about a week earlier than the harp incident. For two days in New York, I had a Paul McCartney song, *The World Tonight*, playing in my head. I was awakened early on the second day and when I turned on the television, he was on The Today Show talking about his wife Linda's cancer and his mother's death from it. I decided to apply the same rules to solving this sign as the first one. The first marker that must be present is a repeated showing of the same symbol in a short period of time. In this case it was multiple images of Paul McCartney and his music appearing around me in two days.

The second marker was that there had to be a connection to cancer and preferably women's cancer, breast or ovarian. That was clearly shown to be the case as the story on the Today Show was Paul McCartney talking about his wife Linda's breast cancer and his mother's death from it. Now all that was missing was the third marker. How did Paul McCartney tie into the birth of my son? Whenever I felt confused, I always went to my book shelf for the answers. This time would be no different. I had a book in my library that listed birthdays of famous people. As I turned to the date June 18th, there was my Paul McCartney connection. He and Kyle shared the same birthday. I had that sign shown to me four months before I ever even met his mother.

I could always feel that a big change was coming. I did know it would involve a reincarnation. Someone had clearly pointed that out to me in multiple events beginning with *The Secret Garden* opening to, "I will cum bak." When I looked back at the story in detail I found that the message included a cryptic drawing of a missel thrush sitting on her nest. More clues missed that a new life was on its way. I also was firmly sure that the event that was coming would have something to do with harps and Paul McCartney. In the end, both these things proved to be true.

The key synchronicity that brought Michele into my life was a movie about reincarnation, *Kundun*. I would've never met her if not for that movie. If not for all my spiritual growth through the acupuncture sessions, I would never have been able to see these signs, and the re-birth of my soul mate may never have happened.

Finally, Susan played a key role as the ultimate devil's advocate, pushing me away rather that supporting me. I would never have begun an affair if she hadn't played her part to ultimate perfection.

It is for all these reasons that I like to put fate back into the equation and say there was also no possible way for it not to happen. It is happening right now, every day and in each and everyone's lives, synchronistic events laid out in perfect coordination as we each act out the characters we've chosen. All you have to do to find your *key* is open your heart, clear your mind and feel the love that is flowing to you from the other side.

Postscript

February 11th, 2008 was a big day for me. I won't go into a complete recap of all the events of the last ten years but to sum it up, I had been paying dearly for Susan having played the role of my wife. By November of 2007, I had finally had enough of it when I heard she had left her job, rented out her house, moved in with her boyfriend from the yacht club and was now leaving on a multi-month cruise through the Gulf of Mexico on his ship.

I was extremely happy for Susan that her life was doing well, but I also felt it was time now for us to part ways. I contacted her while she was still in Los Angeles but she refused to deal with me on the issue, promising instead to call me the next day. That call never came and after a week of trying to reach her with no response, I called my attorney Barry Friedman. I had him file a modification motion requesting termination of my spousal support payments.

Susan dragged her heels the whole way into court refusing to negotiate with us or even submit the required income and expense declarations on time. She did show up on the day of the hearing, without an attorney. She handed the judge her response to our motion and after reading over the document for a few minutes, he asked her a few select questions. It was very apparent to him what Susan was doing. He gave her a quick lecture on how the law interprets living with your boyfriend. She attempted to have the motion moved to another date but the judge pointed out that he would have the support terminated in the mean time. He then asked us to go outside and make one last attempt at reaching an agreement before he held the matter over into the afternoon for a full hearing. My attorney and I walked out of the courtroom and Barry then approached Susan to see if she would like to talk about ending this amicably.

"I'll talk to you, by yourself," she said, pointing to Barry. Susan completely ignored me, as if I wasn't even in the building.

Barry stepped away from her to come over and talk with me. "Do I have your permission to offer her a deal?" he asked me.

"What do you have in mind?" I said, already knowing what I wanted to do.

"I'd like to tell her that we won't request any of the support back that you've already paid to her and you'll give her two or three more months of alimony and then that's it – forever."

I wasn't really happy about paying her more support. I was entitled to ask for the money back through November but I also knew from past experiences that some type of "carrot" approach may work better than nothing at all. I agreed to the offer and a few minutes later, in the cafeteria of the courthouse, Barry convinced her that a deal was in her best interest. Ten minutes later, we were in front of the judge again and the whole thing was finally over, forever. Ever the actress, Susan briskly walked out of the courtroom ahead of us, ignoring a call from my attorney with a wave of her hand and a quickly blurted remark to put anything further we had to say in writing. Our request was just to ask her where we should send the final documents, as she had given no new address in her declaration.

"To my office," was her fleeting response as she bolted out of the courthouse.

I left Torrance that morning feeling like a new man. I was sad Susan wouldn't end this on more friendly terms but happy to be free from ten years of a weight dragging my life along the bottom of some muddy river. I could never get a clear picture of what it would be like to finally rise to the surface again and get an unobstructed view of the possibilities that lay ahead. Now I was driving up into Hollywood on a gloriously sunny day with my manuscript next to me in the car, on its way to the copyright process and then hopefully into the hands of a good editor and publisher. It was a perfect day and one that would be neatly tied into my book when I returned home later that evening.

Monday evening the NBC Nightly News threw out this interesting bit of tabloid news. Sir Paul McCartney was in court today, in London, battling with his ex-wife Heather Mills over alimony payments. He showed up with his attorney and she came alone representing herself! I just about fell out of my chair. I couldn't have even imagined this synchronicity resurfacing to close out this final chapter of the story. Of course, in typical grand fashion, this wouldn't be the only sign lighting the way. There would soon be others to follow.

The next day I was working on my stage helping a client with a shoot for the Oxygen channel. They were shooting promos and host wraps for a segment on women's issues dealing with forced slavery, rape, prostitution and other acts of violence committed in various parts of the world. During a break in the shooting, the host was talking about a place near UCLA that has the largest sperm bank in the world. She couldn't remember the name of the company and repeated several times I can't remember the name of it. Overhearing her talking about it, I cut in with a reply, "It's the California Cryobank. I shot a video for their cord blood collection services." Yesterday it was a Paul McCartney synchronistic event, today a request to remember the Cryobank video all coming while I was working on a promo for women's issues that had been growing like a cancer in recent years. The signs were appearing on cue and this time as a final confirmation to the book I had just finished. A clearly lit pathway now pointed out everything happens when it should. I sensed that there were more signs to come and the next day didn't disappoint me.

On Wednesday afternoon, Michele and I went over to Kyle's grade school to launch his science project with him. We had built several bottle rockets to explore Newton's laws of motion and the affect of changing fuel quantities and air pressure. The entire class came out to help with the exhibition launches and we had several good aerial displays. After class dismissed, I went back to our house to change clothes as I had gotten mine muddy during the launches. I was walking down the hallway when Kyle called out to me from his room.

"Dad, look at my new baseball uniform." He was standing by his bed holding up a blue jersey to show me.

There, emblazoned in bold white type was the number *23.* I asked Kyle if he had picked out the jersey himself.

"No, they just gave it to me Dad," was his reply. I bolted downstairs to find his mother.

"Did you see the number on the jersey they gave him?" I asked when I found her in the kitchen.

"Yes I did," she replied with a smile.

"Did you ask for that number?"

"No, they just handed them out to the kids and that's the one he got," she answered.

"Pretty strange isn't it?" I asked, intentionally prodding.

"Yeah, that's pretty funny," she said, knowing exactly what I was getting at.

The team he had been picked for was the *Twins.* The first past life Kathy had shown me was the one in which we were twins. Kyle was born on June 18th, which also made his sign a Gemini or *twin.* Twins, with the number twenty-three printed on his back; I guess they didn't want this sign to slip past me.

Conclusion

It all started with a thought, and then manifested itself as a dream. Who better to interpret my dreams than Freud himself, brought into my story through my connection to Peter Michalos. I think Freud would've really loved to have taken a run at *The Key of Life*. It's the modern day version of *Gradiva* with one major twist. Everything in it is true. It all happened; nothing was made up, created or altered for effect. Even though Jensen's work, *Gradiva,* was a novel, many of Freud's observations of it can be applied to *The Key of Life* as well.

To begin with, Freud, in his 1907 essay, *Delusions and Dreams in Jensen's Gradiva,* said "The question that first arises is whether dreams have a meaning at all, whether they ought to be assessed as mental events. Science answers 'no': it explains dreaming as a purely physiological process behind which, accordingly, there is no need to look for sense, meaning or purpose: dreams are comparable only to twitchings, not to expressive movements, of the mind."

In contrast to that statement Freud also wrote in the same essay; "Imaginative writers seem to be on the same side as the ancients…they are apt to know a whole host of things between heaven and earth of which our philosophy has not let us dream. In their knowledge of the mind they are far in advance of us everyday people, for they draw upon sources which we have not yet opened up for science."

I'll let you decide which side you fall on in this debate now that you've read *The Key Of Life*.

The similarities between *The Key Of Life* and *Gradiva* are striking in many ways. To begin with both stories revolve around a fascination for a young woman who is clearly out of reach for each of the two main characters, myself and the fictional archaeologist Norbert Hanold. Dreams that manifest themselves in reality are then investigated by both of us, propelling our search for these two women forward until in the end, both Hanold and I find what we're looking for.

Hanold had gone searching among the ancient ruins of Pompeii, looking for any sign that Gradiva, the girl in the bas-relief, had ever really existed. He had a dream of her being there on that fatal August day in 79AD when Mount Vesuvius erupted. Hanold followed his dreams, signs and synchronicities in search of the truth. He found Zoe, a friend from childhood, who's memory and love he had repressed his entire life. Hanold's search for the truth revealed a true love that he had within himself all along.

I began searching for Kathy after being driven by a dream that she had perished as well. Recognizing the synchronicities in my life as a pathway to the truth, I picked up each piece as I watched for the next one to show me the way. As I peeled away the layers of my past lives through the regression sessions, they revealed my true connection to Kathy's spirit since the beginning of time. I had repressed my feelings of love for Kathy just as Hanold had for Zoe. Now they had risen to the surface, never to submerge again. In the end I found the *Key of Life* was my unconditional love for Kathy and all the other spirits I had shared countless experiences with over the eons. My new found knowledge and spiritual growth broke down those final barriers of guilt that had me paralyzed, freeing the way for my soul mate to return to me in this life.

On the roadway that lies ahead of you, find the synchronistic events in your own life. Examine each one carefully, if you recognize it as the truth, save it. Let no one help you organize them. Your collection will lead you to your own *Key of Life*.

Acknowledgements

Investigating and writing this story was a project that I never envisioned as I began my professional career in 1970. The only thing I was certain of then was that I was a photographer and would make my living as one. Since that time I have grown both professionally and spiritually, neither of which would have been possible without all the souls I've been surrounded with on my journey. To all of you that have known me, I want to say I love you dearly and thank you for being a part of my life along the way.

In particular I owe special recognition to my mom, Louise Rogers, for giving me life, along with my dad, Robert Rogers, whose spirit continues to surround and guide me. Your support and love will always be the keystone of my life and for that I'm forever in your debt.

In that same vein, to my siblings who accompanied me on this trip, Rosemary, Jeff, Diane and Tom, thank you for filling my mind with such wonderful memories of our childhood together. There is at least one book yet to be written about all our adventures growing up together during the 1950s and 60s.

It would not be possible to list everyone that has helped shape me into the individual that I am today but my ex-wives Judy and Susan are owed a special note of thanks for making those turns in my life when it needed to be turned. To travel down a straight path may be the fastest way to get somewhere but the scenery would get mighty boring in a hurry. Thank you both for making my life interesting.

If someone were to ask me what person helped me the most in my quest for the truth I would have to answer Lucy Postolov. Her skill as an acupuncturist is clearly documented in this story. Beyond that there is an energy and connection between us that can only be explained by our timeless spiritual bond. Thank you for guiding me along the path, Lucy, I look forward to many more sessions with you in the years to come.

As I investigated these events I relied heavily on all the members of the Lynch family for details about Kathy's life. Kathy's sister, Chris Russell, was invaluable with her countless stories of Kathy and also her complete support for my quest. Although Chris too has passed now, I still feel her spirit near me from time to time, thank you Chris for calling when you did.

Sister Carleen, you were my first solid source of information on Kathy and your memory is also held close to my heart. Thank you for believing my story.

To Kathy's brother, Jim Lynch and his wife Carol, thank you for making me feel like part of your family and to Kathy's sister, Lynda Neff, I really appreciate your continued support as well. I look forward to many more visits with all of you.

To my editors Kenneth Brosky and Alan Rinzler, thank you for taking on my manuscript and steering me in the right direction with your advice. Ken, your initial cleanup and guidance helped me immensely and Alan your notes and questions on every page made me relive every event, bringing out the final details my story needed. Thank you both for all your hard work.

To Janet Kerschner, my indexer, thanks for your professional input and organization of all the topics.

To Ginny Weissman, my publisher, true friend and biggest fan, words cannot express my appreciation for all you've done and your continued, unfailing, support. Thanks to you and Transformation Media Books, *The Key Of Life* has now truly come to life. To Paul Burt of Pen & Publish, Inc., thank you from the bottom of my heart for your support in getting my story published.

Of course there would be no conclusion to *The Key Of Life* without Michele Kohse. I always need a devil's advocate to challenge me and spur my life forward. Michele manages to handle that role yet give me the emotional support that I need as well. This whole story would not have been possible without you Michele. Thank you for taking on this demanding role in our lives. Kyle and I are eternally grateful and love you with all our heart.

Finally there would have been no story at all without Kathy Lynch. My memories of Kathy still pull at my heart daily. She was a brave soul on a daring mission in a life filled with hardships. Battling cancer on three occasions in one lifetime is more than should be asked of anyone, yet Kathy did just that. As Kathy's spirit is never-ending so is my love for her and now Kyle. Thank you for coming back into my life and continuing the spiritual growth that makes us who we are. I do feel your spirit and it truly does make us as one.

Photo by Kyle Rogers

About the Author

Randy Rogers is president and CEO of Telefilm, Inc., a Los Angeles production company he started in 1991. His clients have included Disney, Warner Bros., Paramount, Universal, Sony, Dreamworks, MGM and Lionsgate. To date, Randy has worked on the promotion of over 500 movies and continues to be a part of the biggest marketing campaigns in Hollywood. Prior to that, Randy spent two decades in the television news business as a cinematographer with the last five years of his journalism career working for NBC News in Burbank. He and his family reside in Los Angeles.

Visit the author at
www.thekeyoflife.net
www.randolphrogers.com

Works Cited

Dahl, Sophie. *The Secret Garden.* New York: Penquin Group, 1951 (1911)

Eisenberg, Arlene, Murkoff, Heidi E. and Hathaway, Sandee E. *What To Expect When Your Expecting.* New York: Workman Publishing, 1996

Eisenberg, Arlene, Murkoff, Heidi E. and Hathaway, Sandee E. *What To Expect The First Year.* New York: Workman Publishing, 1996

Freud, Sigmund. *Delusions and Dreams in Jensen's Gradiva.* New York: Moffat, Yard and Co., 1917

Gaarder, Jostein. *Sophie's World.* London: Orion Books, Ltd.,1996

Gideon International. *Holy Bible.* Philadelphia: National Publishing Co. 1985

Goldschneider, Gary. *The Secret Language of Birthdays.* New York: Penquin Group, 1994

Jensen, Wilhelm. *Gradiva, A Pompeiian Fancy.* New York: Moffat, Yard and Co., 1918

Michalos, Peter. *Psyche.* New York: Bantam Doubleday Dell, 1993

Redfield, James. *The Celestine Prophecy.* New York: Warner Books Inc., 1993

Rogers, Louis W. *Dreams and Premonitions.* Santa Fe, NM: Sun Publishing, 1992 (1923)

Weiss, Brian L. *Many Lives, Many Masters.* New York: Simon & Shuster, 1988

Who's Who in America. Chicago: A.N. Marquis Co., 1920-1931ed.

Wiegand, Vera Goughnour. *The Goughnour & Bracken Family Tree.* Bozeman, Montana: Self Published, 1978

World Book Encyclopedia. Chicago: World Book Inc., 1990 ed.

Index

LaVergne, TN USA
29 March 2010

177470LV00004B/19/P